The International Dimension of the Israel-Palestinian Conflict

To Lorenzo

Contents

Illustrations

Abbreviations

AKP	Justice and Development Party
BDS	Boycott, Divestment, and Sanctions movement
CFSP	Common Foreign and Security Policy
EC	European Community
ESCWA	Economic and Social Commission for Western Asia
EU	European Union
ICC	International Criminal Court
ICJ	International Court of Justice
IR	International Relations
MEPP	Middle East Peace Process
NATO	North Atlantic Treaty Organization
OHCHR	United Nations Human Rights Council
OPT	Occupied Palestinian Territory
PA	Palestinian Authority
PLO	Palestine Liberation Organization
UK	United Kingdom
UN	United Nations
UNDOF	United Nations Disengagement Observer Force

UNDP	United Nations Development Program
UNEF	United Nations Emergency Force
UNESCO	United Nations Educational, Scientific and Cultural Organization
UNESCWA	United Nations Economic and Social Commission for Western Asia
UNGA	United Nations General Assembly
UNIFIL	United Nations Interim Force in Lebanon
UNRWA	United Nations Relief and Works Agency for Palestine Refugees in the Near East
UNSC	United Nations Security Council
UNSCOP	United Nations Special Committee on Palestine
UNTSO	United Nations Truce Supervision Organization
US	United States of America
USSR	Union of Soviet Socialist Republics

Acknowledgments

This book is the outcome of a two-year-long individual research project funded by the German Gerda Henkel Foundation and pursued at LUISS (Libera Università Internazionale degli Studi Sociali) University in Rome, while also building on my longer research pursued in the past ten years. It takes a comparative look at how seven powers in the Middle East—Egypt, the European Union, Iran, Russia, Saudi Arabia, Turkey, and the United States—have discursively constructed and performed their roles in the region on the Palestine/Israel question over time, and have thereby not only attached meaning to it but also established webs of relationships bound by dominant paradigmatic framings of the conflict. These framings and the role foreseen for international powers and the UN in them are scripts, and the latter amount to orders when actors perform them accordingly; they break down when actors overperform, underperform, or disperform them. Indeed, scripts have changed over time, and this work traces back continuities, ruptures, and transformations of them. It offers a comparative and historical account to show how today's specific international script on the Palestine/Israel question has emerged, what this script silences and sidelines, and what its alternatives could have been. It also highlights how this script has perpetuated the Israel-Palestinian conflict (so defined in this book to highlight the power asymmetry as one actor is a state and occupying power, the other a stateless people being denied their collective and individual rights) and how it has not succeeded in providing security and peace, but has set a context for further upheaval and crisis in the region at large.

This book will interest students and informed lay readers who would like to get an overview over how key powers in the Middle East have positioned themselves regarding one of the longest-running conflicts in the modern era and how the international paradigmatic framing of it has evolved at the United Nations. Furthermore, its theoretical and methodological take contributes to a decentering approach to International Relations and will therefore interest IR scholars working in this direction.

This work would not have been possible without the wonderful shared journey through this life with Lorenzo Kamel to whom I am eternally grateful for always cheering me up and without whom I might never have begun to think outside the standard IR toolbox. You have opened up a world for me. I am also very thankful to my colleagues at the Istituto Affari Internazionali (IAI) and LUISS University for their extensive feedback on earlier versions and their continuous support—most notably Riccardo Alcaro, Andrea Dessi, Raffaelle Marchetti, and Nathalie Tocci. Particular thanks go to Michelle Pace for all her thoughtful feedback on this book, as well as the many empowering discussions beyond. I am also extremely grateful to all the thoughtful input I received from the anonymous reviewers of this book and to the copyeditor who has done an outstanding job in improving the book. It has also greatly benefited from many discussions with friends and colleagues while living in Jerusalem and from the feedback I received from colleagues and students when I presented my research at conferences, workshops, and seminars in Rome, Moscow, Turin, Tehran, Ramallah, and Beirut. Furthermore, my wonderful students in my seminar on International Politics at Roma Tre University provided me with lots of food for thought when discussing the research and findings of this book. It would not have been possible without the generous support of the Gerda Henkel Foundation, which gave me the unique opportunity to focus on research. The usual disclaimer applies: the views expressed in this book are those of the author only.

An immense hug goes to my two children, Niccolò and Valerie, who always spread love and happiness in my life and (almost) never complain about spending long days at kindergarten and school.

Introduction

The Palestine question has been internationalized from its very beginning. More than a hundred years ago, in 1917, the Balfour Declaration—later incorporated in the British Mandate for Palestine—promised to support a "national home for the Jewish people" while ignoring the right to self-determination of the local Arab-Palestinian majority, which it referred to as the "non-Jewish communities." In July 1937, for the first time in history, the British Peel Commission recommended partition, and the related forced transfer of 225,000 Arab-Palestinians and about 1,250 Jews. Ten years later, in November 1947, thirty-three (out of a total of fifty-six) member states of the United Nations General Assembly (UNGA) suggested the partition of Palestine into two states, one Jewish and one Arab. Over fifty years ago, in November 1967, United Nations Security Council (UNSC) Resolution 242, as well as Resolution 338 in October 1973, embodied the land for peace principle. When the General Assembly now began to stake out Palestinian collective rights—including the right to a state—the so-called peace process took off. In November 1977, Egyptian president Anwar el Sadat made his historic visit to the Knesset, and one year later the Camp David Accords were signed under US auspices. Indeed, the US had now become the key power in the region, launching repeated "peace" proposals that crystalized into the Middle East Peace Process (MEPP). This "peace process"—as this book argues—has been a specific script that has attached meaning to the Palestine/Israel question (namely, a prescriptive one that conditioned the return of land not on preemptory norms of international law, but on negotiations), but also included specific roles for all powers involved (but not for the UN). As long as all powers performed this script into being, it was resilient and had an impact on the ground. At the time of writing, US president

Donald Trump is overperforming this script, as he not only sidelines international law but engages in breaking it, for example when moving the US embassy to Jerusalem, implicitly recognizing the city as the capital of the State of Israel, in contravention to international consensus and law. A proceeding has been initiated against the US by the State of Palestine at the International Court of Justice, while the Palestinians in Gaza have begun their "Great March of Return," partially in reaction to this US move.

While this short overview shows the importance of the international layer of the conflict and the key role that global and regional powers play in the conflict, no study exists so far that *comparatively* explores their role in it. This lacuna is puzzling, maybe now more than ever; after almost four decades of peace processes and substantial international diplomatic and economic efforts, the solution of the Israel-Palestinian conflict appears as far away as ever. *This begs the question: What if the efforts of all these powers, rather than helping to solve the conflict, have actually led to its perpetuation? Rather than being external to the conflict, have they been a substantial part of it? What exactly have the roles of these powers been in the conflict?*

The literature has tended to frame the conflict as Arab-Israeli (Sela 1997), representing the Arab states as a bloc of conflict actors. Some parts of the literature also framed the conflict as one seated in a larger conflict with Islam (Bartal 2015), including Iran (Rawshandil and Lean 2011), at times also Turkey (Tür 2012), into the circle of conflict actors. In contrast to this, the three global powers that have historically also been substantially involved in the conflict—European states/the EC/EU, the US, and the USSR/Russia—are generally framed as external actors, mainly as diplomatic brokers, despite the fact that all three of them have been major arms providers in the conflict, much more than, for example, Iran. The literature has so tended to unreflexively repeat how these three global powers have represented themselves. This book observes key powers—Iran, Egypt, Saudi Arabia, Turkey, EU, Russia, the US—as *actors* in the conflict, as parts of the conflict at its different layers, that is the local, regional, and global ones.

With this approach, this book departs from the Euro-centric tendency of the literature on the conflict specifically, but also of the International Relations literature more generally, which has come increasingly under critique for its Euro-centrism (Acharya and Buzan 2010). The latter is ever more at odds with a world that, while still dominated by the US, is becoming more multipolar and which the current IR toolbox fails to understand and address. The calls for a non-Eurocentric literature are therefore accumulating (Keukeleire and Lococq 2016; Onar and Nicolaïdis 2013). Euro-centrism, as Sebastian Conrad and Shalini Randeria have pointed out, can be understood as the more or less explicit assumption that the general historical development that is seen as characteristic for Western Europe and Northern America is a model according to which the histories and social formations of other societies can be measured and assessed (Conrad and Randeria 2013, 35). The IR literature, specifically the one that began to grow in the 1990s, has had the tendency to argue that the European, Western, and transatlantic worlds had succeeded to build Kantian cultures of friendship, while the Middle East was still dominated by Hobbesian—at best Lockean—cultures of enmity or competition. The eminent role of global powers in constituting such "cultures" in order to foster their own political interests and in being an intrinsic, even dominant, part of them in the past and present are hardly identified in IR.[1] Some of the literature from the field of history, specifically from postcolonial scholars, has studied the deep entanglement of Europe in the conflict. This book shows that this entanglement has not ended there, but that it has evolved since the end of the Second World War. It aims at being decentering by exploring how regional and global powers are interwoven in the conflict, how their role performances interacted in constituting its structure and meaning discursively. Through this historical and comparative approach the book also helps to understand dynamics in the Middle East that go beyond the conflict. It shows how the "peace process" script and its performance has set the scene for the current geopolitical rupture in the region and gives more nuance to evolving academic discussion on an implosion of order in the Middle East (Valbjørn and Bank 2012). The decentering approach of this book is not only pursued through a comparative approach that crosses what is often referred to as the Global South and the Global North but also through its conceptual, theoretical, and methodological framework.

How to Read This Book

This book is in two parts. The first four chapters lay out the decentering conceptual (chapter 1), theoretical (chapter 2) and methodological (chapter 3) framework, as well as the categories and key concepts (chapter

4) in the representation of the Palestine/Israel question extracted through grounded theory in the observed UN speeches and documents. The second part of the book consists of the two analytical chapters, which explore the role performances of the seven powers, as well as the meanings and web of relationships they have sustained (chapter 5), and the evolution of the authoritative international normative framing of the conflict at the United Nations (chapter 6). These two chapters identify dominant and alternative scripts, as well as "periods of continuity" in which these scripts were performed (orders) and "periods of ruptures" when they broke down and new scripts emerged.

In more detail, chapter 1 critically explores the state of the art of the literature to which this book relates and, based on this, conceptualizes the conflict, but not the Palestine/Israel question, which is left undefined since the book investigates inductively how the latter is framed by the key powers and in the UN. It argues that by referring to the conflict as the "Israeli-Palestinian conflict," some parts of the literature posits that Israel and Palestinians share equal responsibility for the situation (Collins 2012, 19–20), and downplays or obscures, or both, the reality of a disenfranchised population and the social, economic, and political structures that have ensured that Palestinians remain stateless. Indeed, this book also reveals how the "peace process" has obscured this project. To highlight the power asymmetry, it refers to the "Israel-Palestinian conflict," with one actor being a state and the other a stateless people being denied their individual and collective rights and sovereignty over the Palestinian territory.

Chapter 2 then proceeds with theoretical reflections. Given the high visibility of the conflict in the regional and global arenas, all powers engaged in the Middle East have an incentive to build their regional and global role identities through it, thus in turn contributing to its high visibility and defining its meaning on the international level. The roles they perform establish a configuration of relationships. For example, the Camp David Accords set up a specific structure of relations between the US, Israel, and Egypt, as well as indirectly also with Syria, Lebanon, or the Palestine Liberation Organization, and they bound these relationships with a specific meaning, a normative representation of the conflict. As these powers continuously performed their roles and associated meaning—that is, this script—into being, it remained resilient and constituted a regional "order."

Chapter 3 explains the methodological approach of this book, anchored in grounded theory and critical discourse analysis of all the speeches of representatives of the seven powers at the opening sessions of the United Nations General Assembly between 1948 and 2015, as well as of all United Nations General Assembly and UN Security Council resolutions on the conflict in the same time period. It also reflects on difficulties and challenges when doing research on this conflict.

Chapter 4 links the first to the second part of the book. It identifies categories and key concepts in the representation of the Palestine/Israel question extracted through grounded theory in the observed UN speeches and documents. These relate to the representation of the self, of Palestinians and Israelis, of the Palestine/Israel question, and of the role of the United Nations.

Chapter 5 inquires into the role performances of all seven powers to identify patterns as well as ruptures. It shows that two scripts existed alongside each other in the period from 1948 to 1967: a global one whereby the Palestine question was framed as a "refugee question" and was managed by the superpowers through the United Nations. They legitimized one state, while speaking only of individual refugee rights, not of the collective rights of the Palestinians. The regional script was spearheaded by Egypt, whereby the Palestine question was one of Western imperialism and Zionist colonialism and played a central role in pan-Arabism. The 1967 war was a rupture: the Arab script broke down and a transition period set in, in which a new script emerged, now produced by the US, which eventually became dominant in 1979. This script split the Arab world, which meant that its ability or willingness to produce an alternative script was undermined. Egypt, Saudi Arabia, Turkey, the EU, and Russia were all gradually absorbed into the US script, playing the roles foreseen for them in it, while excluding and marginalizing Iran. Instead of a comprehensive and inclusive security architecture guaranteed by the UN, the script centered around the US as the gravitational power with no mechanisms built in that could have outlived US power in the region. In terms of substance, the script silenced international law and Palestinian rights, ostensibly enabling the occupation to normalize to such a degree that a contiguous Palestinian state is hardly realizable anymore. The lynchpin has been the negotiations paradigm, namely that an occupied people has to negotiate its statehood with the occupying power, which has given Israel a de facto veto over a Palestinian state. The year 2011 is another rupture from the data analyzed in this book. Scripts need to be performed to sustain themselves and since the Arab uprisings, first Saudi Arabia and later on also the US and the EU have changed their performance. The US—the gravitational power of the "peace process" script—and Saudi Arabia are overperforming the script, while the EU seems to have almost stopped performing.

Chapter 6 then analyzes the authoritative international normative framing of the conflict at the United Nations. It shows that in the first period (1948–67), the framing at the UNGA and the UNSC reflected the position of the superpowers. This changed from 1967 onward. The General Assembly became increasingly independent and affirmative as a result of decolonialization. While the US has silenced discussion over its emerging peace process script in the UN Security Council through its vetoes, the UN General Assembly has contested its approach, by confirming the illegality of Israeli settlements and the rights of the Palestinian people, including the right to their own sovereign and independent state. Indeed, the UNGA has set up a powerful alternative script that, however, needs agency—and performance—to sustain itself. This could be seen in the 1990s, when such agency slowed down. This is changing again since the Arab uprisings, as evident in 2012 when a stark majority of the UNGA affirmed the Palestinian non-observer-member state bid.

The conclusions highlight the findings and reflect on them once more in light of the theoretical framework of this book. When looking at the performances of powerful states at the UN, we can see them as theatrical performances, which is also why the cover picture of this book shows the United Nations hall almost as a theater stage. This theatrical play of all actors involved has continued even during outright war, violence, and death on the ground. Rather than solving the conflict, it has bound the performing actors to a shared, collective performance, which has provided them with "meaningful order."

1

The State of the Art and a New Conceptualization of the Conflict

The literature on the Israel-Palestinian conflict is enormous and has emerged in various disciplines including political science, anthropology, economy, international law, political geography, and history. In light of its sheer size, a book would be needed to analyze this literature and the discursive directions it has taken. As Neil Caplan has pointed out, the academic literature itself has been placed in and contributed to specific narratives of the conflict. He shows how the naming and defining of the conflict is already the first foundational step in taking a position on it (Caplan 2011, 4), that is, calling it Zionist-Arab or Jewish-Arab and so stressing either a national or religious dimension, or Arab-Israeli/Israeli-Palestinian, so either focusing on the regional or local dimension of the conflict. It should be noted that Edward Said's book *Orientalism* (Said 1988) has been a defining moment in the literature, triggering a crucial and intense debate on Orientalist approaches toward the Middle East in general and the Israel-Palestinian conflict in particular. While a review of the whole latter literature lies outside the framework of this book, it will briefly revisit the strictly related International Relations literature on (1) the conflict's international dimension, including at the UN level, and (2) the role of powerful states in it.

Itamar Rabinovich has defined the conflict as a "cluster of distinct, interrelated conflicts," namely the core conflict between Israelis and Palestinians, the broader dispute between Israeli and Arab nationalism, a series of bilateral disputes between Israel and the neighboring Arab states, and, finally, a subset of broader international conflicts (Rabinovich 2012,

2–3). While this conceptualization is useful for this book in highlighting diverse—including the international—levels of the conflict, it remains nonetheless Euro-centric. It groups all Arab states into one unit, which does not reflect the complex reality in the Arab world, and sees them as part of the conflict, while it does not do the same for global powers in the region, as on the international level the definition speaks about "subsets" of conflicts, rather than the actors involved. This conceptualization, hence, sits in line with the larger literature that has presented the conflict as either Israeli-Palestinian or Arab-Israeli, while actors such as the US, Europe, and Russia have been presented as outside diplomatic actors to the conflict.

This type of Euro-centrism, it should be mentioned, is less prevalent in three seminal International Relations books that have dealt with the regional level of the conflict (Walt 1990; Barnett 1998; Hinnebusch 2003). In addition, Dietrich Jung has, for example, identified four dimensions of the conflict: the Israeli-Palestinian, Arab-Israeli, Jewish-Islamic, and colonial/Western dimension (Jung 2004, 14–15), thus including a non-Eurocentric dimension of the conflict. His edited volume focuses on the international paternity of the Palestine conflict, arguing that the "coordinates of the Palestine conflict have been shaped by the dynamics of overlapping international and regional state systems" (Jung 2004, 27). John Collins turns the question around and inquiries into "a Palestine that is globalized and a globe that is becoming Palestinized," arguing that "the same forces operating to produce Palatine's troubling realities are also operating globally in ways that have implications for all of us" (Collins 2012, ix–x).

Regarding the UN level, Nuseibeh (1982) has focused on "Palestine and the United Nations," and substantial chapters of Makdisi and Prashad (2016) deal with issues related to the Palestine question at the UN and have been an invaluable source for this book, which contributes to that literature with a comprehensive effort to reconstruct how key powers have discursively constructed the Palestine/Israel question at the United Nations. Indeed, with its discursive focus, this book also adds the international side to the rather substantive literature that has followed the discursive production of the conflict at the local level (Tessler 1990; Gavriely-Nuri 2008; McKinlay, McVittie, and Sambaraju 2012; Ish-Shalom 2011; Jaspal and Coyle 2014; Matthews 2011; Pappé and Hilal 2010; Berry and Philo 2006; Scham, Salem, and Pogrund 2005; Adwan and Bar-On 2004; Mitrani 2013) and less so on the regional level (Barnett 1998; Stein 2012).

Regarding powerful states and the conflict, on the US, seminal books have dealt with an analysis of the US as a broker (Quandt 2005; Kurtzer and Lasensky 2008), or with the domestic roots of its policy in Israel and Palestine (Spiegel 1985; Mearsheimer and Walt 2007), with only a few books seeing the US as actually centrally engaged in the conflict, not least through the provision of weapons (Chomsky 1999; Rashid Khalidi 2013; Aruri 2003). In contrast, Ussama Makdisi (2010) has explored the Arab faith in and then disenchantment with the US. Compared to the literature on the US, the literature on the USSR/Russia and the Israel-Palestinian conflict is much more limited, which is indicative of the role the literature assigns to Russia (and previously to the USSR) in the conflict. Galia Golan (1990), Andrej Kreutz (2007), and Joseph Heller (2016) have been leading the field here.

The EU has been assessed in light of its conflict resolution capacities (Yacobi and Newman 2008; Pace 2008; Diez and Pace 2011) and its normative power (Pace 2007, 2009; Gordon and Pardo 2015b, 2015a; Harpaz 2007; Harpaz and Shamis 2010; Persson 2017; Manners 2018), whereby a gap between the EU discourse on the conflict and its practices has been highlighted (Tocci 2009; Bicchi and Voltolini 2018; Bicchi 2014; Bouris 2014). One strain of this literature has investigated how internal politics (Voltolini 2015; Pardo and Gordon 2018) or memory (Pace and Bilgic 2017) determine the EU approach. Another strand of this literature has explored EU practices in the conflict, including practices of recognition (Azarova 2018; Bouris and Fernández-Molina 2018; Martins 2015; Serralvo 2016), multilateral practices (Tocci 2013; Mueller 2013; Musu 2010; Pace and Sen 2019; Asseburg 2003), and neoliberal peacebuilding (Pogodda et al. 2014), from a state-building perspective (Sayigh 2007; Bouris 2014), a security perspective (Bouris and İşleyen 2018; Tartir 2018; Tartir and Seidel 2018; Müller and Zahda 2018), and a development perspective (Wildeman 2018), in the framework of which some of its practices resemble colonial ones (Turner 2012, 2016). Indeed, increasingly the literature sees the EU as a direct participant in the conflict, as being complicit in the occupation (Cronin 2010; Huber 2018) or a central part in the management of its "borderlands," of which Palestine/Israel constitutes a particular part (Del Sarto 2015). This book contributes to the latter literature, as well.

Turning to the literature on Egypt and Saudi Arabia, in contrast to the other actors, they have been represented as part of the conflict in a wide array of books on what is called the "Arab-Israeli conflict" (Sela 1997; Laqueur and Rubin 2008). Interestingly, as Caplan points out, "While most discussions from 1948 to 1973 accurately speak of a wider Arab-Israeli conflict, in the period since 1973, and more so since 1993, many people came to see the conflict as being at its core a narrower Israeli-Palestinian conflict for sovereignty and self-determination on the same territory—albeit one with broader Arab dimensions" (Caplan 2011, 5). Thus, as soon as Egypt changed its role representation from a spearhead of the Arab cause to the spearhead of peace diplomacy, the literature tendentiously spoke of an end of the Arab-Israeli conflict (Sela 1997) and renamed the conflict from "Arab-Israeli" to "Israeli-Palestinian," again neglecting the key role that regional powers are still playing in the conflict. It also ignores the fact that there is much solidarity with Palestine in the societies of all Arab states, as became clear during the first and second waves of the Arab uprisings in which often a Palestinian flag was displayed. Furthermore, the literature has hardly explored the impact of the conflict on single Arab states, which has perpetuated the representation of the Arab world as a whole as being posed against Israel. A notable exception to this is the study of Ewan Stein (2012) on *Representing Israel in Modern Egypt*. While some studies on Israel and Egypt—specifically, the three wars between them as well as on peacemaking in Camp David—do exist (Gat 2012), no comparable book exists on Saudi Arabia's role in the conflict. Regarding Turkey, most research has gone into Turkish-Israeli relations (Bengio 2004), less into Turkish-Palestinian relations (Aras 2009) or Turkey's involvement in general. Iran has been mainly presented in the context of an Israeli-Iranian or US-Israeli-Iranian conflict (Rawshandil and Lean 2011), while Seyed Ali Alavi (2019) examines the pro-Palestinian stances of postrevolutionary Iran.

To conclude, what can be found is that parts of the literature on the role of powerful states in the conflict are characterized by three Euro-centric features. First, the US, Russia, and the EU are represented as outside diplomatic actors. This, it should be noted, reproduces the political self-representations of these actors and ignores their historically deep involvement in the conflict. It is thus unable to show the involvement of Europe, the US, and Russia in the conflict, or how—in turn—it might have affected them. Second, Arab states at large have been described as part of the conflict in one single unit, even though this representation has changed over time. Third, in contrast to the rather massive research on the US, the EU, and the Arab world as a group-like entity, single Arab states, as well as other global and regional powers including Russia, Iran, and Turkey, have been underresearched.

This book departs from this Euro-centrism in several ways. First, it sees all powers observed as *actors* in the conflict's global layer, and does not label them differently as broker, aggressor, and so forth. Rather, and second, it asks how these actors represent their identity through the conflict and attach meaning to it. Third, through its comparative perspective—so far unique in this literature as no similar comparative investigation exists—it can also dig deeper into which types of relationships have been built over time in the framework of which paradigmatic representations of the conflict have emerged; it asks how meaning and roles amount to a script that needs to be continuously performed to sustain itself. This script does not necessarily reflect what is happening on the ground, and may actually be meant to gloss over it. To capture both dimensions, this book makes, fourth, a conceptual distinction between the *Palestine/Israel question* and the *Israel-Palestinian conflict*. The first is discursively constructed and thus left undefined. Regarding the second, this book is based on a critical conceptual approach that will now be introduced.

Conflict is typically defined as "incompatibilities of positions," a definition that also assumes conflict as "normal, ubiquitous, and unavoidable" (Bercovitch, Kremenyuk, and Zartman 2008, 3). While such a definition might be applicable to many conflicts in the world, its application to the Israel-Palestinian conflict would—as John Collins (2012, 19) has pointed out—encourage "the belief that the relationship between Israel and the Palestinians is, in some basic ways, a relationship between two sides that share equal responsibility for the situation," glossing over the "great imbalance in the relative ability of each side to inflict violence." Furthermore, the conflict can also not be seen as a "normal" conflict since this downplays or obscures, or both, the reality of a disenfranchised population and the social, economic, and political structures that have ensured that Palestinians remain stateless. Thus, the Israel-Palestinian conflict is defined as an abnormal situation in which the individual and collective rights of Palestinians are systematically violated through an asymmetric power relationship as Israel is a state while the Palestinians have been occupied for more than fifty years by that state (therefore, the *Israel-Palestinian* conflict). This conceptualization of conflict implies that peace would then be defined as the normal relationship in which human dignity, the right to self-determination, and all individual and collective human rights, are protected.

The asymmetric power relations that run through the local-regional-global levels will now shortly be further discussed. Power is defined as "the production, in and through social relations, of effects that shape the capacities of actors to determine their circumstances" (Barnett and Duvall 2005, 39). Based on this definition, Michael Barnett and Raymond Duvall developed a "taxonomy of power" with four types of power:

> The first type is power as relations of interaction of direct control by one actor over another—Compulsory Power; the second is the control actors exercise indirectly over others through diffuse relations of interaction—Institutional Power; the third is the constitution of subjects' capacities in direct structural relation to one another—Structural Power; and the fourth is the socially diffuse production of subjectivity in systems of meaning and signification—Productive Power. (Barnett and Duvall 2005, 43)

We can find diverse configurations of these types of power at different layers, involving different actors, in different venues. The *local layer* takes place in venues located in the geography of what had been designated by the League of Nations as the mandate of Palestine, including, for example, checkpoints, demarcations, parliaments, or courts with its actors including local politicians, judges, soldiers, and so on, but also states that provide, for example weapons, information, or aid to these actors. Types of interaction on this level include violent (military acts, state and nonstate terror, torture and other systematic violation of human rights), economic (trade, finance, currency, taxes, labor), social (people-to-people), legal (court decisions), or political (negotiations, security coordination) interactions. The local layer is characterized by a stark power asymmetry between the stateless Palestinians and Israel as a state in the pre-1967 borders and as the occupying power of the Palestinian territory. There have been several turning points for today's power structure. The 1948 war had a major impact on the size of the territory originally assigned by the UN's partition plan to the State of Israel. Moreover, about 760,000 Arab-Palestinians were evicted by Israel in a matter of a few days and then forcibly denied the right to return. There were also twenty thousand Jews expelled by Arab militias from Hebron, Jerusalem, Jenin, and Gaza. With the 1967 war, the Israeli occupation of the West Bank, including East Jerusalem, and the Gaza Strip began, and—as Neve Gordon has pointed out—for "the first time since the 1948 War, one . . . power ruled all of Mandatory Palestine" (Gordon 2008, 4). The next significant change for today's structure came with the Oslo

Accords when the responsibility for the Palestinian population under occupation, but not for the Palestinian territory, was outsourced to the Palestinian Authority (PA) and in some respects also to the international community.[1] While negotiations between Israel and the PA were ongoing over decades, the occupation continued to expand as both a legal and territorial structure of domination (Newman 1989, 1996; Weizman 2012; Pallister-Wilkins 2015; Parsons and Salter 2008). First, there is compulsory power—direct control of one actor over another—through the occupation, an example of which is the military court system and its regime of arrest, treatment, access to justice, sentencing, release, and imprisonment, which allows Israel to administer direct control over (rather than providing justice to) Palestinians in the West Bank,[2] which particularly also applies to the economic area (Roy 1995). Second, there is institutional power as relations of interaction between Israel as an occupying power and the Palestinians are regulated through the application of diverse legal regimes in the Occupied Palestinian Territory (OPT) by Israel, whereby it operates at least four different legal regimes in the whole area under its control in a situation that can be described as apartheid (ESCWA 2017). In the West Bank, specifically, it applies a mixed military/civil regime that discriminates between settlers and Palestinians whereby Palestinians do not enjoy the legal protections accorded to settlers (Tilley 2012, 66–69).[3] Third, there is structural power in the constitution of the Palestinians as occupied subjects and Israel as the occupying power, which also involves a process of normalization that Abdel-Sattar Qasim described as the process of building an "ordinary (or ostensibly ordinary) relationship between two sides that have different powers, in a way that the weaker will be acting on the service of the stronger" (Salem 2005). Specifically, the Palestinian Authority has increasingly become invested in this normalization process, arguably acting more in the interest of the occupation forces than the Palestinian population (Tartir 2017). Finally, there is productive power in so far as the occupation is represented as temporary and as the Palestinian Authority is represented as a state-like entity, thus being perceived as outside of the occupation rather than subject and functional to it, that is, inside of what Ariella Azoulay and Adi Ophir have referred to as a "one state condition" whereby, over the past 50 years, the occupation has evolved from a "temporary situation" to a "regime" where "Israelis and Palestinians have been governed since 1967 by the same ruling power" (Azoulay and Ophir 2012, 12) in the whole area of what had once been Mandatory Palestine (as well as the illegally annexed Syrian Golan

Heights). The productive power of an imaginary Palestinian state is also well evidenced in the book of Michelle Pace and Somdeep Sen (2019) that shows how stateless Palestinians and internationals are investing in the theatrical performance of a Palestinian state. Indeed, in many respects, this book is complementary to Pace and Sen's research endeavor as it evidences the performance of the script by international and regional powers over the past decades. Furthermore, this productive power directly links to the international level. As Mark LeVine has pointed out,

> The powerful contemporary role of colonial discourse (as generated by the policies of the Israeli government in the Occupied Territories) and imperialism (as epitomized by the economic and strategic policies of the United States, major European countries, and international institutions such as the World Bank in the Middle East more broadly) has meant that today, as a century ago, the 'West's' promises of freedom, prosperity and modernity remain an impossible dream, one that recedes farther into the distance the closer people think they are getting to it. . . . This illusion remains hard to spot. (LeVine 2009, 7)

The *regional layer*'s venue includes borders, border crossings, embassies, or regional organizations such as the Arab League or the Organization of Islamic Cooperation, while its actors include heads of states, ambassadors, armies, and nonstate actors. Interactions can be violent ("traditional" warfare), economic (trade, investment), political (diplomacy), or social (people-to-people). Power on the regional level is diffused in a more ambiguous way than on the local level. The regional security complex (Buzan and Wæver 2003) has been dominated by the US and Israel as the overshadowing military powers whose compulsory power has to a large degree been further boosted by Egypt's separate peace with Israel. However, in the wake of the US-led Iraq invasion, the assertiveness of other powers in the region has been growing, including Russia, Iran, and Hezbollah. Nonetheless, Israel's compulsory power remains evident in the continuing occupation of the Syrian Golan Heights. In terms of institutional power, it should be noted that Israel is not part of regional organizations such as the Arab League or the Organization of Islamic Cooperation due to their nonnormalization policy in the face of Israel's ongoing occupation; the effectiveness of these institutions has been debated (Barnett and Solingen 2007; Pinfari 2009). Even though the nonnormalization policy of the Arab League is increasingly relaxing as Saudi Arabia and Egypt are in a de facto alliance with Israel against Iran, Israel remains socially and economically more closely integrated with Europe and the US than with the Middle East (Huber 2017). The Palestine Liberation Organization—initially established by the Arab League to control the Palestinians—became independent after the 1967 war. Fatah, as well as other Palestinian actors such as Hamas, have ever since been maneuvering through regional politics in trying to find alliances and support. In terms of structural power, as this book argues, self-images of key powers in the region—Saudi Arabia and Egypt—have changed in a way that has enabled the so-called Camp David Order. One could even go one step further than this book and analyze the Camp David Order as a form of imperialism as Johan Galtung (1971) has conceptualized it.[4] Finally, in terms of productive power, it should be noted that the Palestine/Israel question has been a leading issue in regional politics and has deeply influenced regional dynamics, due to the importance the issue holds in what Marc Lynch has termed a suprastate public space (Lynch 1999, 2006) in the Arab world where supra/trans-state identities such as Arabism or Islam remain important (Hinnebusch 2003, 299). The issue, therefore, played a key role during the so-called Arab Cold War (Kerr 1971) and continues to play a role today in what Morten Valbjørn and André Bank have termed the "New Arab Cold War" (Valbjørn and Bank 2012) or in the continuing uprisings in the Arab world where people have voiced support for the Palestinians. This book also adds to this perspective, since it highlights how the continuing role performance of Saudi Arabia and Egypt within the Camp David Order has kept the US script of a Middle East Peace Process alive despite its obvious failure to achieve peace for forty years.

On the international layer, the main venue has been the United Nations, with the key actors being heads of state/foreign ministers/ambassadors and the main instruments economic (so-called development aid), political (diplomacy), and legal (in the confines of international law, involving the International Court of Justice (ICJ) and the International Criminal Court (ICC). Also at this layer power is unequally distributed. There is compulsory power, as some members (notably the US and the EU member states) are main financial contributors to the UN and can threaten the UN and its agencies with the withdrawal of these contributions. The US has, for example, used this power as a punitive measure when the UNESCO (United Nations Educational, Scientific and Cultural Organisation) accepted the PLO as a full member in 2011. In 2017, the US and Israel exited UNESCO. There is institutional power, as some members are veto powers (US, China, Russia, France, UK) in the United Nations Security Council while about sixty UN member states have never been part of the UNSC. There is structural power, as Israel has been a member state since 1949, while Palestine is not. This not only means that Palestine lacks the ability to vote and to propose resolutions (lack of institutional power), but—despite being recognized by the majority of the international community (Bouris and Huber 2017)—it lacks recognition as a state by the UN, mainly by Western nations, the majority of which deny a Palestinian right to statehood and make the latter subject to negotiations, ultimately giving Israel a veto over it. The PLO received permanent observer status at the General Assembly in 1975; in 2011, its application for full membership in the UN was blocked by the US (an application for full membership needs a two-thirds majority in the UNSC and the UNGA and can be vetoed in the UNSC); and in 2012, it received nonmember observer state status as a result of UNGA Resolution 67/19. UNGA Resolution 67/19 enabled the PLO to join treaties and UN agencies, as well as the International Criminal Court, which it did in 2012, initiating a proceeding against Israeli individuals. Finally, there is productive power. The dominant international normative framing of the Palestine/Israel question is staked out at the United Nations through UNSC and UNGA resolutions, but also in the activities of other UN agencies, which have concrete effects on the conflict at all levels. Some states are more powerful than others in terms of productive power. In 2017, for example, the UN's Economic and Social Commission for Western Asia (ESCWA) published a report that argued that Israel had established "an apartheid regime that oppresses and dominates the Palestinian people as a whole," suggesting that the UNGA should seek an advisory opinion from the International Court of Justice "as to whether the means used by Israel to maintain control over the Palestinian people amount to the crime of apartheid" (Economic and Social Commission for Western Asia 2017). Under pressure mainly from the US, ESCWA was forced to remove the report from its homepage, as a result of which UN Undersecretary-General and Executive Secretary for ESCWA Rima Khalaf stepped down in protest to what she perceived as censorship. Thus, some states have more productive power at the United Nations than others. This book, furthermore, shows how the UN has been sidelined in the conflict by the US, which in the framework of the Middle East Peace Process has produced a script on the conflict that prioritizes bilateral negotiations while silencing Palestinian rights.

2

Theoretical Background

Roles, Meanings, and Scripts

All powers observed in this book have built specific role identities on the Palestine/Israel question at the UN level, not only setting up webs of relationships but also attaching meaning to it. Indeed, theory on role identity is helpful in shedding light on the agency of the seven powers involved and how they might have perpetuated conflict.

Role theory entered the field of foreign policy studies in the 1970s with Kalevi Holsti's pathbreaking work on national role conceptions (Holsti 1970). For Holsti, such role conceptions could explain general foreign policy choices and were rather stable, being mainly rooted in the domestic and cultural/historical context. This was contested by realists who saw role identities as an ephemeral phenomenon that would change with the distribution of power in the international system. Role theory received a further boost in the 1990s in foreign policy analysis. Sebastian Harnisch defines roles as "social positions . . . that are constituted by ego and alter expectations regarding the purpose of an actor in an organized group. . . . Whereas some roles are constitutive to the group as such, e.g. recognized member of the international community, other roles or role sets are functionally specific, e.g. balancer, initiator" (Harnisch 2011, 8). Role theory distinguishes conceptually between

1. self-defined role conceptions (Holsti 1970), normative expectations that the role beholder expresses toward itself (Aggestam 2006), or "an actor's perception of his or her

position vis-à-vis others . . . and the perception of the role expectations of others . . . as signaled through language and action" (Harnisch 2011, 8);

2. role performance, that is, attitudes, decisions, and actions taken to implement role conceptions (Holsti 1970), or actual foreign-policy behavior in terms of characteristic patterns of decisions and actions undertaken in specific situational contexts (Aggestam 2006);

3. role prescriptions from the other and the external environment (Holsti 1970) or role expectation that other actors prescribe and expect the role-beholder to enact (Aggestam 2006), and

4. position, that is, a system of role prescriptions (Holsti 1970) or role sets, that is, a general role that includes several specific roles (Aggestam 2006, 17–20).

Roles, so defined, are rather stable, and change occurs either internally as a result of role conflict when dominant role conceptions within a role set are incompatible, or externally, "when the conditions and context within which they were originally formulated change" (Aggestam 2006, 23). Role theory has thus developed to examine not only the internal but also the external foundations of roles. However, the distinction between role conception and role behavior might be difficult to uphold as the voicing of a specific role conception is already a role behavior, not least since it not only reproduces an identity but also shapes the perception of the self by the other.

Besides the field of foreign policy analysis, International Relations as a larger field became increasingly invested in role theory, as the concept of role identity became key in constructivist work. While Holsti had looked at the internal roots of identity, constructivists looked at identity in a relational way. The paradigmatic definition of Ronald Jepperson, Alexander Wendt, and Peter Katzenstein, for example, maintains that identity "comes from social psychology, where it refers to the images of individuality and distinctiveness ('selfhood') held and projected by an actor and formed (and modified over time) through relations with significant 'others.' Thus the term (by convention) references mutually constructed and evolving images of self and other" (Jepperson, Wendt, and Katzenstein 1996, 59). Constructivists also examined the larger constitutive effects of role identities on the international system. In his seminal book *Social Theory of International Politics*, Alexander Wendt identified "different kinds of roles in terms of which states represent Self and Other," concretely three of them (enemy, rival, and friend) that are constituted by and constitute three cultures of international politics, namely Hobbesian, Lockean, and Kantian (Wendt 1999). As already elaborated in the literature review of this book, this theory has lent itself to Euro-centric approaches to the study of the Middle East.

Besides constructivism, critical theory has contributed substantially to theory on identity, but much of the work in this respect has been rooted in an inside-out perspective. Thus, while critical, this literature has in a way perpetuated a Euro-centric perspective that neglects the intersubjective side of identity and the impact the outside has on it. David Campbell, in his seminal work on *Writing Security*, has argued that foreign policy is a "political practice that makes 'foreign' certain events and actors," and is thus a "specific sort of boundary-producing political performance" (Campbell 2013, 69). For Campbell, therefore, state identity is understood as the "outcome of exclusionary practices." Thus, identity is all internally rooted and cannot explain how the other has impacted on the self—the other remains conceptually excluded. This sits, in fact, in a specific hierarchic image of self and other: it is highly critical of this image, but it cannot escape it, as it is not conceptually open to another image of what could be termed an "entangled relationship."

What is notable indeed about all these concepts of identity is that they are tendentiously placed in a specific hierarchic image of a relationship. Carol Gilligan in her pathbreaking book *In a Different Voice* has described two images of self and other. The first image—hierarchy—places the world in relation to the self whereby the self is defined through separation from the other. Thus, the sense of self in the former is organized around maintaining the position of the self at the top of an hierarchy whereby the rise to power of the other is seen as a threat. This view is rather deeply entrenched in realist theory, but it can also be found in liberal theory, constructivism, and critical theory. In this image, while aggression is always present, disagreement can (and should) be mediated through systems of logic and law (Gilligan 1993, 29). Thus, the self is separated from the other, whereby the other takes the form of what George Herbert Mead has called a "generalized other" (Mead 1967), that is, the expectations toward the self and the other in a shared social system. In contrast to this, the second image raised by

Gilligan—a web—places the self in relation to the world whereby the *self is delineated through connection to the other* (Gilligan 1993, 35). As a result, the sense of the self is "organized around being able to make, and then to maintain, affiliations and relationships," which implies that the "disruption of an affiliation is perceived not just as a loss of a relationship but as something closer to a total loss of self" (Miller 1987, 83). In this view disagreements are mediated through *communication in a relationship* (Gilligan 1993, 29). This image "fosters the development of the empathy and sensitivity necessary for taking the role of 'the particular other' " (Gilligan 1993, 11). As Gilligan has pointed out,

> As the top of the hierarchy becomes the edge of the web and as the center of a network of connection becomes the middle of a hierarchical progression, each image marks as dangerous the place which the other defines as safe. Thus the images of hierarchy and web inform different modes of assertion and response: the wish to be alone at the top and the consequent fear that others will get too close; the wish to be at the center of connection and the consequent fear of being too far out on the edge. (Gilligan 1993, 62)

The image of web is based on a "relational ontology which understands human existence in the context of social and personal relations," as we are "literally constituted by the relationships of which we are part" (Robinson 2006, 222).

Two academics, Jennifer Mitzen and Janice Bially Mattern, have begun to develop theory on role identity in a way that sits in such an image of relationships. Mitzen has pointed out that roles "locate and define the individual with respect to a social context," while role identities "are internalized roles, aspects of an actor's sense of self that reflect the appropriation of roles and motivate behavior (the 'I')." Role identity so defined employs the notion of *identity as a social relationship*—it is "formed and sustained relationally" and "depends on others do be realized" (Mitzen 2006, 357). She further argued that routinized relationships, even if dangerous, provide actors with ontological security, and applied this to the case of the Israel-Palestinian conflict, arguing that during and after Oslo, it was "easier to act on old, concrete fears than on new, untested hopes" and to "break with routines would be fraught with ontological fear" (Mitzen 2006, 363). This approach, it should be noted, still centers on one side (the self) of the agency and so cannot really account for the relationship of both (or several) sides. From a decentering perspective, an approach is needed that takes all sides into consideration.

What comes closest to such an approach maybe Janice Bially Mattern's work on identity, which she sees as a *relationship in process*, arguing that the web of relationships through which identity is constituted and which it constitutes is a source of order in international relations. International identities "amount to knowledge shared among states—intersubjective knowledge—about their situation relative to each other," including positive (friends) and negative (enemies) bonds. Rather than being fixed, "identity is a relationship that is always in process, whether that means emerging, evolving, or breaking down. . . . Crucially, whenever states are collectively involved in the process of an international identity (no matter what its content), they are also collectively implicated in an international order" (Mattern 2004, 4). She shows how after the breakdown of identity (and thus of a relationship) during crises, the latter can be reproduced if actors choose to do so. Or it cannot be reproduced, which would then lead to disorder until new identities and webs of relationships are established. As opposed to constructivist accounts, where identity is formed and maintained through socialization and learning, this view sees identity as formed and maintained through language (Mattern 2004, 71) and is also open to bringing purposeful action by political actors back in. Such purposeful action can be assessed through different perspectives, including an "Austinian move" that sheds light on the performative potential of language, a "Foucauldian move" regarding the implications of such language, and a "Derridarean move" that opens up space for alternatives (Diez 2014).

Mattern's approach can also be applied to study multiple relationships (instead of only bilateral ones) as in the case of this book. For the powers observed here the Palestine/Israel question—due to its internationalization (Busse 2017) and in turn contributing to it—has become an ideal outlet to project certain images of themselves onto the international arena by performing certain roles. For all these powers, the conflict has—to paraphrase Roxanne Doty—"provided the context within which identities have been constructed and reconstructed. In the process of attempting to formulate policy, resolve problems, and come to terms with various issues, subjects and objects themselves have been constructed" (Doty 1996, 2). This has been valid, for example, not only for Iran or for Egypt, for which the relationship with Israel became "an inextricable part of its collective imagination and self-perception (Stein 2012, 23), but also for the European Community, later the European Union, for whom the Palestine/Israel question has been one of the first fields of common foreign policy action, and thus even constitutive for its actorness in foreign policy in the first place. By mobilizing a specific identity through foreign policy discourse at the United Nations, actors not only reproduce it but also attach meaning to the conflict. They construct the conflict in terms of who are its actors, what it is about, how it should be solved, and through which program of action.

Such role performances are, however, not to be seen only singularly. Rather, together, they (re)produce specific webs of relationships bound by meaning through a dominant framing that might sideline or silence conflicting or competing framings. This whole setting could also be described as a theatrical performance (Pace and Sen 2019) as each actor performs not only a specific role but, through performing together, all actors also produce a common script. *These scripts define an international "theatrical play" on the Palestine/Israel question, denoting paradigmatic meaning on what that question is about, how it should be solved, and what the role of the observed international powers and the UN in that play should be.* Such scripts do not necessarily respond to any "reality" on the ground, but rather produce a certain reality. *They bind the performing actors to a shared, collective performance, which—if continuous—amounts to order. As soon as actors in the script under-, over-, or disperform, the script—and with it the order it implied—breaks down.* In such periods of rupture, we might witness discursive struggles on new scripts.[1]

This book takes the UN as the main venue for observing all these dynamics. The UN most authoritatively embodies the "international community" as an imagined community (Allen 2016, 59)[2] and serves as the "theater" (in terms of venue) where actors perform their roles. Investigating the performances of the seven powers thus unveils not only the role identity they produce and meaning they attach to the Palestine/Israel question, but also patterns across these powers and time, that is, patterns of dominant meaning attached and webs of relationship set up. Dominant meaning, however, does not only exist through the performance of the seven powerful states observed. Most authoritatively, it resides normatively in UN resolutions, most evident in landmark resolutions such as 181 (partition plan), 242 (land for peace), or 67/19 (Palestine as nonmember observer state) with concrete effects on the conflict. As Richard Falk has pointed out, the UN is a "relevant arbiter of the legitimacy and illegitimacy of competing claims" and the "UN is a crucial player in legitimacy war settings, as it has great influence on international public opinion and global discourse by the way in which it processes claims of right and wrong" (Falk 2016, 88, 91). Thus, following the exploration of role performances and the script they amount to, the book contrasts this with an investigation into the authoritative normative framing in the form of UN resolutions, as well as the discursive struggles around them, which also involve states other than the seven powers and can therefore serve to explore potential alternative scripts, as well. Thus, this theoretical lens ensures an approach that is decentering as it allows an accounting for the observation of continuities, ruptures, and alternatives.

3

Methodology

This book is based on a rather complex analytical approach to study the international dimension of the Israel-Palestinian conflict, conceptualized as being produced by scripts. Through their discursive practices, states not only define the conflict and produce their role identities but also a web of relationships bound by a dominant normative framing of the Palestine/Israel question. The methodology needs to be able to capture this complex definition. Furthermore, the book is also based on a comparative approach in terms of time and actors, covering a rather extensive historical period (1948–today) and a substantial number of actors, namely three global (Europe, Russia, US) and four regional powers (Egypt, Iran, Saudi Arabia, Turkey). Grounded theory is a methodology that is able to capture this analytical and empirical complexity by developing theory closer to empirical data. Furthermore, grounded theory sits well with a decentering analytical approach. While the calls for decentering the study of IR (Nayak and Selbin 2010; Tickner and Blaney 2012; Acharya and Buzan 2010), of democracy (Morozov 2013), of EU foreign policy (Onar and Nicolaïdis 2013), or of the Arab world (Huber and Kamel 2016) have increased, Keukeleire and Lecocq (2016) have pointed out that this program has not yet been translated into a systematic decentered analytical praxis; grounded theory could be a first step in this respect.

Grounded theory is the "discovery of theory from data systematically obtained from social research" (Glaser and Strauss 1999, 2). Theory is derived from data in a process that moves from describing data, to their conceptual ordering into categories with properties and dimensions, and, finally, to developing theory whereby all steps stand in close relationship to each other. This book is guided especially by the research techniques developed by Corbin and Strauss (1997), as their approach is sensitive to the agency-structure divide, which is useful when dealing with a concept such as "role identity" that bridges structure and agency in International Relations. Grounded theory, as Juliet Corbin and Anselm Strauss have pointed out, allows the researcher to be aware "of the interrelationships among conditions (structure), action (process), and consequences" (Corbin and Strauss 1997, 9–10). Grounded theory can also be combined with discourse analysis as a method. Discourse analysis is both a theory and a transdisciplinary method that has gained in prominence in IR since the 1990s. A variety of diverse approaches exist (Dijk 2011; Wodak and Meyer 2009), whose common ground is that discourse is not just a description of reality, but "the layer of reality where meaning is produced and distributed" (Waever 2009, 199). Discourses—systems of meaning production—"provide the categories through which the world is understood" (Rowley and Weldes 2012, 181). This chapter describes how grounded theory and discourse analysis were operationalized in terms of research design, samples, and analytical procedure. It closes with reflections on the positionality of a researcher on the Israel-Palestinian conflict.

3.1. Research Design

In light of the vast empirical data available on the issue observed in this book, a choice to limit the analysis to a specific set of data had to be taken. This study has been informed by the method of Lene Hansen who developed a systematic approach for research designs in discourse analysis, focused on the study subject, the numbers of selves observed, the intertextual model, the temporal perspective, and the number of events (Hansen 2006, 66–73).

In terms of the actors observed, this study has applied three criteria based on the theoretical and conceptual framework adopted in this study. It focuses on those actors who, first, have been or are employing the Palestine/Israel question in building their international role; second, had or have considerable compulsory, institutional, structural, or productive power in the Middle East to give sufficient weight to their representation of the conflict; and third, have a voice in the international discursive struggle on the Palestine/Israel question. This clearly applies to three global powers—the US, the USSR/Russia, and the EC/EU—and four regional powers—Egypt, Iran, Saudi Arabia, and Turkey. It excludes weaker regional states (Syria), emerging powers that are only recently taking a somewhat more exposed position and therefore a role on the conflict (China), emerging powers that do take positions rooted in their own experience but seek to assume less of a role in the region (South Africa), or nonstate actors that are building a role identity on the conflict, but play less of a role in the international discursive struggle over it (Hezbollah).

It should be noted here that while Egypt, Iran, the USSR/ Russia, Saudi Arabia, Turkey, and the US are all states, the EC/EU is not. The latter has evolved substantially over the time period observed here and has been diversely defined as a quasi-federal state (Sbragia 1992), a "multiperspectival polity" (Ruggie 1993), a "postmodern state" (Caporaso 1996), a "multilevel polity" (Hooghe and Marks 2001), a "fusionist state" (Wessels 1997), a "hybrid polity" (Manners and Whitman 2003), or "a polycentric 'polity' possessing a multilevel governance 'regime' " (Bellamy and Castiglione 2004). Following Jupille and Caporaso (1998), actorness in foreign policy can be assessed with four criteria: recognition, authority, autonomy, and cohesion. The EC/EU has been recognized as a distinctive actor in the conflict, even if reluctantly by the US and Israel (Harpaz 2007; Harpaz and Shamis 2010). The EC/EU has over time also developed the legal capacity to act on the conflict.[1] The EC/EU also developed its autonomy to act, as evident in the leading role the High Representative plays in the Middle East Quartet, as well as directive policies such as the differentiation policy mandated by the European Council. What the EU mainly lacks on the conflict up until today is cohesiveness as member states are prone to undermine EU policy (Pardo and Gordon 2018). However, as Tanja Börzel et al. argue, cohesiveness is not necessarily an ingredient for assessing actorness. "Whether an actor pursues an inconsistent and incoherent foreign policy is an empirical question, not a definitional criterion" (Börzel, Dandashly, and Risse 2015, 12). They propose capability as a fourth criterion, and, again, the EU has acquired most of the traditional foreign policy tools, as well as specific EU ones that nation-states do not possess (Smith 2003, 67; Keukeleire and MacNaughtan 2008, 33).

Furthermore, if one scratches beyond the surface, it becomes clear that the EU today might be more similar in actorness to the US (where foreign policy, specifically also concerning the Middle East, has been subject to virulent infighting between the White House, the Department of State, the Pentagon, and the Congress) than to an autocratic and centralized decision-making system such as the Egyptian one would be to the US. Furthermore, just like all the other states observed here, the EC and then the EU have in fact tried to build foreign policy actorness on the Palestine/Israel question (see chapter 5), and this has defined its identity, its relationship as an actor to the other powers, as well as the conflict as such. Finally, in terms of widening and deepening, the EC/EU has gone through a substantial change, but so has the USSR/Russia. By conceptual and theoretical choice, this book focuses on role performances at the international level, and while it does contextualize these in domestic developments, *the focus is on how these role performances have given meaning to the Palestine/Israel question, building up a script on it*; thus—by and large—state and state-like entities are treated as black boxes. However, the book also provides the local and regional context when presenting each case study.

In terms of the intertextual model, this book observed the official discourse at the United Nations, and the UNGA and the UNSC specifically. The United Nations was chosen because it has been the key international venue of the conflict where states not only perform their international role identities but where the *international authoritative framing of the conflict is established normatively*, notably in UNSC and UNGA resolutions. Within the UN, the UNSC and the UNGA are the main organs responsible for decision-making. This is not to argue that official discourse and debate in other venues—for example, in the United Nations Human Rights Council—are not relevant or do not influence the international normative framing of the conflict. They do not, however, enjoy the same decision-making powers as the UN's two central organs. At the UNGA, all speeches of the respective seven country representatives at the annual opening sessions were analyzed, as well as all resolutions passed on the conflict. At the UNSC, all resolutions—passed or vetoed—were analyzed, as well as the debate surrounding specifically the resolutions that had been vetoed since, as opposed to the passed resolutions, they indicate dissension and debate in the international arena. All these documents were analyzed inductively through a four-step procedure, that is, categorization, open coding, conceptualizing, and axial coding (see below in detail on analytical procedure).

In terms of the temporal perspective, the time period was 1947–48 until 2015 (at times extended up until 2018). This choice excludes the time period before 1947–48 in which milestone decisions regarding the conflict had been pursued at the UN and the League of Nations. However, it has been chosen as the year in which the structure of the conflict changed decisively locally with the Nakba and the founding of the State of Israel; regionally with the loss of the 1948 war; and internationally as the UK dropped and the United Nations assumed responsibility for the Mandate for Palestine. Furthermore, by covering more than eighty years, this study is able to take account of ruptures and continuities (Walker 1993) in the reconfiguration of roles of the observed actors in the conflict, as well as the dominant international framing of it.

Finally, in terms of the number of events, the analysis focused on those parts of the speeches that were dedicated to the conflict (even though other parts of the speeches were taken into consideration) and on resolutions that strictly dealt with the conflict in its local dimension, that is, the geography of today's Israel and the Occupied Palestinian Territory, rather than on resolutions related to Israel and Egypt, Israel and Lebanon, Israel and Iran, or Israel, Syria, and the occupied Syrian Golan Heights. This choice was taken in line with the larger conceptual approach of this study to the conflict. This research design is visualized in figure 3.1.

3.2. Sample

The sample includes all speeches of the seven powers at the opening of the United Nations General Assembly in September each year from 1948 through 2015. In terms of the participants, this study focuses on

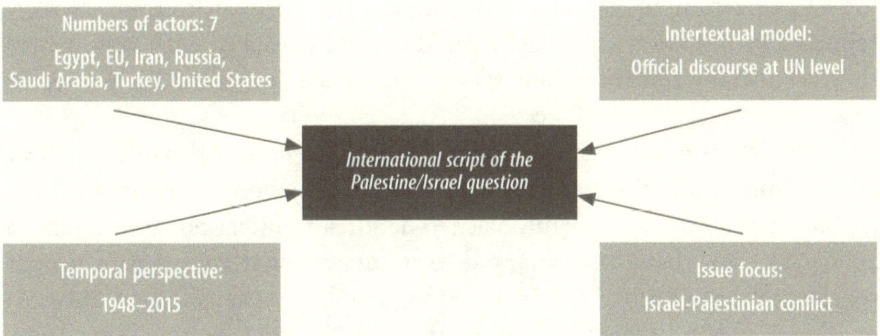

Figure 3.1. Research design.

representatives of states. It is useful to conceive of such political actors as nodes (Diez 2001, 17) between the local, regional, and global discursive contexts. For all these representatives, as Mor Mitrani has pointed out, the UNGA—and the opening sessions specifically—is an "arena in which states present their stands," serving as "the formal and broader public sphere where members . . . gather in order to communicate and deliberate on issues and matters that concern them as states and which they seek to govern" (Mitrani 2017, 10).[2] These speeches have the general intention of giving a concise representation of the role understanding of a country, as well as its related direction for action in terms of key international issues for the year to come. The opening debates of the UNGA each year give all member states, as well as some nonstate actors such as the Palestine Liberation Organization (PLO), the opportunity to address all other member states. The speeches observed in the framework of this book were either by the ambassadors of the countries at the United Nations or by the foreign ministers or heads of states. In the initial decades of the UN, heads of states came to the opening session of the UNGA at specific occasions, as for example, Egyptian resident Gamal Abdel Nasser in 1960 or President Anwar el Sadat in 1975. Since the end of the Cold War, the speeches have, however, been increasingly made by heads of states or foreign ministers. In the case of the US, for example, since 1990, it has always been the president who came to the opening session and who was only in singular cases substituted by the secretary of state. The same applies to Iran since the Mahmoud Ahmadinejad period (previously mainly represented by the foreign minister). The opening speeches at the UNGA aim at several diverse discursive arenas. They speak to the other member states at the United Nations and therewith also to those states that are members of regional organizations such as the Arab League or the Organization of Islamic Cooperation. They are furthermore widely reported in the media, primarily the domestic media of each state where they are usually reprinted, but also in the international media in specific cases.

These speeches therefore meet Hansen's criteria of providing a clear articulation of identities and policies and being widely read and attended to, thus having the formal authority to define a political position (Hansen 2006, 76). They have the potential to influence what counts as a proper representation within a particular foreign policy issue (Hansen 2006, 6) on the domestic, regional, and international levels. At the same time, they need to take into account the limits that the discourse on all these levels presents for their own articulation. On the international level, while there is a discursive struggle on the conflict, some positions are "shamed" by walkouts, as happened for example in 2011 when the delegations of France, Germany, the UK, and the US walked out during Iranian president Mahmoud Ahmadinejad's speech. Beyond the "international community," state representatives also speak to their regional peers at the UNGA. Notable in this respect has been, for example, Egypt, which sought to justify its peace treaty with Israel at the UNGA as it was expelled from the Arab League and therefore deprived of highlighting its discursive position in that forum. Other actors—the EU, for example—can similarly represent their positions to other states from the region through the UNGA. Finally, state representatives also need to keep their domestic audiences in mind. It would, as Hansen has pointed out, be politically unsavvy "for politicians to articulate foreign policy without any concern for the representations found within the wider public sphere as they attempt to present their policies as legitimate to their wider constituencies" (Hansen 2006, 6–7). This applies to the democracies and autocracies observed in this book, as the Palestine/Israel question is internationally and regionally highly exposed. Representation of the conflict and the role of the self at the United Nations should, therefore, not only be seen as seated in the domestic discursive context, but they are an active part of it; they (re) produce domestic discursive positions.

All speeches have been accessed at the UN portal in English. As a standard, the speeches are delivered in the respective languages and the delegation then provides the English version to the United Nations. This raises the problem of translation. Languages are situated in a culture, represent specific "shared lifeworlds," and have linguistic and epistemological codes. Languages often include words that cannot be properly translated into another language. The logical conclusion of this is that communication in the UNGA is impossible with actors speaking in different sign systems, and thus not able to truly communicate with each other. However, one can assume that over the course of the existence of the UN, such a shared lifeworld has evolved to some degree, even if it might be somewhat hampered through the translation issue. Therefore, while the issue of translation is problematic, it remains an issue that is inherent to this research. That also means that it remains unresolved in and at the same time addressed through this research.

Another issue was that not all speeches of the seven powers in the time period 1948–2015 are available. A specifically difficult case was the

EC/EU in this respect, as it came into being in the observed time period only. Thus, in this case, speeches were observed only from 1958 onward, when the Council of the European Community came into being. From 1958 to 1976, the speeches of the two countries that presented the presidency of the Council in that year (half-yearly rotation) were observed. It should be noted that West Germany and East Germany became full members of the UN in 1973 only, so that the speeches of West Germany (EC member as opposed to former East Germany) could be observed only from then onward. In 1975, the speech of the country holding the presidency of the Council was supposedly on the EC position—and this was explicitly implemented from 1977 onward. Thus, from 1977 until 2011 only the speech of the country holding the EC presidency during the opening session of the UNGA was observed. Since 2011, the EU president has addressed the General Assembly on behalf of the EU. All the analyzed 454 speeches are summarized in figure 3.2.

There are some years in which speeches are missing. This is either related to the fact that the speech was not archived by the UN Dag Hammarskjöld Library online or was not given. For example, Saudi Arabia did not give its annual UNGA speeches in 2013 and 2014 out of protest, stating that the "Saudi decision . . . reflects the kingdom's dissatisfaction

Country	Number of speeches observed	Years of speeches missing
Egypt	69	2003
Iran	66	1947, 1950, 1953, 1954
EU	57 (of which 27 from 1958 to 1976, 25 from 1977 to 2011, and 5 from 2011 onwards)	After 1977: 1984–1986, 1990–1992, 1995–1997, 2003
Saudi Arabia	54	1948–1956, 1995, 1997, 2007–2011, 2013, 2014
Soviet Union / Russian Federation	69	1970
Turkey	69	1949
United States	70	——

Figure 3.2. Number of UNGA speeches observed by country. Source of all speeches: United Nations (2019).

with the position of the UN on Arab and Islamic issues, particularly the issue of Palestine that the UN has not been able to solve in more than 60 years, as well as the Syrian crisis" (Reuters 2013).

3.3. Analytical Procedure

These sources were examined through an analytical procedure characterized by four steps: categorization, open coding, conceptualizing, and axial coding (Corbin and Strauss 1997). Given that this research has been pursued by an individual rather than a group of researchers, no computer software has been used.

Initially, I began to read speeches across countries and years randomly. Relatively quickly four categories emerged, as they were continuously addressed by all powers over time: the representation of the role of the self, the representation of Israelis and Palestinians, the representation of the substance of the conflict (diagnostic representation of the conflict) and its potential solution (prognostic representation of the conflict), and the role the UN should play in it. These, therefore, emerged as the main themes of the discourse at the UN level. Having identified these categories, I began to read speeches alongside them systematically by country, beginning from 1948 through 2015 (at times extended to 2018). I analyzed how each of the actors represented their role and the conflict through historical periods and at key turning points. To explore the discursive strategies deployed in the texts, the analysis was driven by the following key questions, identified by Senem Aydin-Duzgit:

> How are the chosen subjects named and referred to linguistically? What traits, characteristics, qualities and features are attributed to them? By means of what arguments and argumentation schemes are certain representations of the subjects justified, legitimized and naturalized in discourse? From what perspective are these nominations, attributions and arguments expressed? Are the respective utterances intensified or mitigated? (Aydin-Duzgit 2014, 137)

I read each speech once, before extracting key concepts of the speeches into an Excel document by year with a tab for each country, under the categories of the representation of self, other (Israelis and Palestinians), conflict diagnosis and prognosis, and the proposed governance of the conflict through the United Nations. Once I had finished this process for each country, I went into open coding of properties and dimensions of these categories. For example, the representation of the self as a spearhead or the representation of the self as a coordinator are properties of the representation of the self, while the representation of the self as a spearhead of the Arab cause or as a spearhead of peace are two diverse dimensions of the property of representing the self as a spearhead. The result of this step can be found in chapter 4, which conceptualizes the categories of self, other, conflict, and UN role.

The next step was axial coding. The purpose of axial coding "is to begin the process of reassembling data that were fractured during open coding" (Corbin and Strauss 1997). I used axial coding in two ways.

First, there was coding for process, pursued on the level of the single discursive positions of the representatives of the respective states across time to show how they represented the self, the other, the conflict, and the role of the UN over time and to situate their representations in the respective local, regional, and global context in which they evolved by country across time. It focuses on agency, but situates agency. It responds to the questions how do regional and global powers represent their role and the conflict at the UN level, and in which domestic, regional, and global contexts did these representations emerge? This allowed for observing change in response to a situation or problems while taking account of the "complex ways in which . . . conditions/consequences intersect to create a context for action" (Corbin and Strauss 1997). At the end of this process, patterns, continuities, and ruptures were identified, exploring scripts or the various webs of relationships that emerged bound by a dominant normative international framing of the conflict. It also focuses on agency, but rather than situating it in structure, it observes how structure is a consequence of agency. It responds to the questions how representations interact, which relational configuration they set up, and what dominant framing of the conflict has emerged as a result.

Second, there was coding for consequences. This was pursued at the collective level, examining all UNSC and UNGA resolutions on the Palestine/Israel question as international authoritative framings of it. This inquired more substantially into normative dimensions, the discursive struggles surrounding them, and the potential alternatives they constituted.

Finally, the conclusions discuss what these findings mean for role theory. In the language of grounded theory, the conclusions therefore engage in "selective coding," that is, the "process of integrating and refining the theory" (Corbin and Strauss 1997).

3.4. Reflections on the Position of a Researcher on the Israel-Palestinian Conflict

The Israel-Palestinian conflict is highly politicized not only in politics but also in academia; indeed, it has lately become increasingly securitized. In reaction to the growth of the Boycott, Divestment and Sanctions (BDS) movement on campuses in the US and Europe, which—as Federica Bicchi (2018) has pointed out—sparked "a (re)politicization of debates about the occupation," counterinitiatives that securitized these debates emerged. In Germany, for example, the parliament has passed a resolution that has equated BDS with antisemitism and in which a passage that critique of Israel is not antisemitic was cut out. This securitization intimidates academics and limits freedom of thought and speech.[3] In this politicized and securitized context, it is challenging to write about the Israel-Palestinian conflict and, therefore, important to reflect on the researcher's background and position, as it affects what she chooses to investigate, the angle of investigation, the methods judged most adequate for this purpose, the findings considered most appropriate, and the framing and communication of conclusions.

As evident in the conceptual section of this book, this study attempts to contribute to the non-normalization of the decades-long denial of individual and collective rights to the Palestinians, and to reveal a specific international script that has enabled it and prevented peace to unfold in the larger region. While analyzing this, the book sits within the framework of international law and paradigmatic UN resolutions, which—besides being the object of research here—also provide protection for research in such rather difficult times.

Theoretically speaking, it leans toward critical approaches that involve "a commitment to heterogeneity, plural and non-nationalist conceptions of political community or the principle of not inducing harm in foreign policy," serving "as yardsticks in the interpretations of texts upon the condition that self-reflexivity (of the researcher's own normative assumptions) is constantly present throughout the analysis" (Aydin-Duzgit 2014, 136). To ensure and "acknowledge the importance of this reflexive dimension" (Nicolaïdis, Sèbe, and Maas 2015, 9) in this book, I include epilogues at the end of each chapter, in which I present particular conclusions from the book, while the reader might arrive at different ones. I, therefore, would like to engage the reader, asking her or him to empathize with my reading, but also enter into a dialogue with me. Both author and reader would be engaged in a dialogue that refuses to treat the conflict "at arm's length," without comprising academic vigor (Sen 2018, 102).

4

Categories and Key Concepts in the Representation of the Palestine/Israel Question at the UN

In the process of categorization and open coding of the speeches of all seven states, the following categories emerged: the representation of the self, the other (Israelis and Palestinians), the conflict (diagnostic and prognostic), and a related plan of action at the UN level/the UN role in it. The self has been represented in diverse images that include a relational and a perspectival component. The representation of the other has not taken place in a binary distinction as usually argued in the literature, but instead in more complexity that has also allowed for various positive representations of the other, or the removing of the self-other distinction. The representation of the conflict in terms of its substance and solution has evolved over time and all roles related to what they term "peace" have tended to drop the diagnostic part and have singularly concentrated on the prognostic part of the conflict. As for the part foreseen for the United Nations in the conflict, roles in hierarchic images have developed a story line that foresees no role for the UN and roles in vertical images have come forward with a story line that does foresee such a role.

4.1. The Representation of the Self

Two components of representing the self have been found, a relational component and a perspectival component. The relational component refers to the image of a relationship as either hierarchic or vertical in line with Gilligan's approach, which was referred to in the theorical chapter of this book. The perspectival component relates to an insider or outsider perspective, that is, of seeing the self as part of the conflict or as outside of it. As the postcolonial literature has pointed out, this insider/outsider perspective has addressed the other in a specific way, seeing the self in the role of the spectator, while the other became the object of study (Mitchell 2013; Tawake 2000), but also targeted action. On the outside/inside component, the roles that see the self as outside of the conflict are first and foremost those that do not see a role for themselves or present themselves as concerned bystanders. These roles imagine neither a hierarchic nor a vertical relationship—they are outside any web of relationships. Also the roles of brokers, mediators, contributors, and supporters for peace all see themselves as outside of the conflict, which is the object of their action. In contrast, there are also roles that see the self as inside of the conflict such as being the spearhead or defender of the Arab or Islamic cause. The role of opponent to peace initiatives sits somewhere between inside and outside of the conflict and can be directed against both, a hierarchically or vertically organized system of relationships.

On the hierarchic/vertical component, there are spearheads (e.g., of peace diplomacy or of the Arab cause) that assume a leadership position for themselves in achieving a certain political purpose, and there are supporters (for example "supporter of the Arab cause" or "supporter of peace diplomacy") who accept that leadership, its claim to power, and the associated political purpose and so actually enable this role, as a spearhead could not lead a system without supporters. Both of them, spearheads and supporters, set up a hierarchic system of relationships. More vertically organized are coordinators (for example "defenders of the Arab cause" or "mediators/facilitators of peace diplomacy") whereby this role implies coordination from the middle of a web rather than the top of an hierarchy. A coordinator seeks to build a network of local, regional, and international actors that increasingly ties them into binding relationships. This role is reinforced by contributors who do not place themselves in the middle of a web but rather on the sidelines, so sustaining the role of the contributor. Both contributor and coordinator set up a vertical system of relationships. Concerned bystanders and no roles stand outside such systems of relationships, while opponents actively resist any such system (but arguably also play their own role in it).

4.2. The Representation of Palestinians and Israelis

The critical discourse literature tends to juxtapose binary categories (Campbell 2013). Thomas Diez has suggested four different forms of othering: the representation of the other as different; the representation of the other as violating universal principles; the representation of the other as inferior; and the representation of the other as an existential threat, that is, the securitization of the other as a security threat, legitimizing extraordinary measures such as war (Diez 2005, 628). There are other traits of seeing the other, however. When Egypt left the Arab League after the Camp David Accords, the Jordanian king noted that the Arab League had lost its "father" (Barnett 1998). Egypt, as observed in this research, often referred to the Palestinians as "brothers." Self-other relationships might be more complex than usually assumed in the literature. This is not to say that othering is not there: it clearly is, but that one should look more into the relationship that this establishes and perpetuates. What has emerged from grounded research pursued in the framework of this book is that while role identity has been constructed in relational terms, this has not necessarily fallen into binary categories, and it is continuously evolving over time. Concretely, the representation of the other has always happened in relation to the specific representation of the self that they are meant to sustain.

Concretely, four representations of the other have been found, that is, the other as an aggressor, a violator of universal principles, a legitimate state/actor, or a protectee. Furthermore, all four representations were quite complex and included diverse subcategories.

Aggressor: Aggressor is an "in vivo code" that has repeated itself continuously, specifically up until the end of the Cold War. It has been used in the form of a noun (aggressor), as well as an adjective (aggressive), and has typically come along with other adjectives, namely imperialist, colonial, expansionist, brutal, ruthless, provocative, barbaric, or terrorist. This representation has been mainly applied to Israel (in singular cases also to the Palestinians represented as "terrorists") and coincided with the roles of Spearhead or Defender of the Arab/Palestinian/Islamic cause. At specific periods of time, particularly during periods of war (the 1967 war, the 1973 war, the 1982 war), this representation has tended to divert to representing Israel as an *existential threat*, that is as genocidal, Nazi, or a cancer.

Intransigent violator of universal rights: The intransigent violator of universal rights also is an "in vivo code" that has been frequently used for Israel. The adjective intransigent is typically used together with violator of rights and norms codified in international law. It has, furthermore, also often come together with impediment to a nuclear weapons regime, with defiant of international law and peace proposals, with unilateral actor, and obstacle to peace. At the same time, this representation has an inherent tendency to acknowledge Israel as a legitimate state in the international community that should adhere to its principles.

Legitimate state/actor: Legitimate state/actor has been applied to both Israel and the Palestinians with increasing currency after the 1967 war. This framing comes together with rights, needs, and obligations that being a legitimate state or actor in the international community means. For example, in the case of Israel, this frequently mentioned its security needs and right to exist/to peace, but also its obligations, specifically as an occupying power that has signed the Geneva Conventions. In this latter respect, it is not far from the representation of Israel as a violator of universal norms, but it puts more stress on the rights and needs of Israel.

Regarding the representation of the Palestinians, this framing has acknowledged their distinct personality as a people, and represents the Palestinians as their own nation that has rights, such as the right to self-determination and to their own state. It shifts responsibility to the Palestinians as being agents of their own fate despite their stateless-ness and it also implies obligations such as the rejection of violence or the obligation to democratic reform.

Also in this category falls the representation of Israel and Palestinians as friends, or as peace seekers (especially frequent during the peace process in the early 1990s), as it represents both as being placed in the community of peace-loving nations. Neutral mention of Israel and the Palestinians (without adjectives and nouns) also falls into this category. This framing of Israel and the Palestinians as legitimate state/actors has tendentiously come together with all roles associated to "peace."

Protectee: Protectee represents the other as positive and as having shared "baggage" with the self, such as values, language, and history. In some cases this goes as far as removing the self-other distinction to a certain degree. For example, the framing of the Palestinians as Arab or Muslim brothers by Nasser's Egypt or early revolutionary Iran evokes a shared identity, but at the same time has a substantial paternalizing tendency, with the self being the more powerful protector of the weak victim for whom the first speaks without necessarily listening to the latter's own needs. For the case of Israel, the US has at times framed it close to something like a US protectorate. The US has frequently pointed out that they share the same values with Israel, which—at the same time—has never been applied to the Palestinians, implying that they do not, so setting up a superior-inferior relationship. This representation of the other has in fact only been employed by states that have imagined themselves in hierarchic modes of relations, that is, spearhead of a cause, spearhead of peace, and so forth.

All representations of the other have, therefore, been directly linked to the representation of the self in its relational as well as perspectival components. Furthermore, the representation of self and other have also been closely linked to the diagnostic and prognostic representation of the conflict.

4.3. Diagnostic and Prognostic Representation of the Conflict

Diagnostic and prognostic representations of the conflict are necessarily related, as evident below, but what has been notable is that all roles associated with "peace" have tended to drop the diagnostic part and to solely focus on the prognostic part of the conflict, that is, its solution.

The conflict as a refugee, humanitarian, and development issue and the "economic peace" solution. This representation of the conflict was dominant in the West up until the 1967 war. It was contested by Arab countries that criticized it as a concept that sought to depoliticize the conflict and the ongoing role of key Western states (the US, the UK, and France) in it. After 1967, this representation continues to exist but has not been dominant. Today, it usually finds expression in the concept of "economic peace," that is, peace through prosperity and economic development, as well as regional economic cooperation, and evades final status questions, including the Palestine refugee question. Lately, it has had a comeback with the ultimate deal of President Trump and the "peace to prosperity" workshop held in Bahrain.

Israeli expansionism and the "undoing" of Zionism. The framing of Israeli expansionism over all of Palestine (stealing of land, driving lawful inhabitants out, displacement, violation of their rights) and Israel as a tool of imperialism was the dominant framing of the Arab states until the 1967 war. It was frequently matched with the solution to the conflict being the "undoing" of Zionism. Iran has also employed it, mainly in the early 1980s.

Israeli occupation and the two-state solution. After the 1967 war, the dominant framing of the Arab states, Turkey, Russia, Iran, and the EC/EU has become the Israeli occupation of the Palestinian territory (settlements, unilateral measures to change the status of Jerusalem, repression and violation of human/basic/political rights of Palestinians, forced demographic change). This representation has been matched by the land for peace solution and, as a specific version of it, the two-state solution:

- "Land for peace": this is embodied in Resolution 242 and 338. It qualifies international law, as it conditions the "inadmissibility of the acquisition of territory by war"[1] on negotiations. It is biased toward states as it requests respect for their sovereignty (the right of all states to exist within secure, recognized, and guaranteed borders), while not mentioning the rights of the stateless Palestinians. It mentions the withdrawal from (the) territories occupied, without, however, determining who will govern the Palestinian territory.
- "Two-state solution": the "two-state solution" is the application of the "land for peace" formula and its negotiations paradigm to the OPT. Two principal versions of the two-state solution exist. The Arab version frames it as the full withdrawal of Israel from all the territories occupied in the 1967 war (including the Syrian Golan Heights), the establishment of a sovereign independent Palestinian state in the West Bank and Gaza with East Jerusalem as its capital, and a just solution to the refugee question based on Resolution 194 (Arab League 2002). The Western version calls for a "settlement, negotiated between the parties, [which] will result in the emergence of an independent, democratic, and viable Palestinian state living side by side in peace and security with Israel and its other neighbors. The settlement will resolve the Israeli-Palestinian conflict, and end the occupation that began in 1967" (Middle

East Quartet 2002, 1). The major differences between these versions include that the Western one does not explicitly mention a full withdrawal to the 1967 borders, mentions an "agreed, just, fair, and realistic solution to the refugee issue," and so does not take Resolution 194 as a basis for negotiations, and includes a "negotiated resolution on the status of Jerusalem" rather than accepting East Jerusalem as the capital for a future Palestinian state.

- "Rights as peace": this is embodied in international humanitarian and human rights law, as well as in specific resolutions such as UNGA Resolution 191 on the right to return. It seeks to realize the rights of the Palestine refugees since 1948, and Palestinian individual and collective rights since 1967.
- "Apartheid and the one-state solution": While the issue of apartheid has been discussed at the UN—notably, the UN Economic and Social Commission for West Asia (ESCWA) has published a report on it (ESCWA 2017)—of the observed powers only Iran has referred to the situation in Palestine as apartheid. Two formulas have been related to this, one is the "rights as peace" one already mentioned. The other formula is the "one-state solution," which is increasingly discussed both locally and internationally. Of the observed powers, it has been proposed by Iran (see analysis of Iran in this book, chapter 5).

4.4. The Representation of the United Nations

Finally, the United Nations has been represented in two types of narratives or story lines, whereby—tendentiously—roles in hierarchic images have developed a story line that foresees no role for the UN and roles in vertical images have come forward with a story line that does foresee such a role.

The first story line is that the UN is part of the problem, that it is biased, blocked, and ineffective. It argues that the UN has not only failed to provide security, but is an immoral and ideological actor. UN diplomacy is seen as leading nowhere and that deals in the framework of the UN Charter might not hold in practice. Peace-keeping missions are seen as complete failures; humanitarian support, most famously the United Nations Relief and Works Agency (UNRWA), is seen as an anti-Israel entity. Correspondingly, this story line denies the UN as it currently stands the duty, right, and competence to act. The second story line is that the UN holds substantial responsibility for the conflict through the actions of its predecessor—the League of Nations—as well as through UN actions throughout time. This narrative does not deny that the UN has been biased and ineffective, but it also sees a duty, right, and a capacity for the UN to act in line with its charter and its norms as the basis for a just solution of the conflict rooted in international law.

5

Continuities and Ruptures in the Role Representations of the Seven Powers

This chapter presents the performances of each of the seven powers observed at the UN General Assembly from 1948 until 2015 and beyond. For each, after highlighting the representation of the self, the other, the conflict, and the role of the UN in specific time periods, these are then also situated in the respective local, regional, and global context in which they evolved. The chapter concludes with a synthesis that shows how these performances amounted to scripts, when they were stable, and when they transformed.

5.1. Egypt and Saudi Arabia

Egypt and Saudi Arabia are discussed together here as the two key Arab players in the conflict. Their respective representations have clearly been impacted by their relationship with one another, as well as by their relationship with the US. While initially opponents in the Arab Cold War (see below), with Egypt dominating through its pan-Arab leadership, their relationship changed after the 1967 war. Saudi Arabia became the key Arab player, without, however, being hegemonic. After 1967 and specifically since 1979, as Egypt moved into the US alliance system in which Saudi Arabia had already been seated, both states faced a similar context. On one hand, there are domestic constraints to their international representation of the Palestine question; on the other hand, as backbones of the US alliance system in the Middle East, they have similar international constraints. Furthermore, both remain the two key Arab players today and have taken a harshly revisionist direction. Following the disintegration of Iraq and the Arab uprisings, they have both been central in a revisionist axis that has clamped down on these uprisings.

5.1.1. Up until the 1967 War

Egypt initially represents itself as a "concerned protestor" until 1951 when it changes its self-representation to "spearhead of the Arab cause," which remains rather stable until 1968. Thus, this change in role performance takes place just before the coup d'état in 1952. Israel is framed as an instrument of Western imperialism and as a lawless, expansionist invader, and in the two war years, 1948 and 1956, as a colonial and racist aggressor. Throughout this period, the Palestinians are represented as brothers and as the Arab people of Palestine in need of help. This changes in 1964—the year the Palestine Liberation Organization (PLO) was founded under the auspices of the Arab League—when Palestinian agency is increasingly acknowledged. The Palestine question is described as an issue of imperialism, stolen land, and Israeli expansion, whereby the proposed solution is the self-determination of Palestine's original inhabitants and their right to return. The UN is seen with reservation. A good example that exhibits almost all these elements is Egyptian resident Gamal Abdel Nasser's speech at the UNGA in 1960, in which he stated that

> in our part of the world, the Arab East, the United Nations has forgotten its Charter and disregarded its responsibilities towards the rights of the people of Palestine. . . . The logic of imperialism, as manifested in its crime against the people of Palestine, has been to break the geographical unity of the Arab world, on the one hand, and, on the other, to create for itself in the very heart of the Arab world a base from which to threaten the Arab peoples. . . . It is certain that the determination of the Arab peoples to restore the Arab rights in Palestine has since this aggression become one of the major driving forces in the Arab East. But now, what is the solution? The only solution to Palestine . . . is that matters should be restored to normalcy and should return to the condition prevailing before the error was committed. . . . As for Palestine, the United Nations has to bear its responsibilities towards Palestine and the Arab

> people. . . . we demand the restoration of the full rights of the people of Palestine. . . . Justification based on acceptance of the "fait accompli" is sinful and harmful to principles; should we accept such a pretext, we would have no right to pursue the thief to recover from him what he has stolen and to make him pay for his crime in accordance with law, for, once committed, his theft would become a "fait accompli." The "fait accompli" which is not based on justice and the rule of law is a perversion which society must remedy. (Nasser 1960, 47)

Saudi Arabia's early speeches at the UNGA are not available, except for the speech of Amir Faisal al Saud in 1947 where he stated that peace in the Middle East will depend upon the solution of the Palestine question and that "Arabs were protectors of the Jews at all time when the Jews were prosecuted all over the world, especially in Europe. But today the Arabs wish to repel the aggression of a political minority group, namely, the Zionists" whom he then compares to the Nazis (Al Saud 1947, 248–49). From 1957 onward, Saudi Arabia does not represent a role for itself. It only defines the other, the conflict, and the actions the United Nations should take: Israel is represented as an expansionist, colonial, and racist aggressor, and Palestine as an integral part of the Arab homeland. The solution is the "de-Zionisation of Israel," which should be pursued by the UN. For example, in 1958, the Saudi representative at the UNGA, Ahmed Shukairy (later first chairman of the PLO), stated:

> In 1947 Palestine became the problem of the United Nations. . . . Partition was decided upon and Israel was created, but there is no peace in the area. On the contrary, peace has become more remote than ever. . . . Doubtless, we have reached the stage when the United Nations must reconsider the position and the resolutions that gave rise to Israel. We have reached the stage where the United Nations should undo its own doing. . . . The solution lies in the de-Zionization of Israel. It lies in a return to the situation which existed in 1947, when the legitimate Jewish inhabitants lived in a flourishing community as fellow citizens with the Moslems and Christians of Palestine. . . . the United Nations should undertake the necessary steps which will lead to the following five principles: first, the restoration of the geographic and historic unity of

> Palestine; second, the repatriation of Arabs and Jews—this is a principle which must apply to both, a principle of repatriation for every citizen in the world—the Arab refugees to their homes in Palestine and the Jewish newcomers to their former countries; third; the constitution of Palestine as a democratic State, a United Nations Member, where all the inhabitants will have equal rights and duties—Moslems, Christians and Jews alike; fourth, the disarmament and demobilization of all troops, the demilitarization of the whole country particularly Jerusalem. . . . fifth, the appointment . . . of a United Nation's representative to report to the General Assembly on matters pertaining to the status quo of religious shrines and free access to the Holy Places. . . . Palestine is an integral part of the Arab homeland, and such it has been since time immemorial. The Arab nation, now on its march towards final liberation[,] will not give up one single inch of its territory. (Shukairy 1958, 273–74)

When comparing the representations of Egypt and Saudi Arabia, the first in this time period sees itself as the spearhead of the Arab cause, while Saudi Arabia does not define its role through the Palestine question, and so does not challenge the leading role Egypt performs in this period of time.

❧

These observations have to be seen in the larger context of the time in a region in the process of decolonization, where the states and relationships between them were not settled,[1] and where the Palestine question, as Roger Owen observed, had "the same ability both to unite Arabs and divide them" (Owen 2004, 88). The Palestine question and with it the question of how to deal with Israel became one of the key themes—besides unification and the relationship to the West—around which Arab states struggled to define their identities and relationships to one another (Barnett 1998). Due to the support that the Palestine question enjoyed in the publics of the Arab states, it could be easily instrumentalized by politicians not only to gather support at home but also to boost one's regional reach and to undermine other, hostile regimes. The Palestine question played a key role in the Arab Cold War (Kerr 1971).

Saudi Arabia, despite its rhetoric, did not assume a specific role for itself on the Palestine question. Due to its military weakness, Saudi Arabia—initially mainly worried about a territorial expansion of Hashemite Jordan and the security of its dynasty—had entered into a strategic alliance with the US despite the latter's position on the Palestine/Israel question. As Maurice Labelle has pointed out in this respect, the "Saudi kingdom officially aligned itself with the United States in order to safeguard its territory and prioritized its partnership with Washington over Palestine" (Labelle 2011, 280). Thus, from the very beginning, the Saudi regime had to maneuver through a public opinion that set limits to relations with Israel and its alliance with the US, which sought to foster them. Saudi Arabia in this first time period responded to this dilemma by not defining its role identity on the Palestine question and taking no action on it, while at the same time denouncing Israel and the US on the issue (Labelle 2011, 270). Over the decades, as this chapter will show, Saudi Arabia began to perform a role on the question while gradually shifting closer toward the US.

In contrast to Saudi Arabia, Egypt initially emerged as the champion of the Palestine question. This had a domestic and a regional background. On the regional level, the debate on "whether and under what conditions they might have dealings and relations" with Israel "culminated in the normative prohibition against making peace with Israel, codified by the League of Arab States in April 1950" (Barnett 1998, 85–86). More than a general prohibition against making peace with Israel, this was actually a prohibition against making a *separate* peace with Israel, at the time mainly aimed at preventing Jordan from doing so. On the domestic level, the 1952 coup brought the Free Officers to power. Initially, they did not differ much in their foreign policy positions from their predecessors. They did, however, undergo a substantial shift during the 1950s, when Arabism—and with it the Palestine question—became what is defined in this book as a script that Egypt increasingly "wrote" but also performed.

As Andrea Teti has argued,

> While in 1952 the Free Officers displayed a "minimalist" form of Arabism at best, and while they were well-disposed to the West and the US in particular, and had little original involvement in, or concern for, regional politics, 1958 sees Egypt fully engaged in a maximalist Arabism, committed to an understanding of unity as political unification, publicly hostile

> to the West. . . . This radical transformation is the consequence of an incremental but conscious subscription to Arabism as a legitimating narrative of political identity. (Teti 2004, 87)

The 1956 Suez crisis played a crucial role in this respect. It was the last show of the power of Britain and France in the region and while Israel did emerge as a major military power in the crisis, the political victory was with Egyptian president Nasser who became the "undisputed leader of the Arab world in the aftermath of the war" (Shlaim 2014, 186–87) against Western imperialism and Israeli colonialism (Makdisi 2010, 251). The Suez crisis not only heightened Nasser's threat perceptions of Israel, including as an instrument of European imperialism against the Arab world; it also boosted his activism on the Palestine question whose importance for the Pan-Arab movement he understood. As Avi Shlaim has pointed out, in the past Nasser used to talk about the need to find a solution to the Palestine refugee question, whereas after 1956 "he began to talk about the liberation of Palestine. . . . The containment of Israel became a Pan-Arab goal" (Shlaim 2014, 186–87). As Nasser pointed out in his book, the role of the hero of pan-Arabism was out there—it was a "role in search of a hero" (Nasser 1955, 87)—and he would become that hero.

He performed the role intensively, including at the level of the Arab League, the Arab summitry system established by Nasser, as well as at the United Nations. Adopting that role, Nasser shaped it, but was at the same time bound to its script, especially when the script was employed by one of his counterparts, Syria specifically. In 1958, the Syrian Ba'ath Party forced Nasser into setting up the United Arab Republic, trapping him in his rhetorical attachment to "Arab unity." The United Arab Republic (as well as the coup in Iraq in 1958, which increased the fears of the so-called "conservative" regimes in the region that revolution was an unstoppable tide), further fueled what Malcom Kerr has called the "Arab Cold War" (Kerr 1971) between the so-called conservatives and "radicals," as well as within each of these fractions. Saudi Arabia and Egypt were increasingly pitted against each other and the Saudi royal family—more and more hostile toward the Egyptian president and his growing activism in the Arab world—was frequently attacked by Nasser on its inactivism on the Palestine question. Saudi Arabia—despite the kingdom's rhetoric on Zionism—was rather passive in the conflict as they "were more concerned with Soviet penetration of the Middle East and the alliance Moscow forged with Cairo, Damascus and Baghdad than with the threat posed by Zionism" (Bahgat 2009, 181).[2] As, in fact, evident in its representation at the United Nations, Saudi Arabia did not develop a role identity with respect to the Palestine question, and so did not contest the role of Egypt.

Most decisive in regard to the Palestine question, however, was the coup in Syria, which led to the fall of the United Arab Republic of Syria and Egypt and the virtual end of the unity question, forcing both parties to boost their Arabist credentials by turning to the other key pan-Arab issue: the Palestine question. Specifically, the new Ba'athist regime in Syria took a radical posture to legitimize its rule after the coup and entrapped Nasser in his own role as a hero of pan-Arabism, attacking him as inactive on the Palestine question and as reactionary (Kerr 1971, 26). To control the Syrians, whom Nasser feared might press him into military action on the Palestine question, and in an attempt to regain ground with the Saudis, Nasser set up the summitry system. As Michael Barnett has pointed out, the " 'era of summitry'—beginning in January 1964 and ending in September 1965—symbolized the move by Arab states to set aside the debate about unification, embrace sovereignty, and shift their focus to Israel" (Barnett 1998, 123).

Contrary to Nasser's intention, however, the dynamics triggered by this move contributed to trapping him into action on the Palestine question. As the issue progressed to center stage again in the discourse on the regional level, Arab leaders "became increasingly vulnerable to symbolic sanctions regarding their commitment to Arabism as defined by the Palestine conflict" and a "deadly game of outbidding and symbolic entrapment" began (Barnett 1998, 123). Israel, on its part, increased confrontation and violence on its borders. Thus, the emerging discourse—instead of limiting foreign policy action—began to unleash it.

While the road to the 1967 war is disputed by historians (Quigley 2013), Shlaim has argued that of "all the Arab-Israeli wars, the June 1967 war was the only one that neither side wanted. The war resulted from a crisis slide that neither Israel nor her enemies were able to control" (Shlaim 2014, 236). As events on the Israeli-Syrian fronts and rhetoric on both sides escalated, the USSR was concerned that Israel wanted to overthrow its allied regime in Syria and conveyed wrong reports to Nasser that Israel was amassing troops on the Syrian border. The Syrians exposed Nasser's inactivism and, if he wanted to remain credible, Nasser had to act, even though—as historians largely agree—not with the intention of actually going to war, which would overstretch Egyptian capacities as Cairo was already bogged down in a war in Yemen. He demanded the removal of the United Nations Emergency Force from Sinai, sent Egyptian troops into the area, and closed the Straits of Tiran, an act Israel considered a casus belli. Nasser might have hoped that the issue would pass to the United Nations Security Council first or that the US would constrain Israel, but Israel decided to go to war. As Fouad Ajami pointed out, political ideas had created their own realities:

> Often in defiance of logic, they hold men and are in turn held by them, creating a world in their own image, only to play themselves out in the end shackled by routine problems not foreseen by those who spun the myth, or living past their prime and ceasing to move people sufficiently. Or, political ideas turn to ashes and leave behind them a trail of errors, suffering and devastation. (Ajami 1978)

With the loss of the 1967 war an era came to an end in the region. Arabism and the Egyptian role lay in shatters. As Malcom Kerr has pointed out, there "could hardly be competition for prestige when there was no prestige remaining. The old ideological conflicts had lost their meaning" (Kerr 1971, 129). The conflict's regional script had broken down, and a new one was slowly to emerge; this time, however, written by another power.

5.1.2. From 1967 to 1979

After the 1967 war, Egypt enters into a period of struggling with the representation of its role that takes almost a decade. Initially, it does not refer to the role of the self anymore and then slowly begins to present itself as the spearhead of peace in the region. In his address to the General Assembly in 1975, Egyptian president Anwar el Sadat stated that Egypt had reacted positively to US mediation efforts, which, according to Sadat, were

> thwarted because of Israel's intransigence and its inability to accept the challenges of peace. Notwithstanding this, Egypt did not lose its enthusiasm for peace nor its belief in it. For us, peace is a strategic objective, a genuine commitment. . . . Therefore, I find it incumbent upon me to speak to you frankly, and in the

> same spirit which you found in me when I took the decisions for peace. As you are aware, I took a historic decision to begin the battle on 6 October 1973. It was not a decision to wage war for the sake of war; the objective was to blaze the trail towards peace anew, so that the world should be made aware that the Arab nation could never accept an occupation or even accept the curbing of the Palestinian people's rights or their deprivation of those rights. It was imperative, therefore, to take this historic decision so that events should resume their normal course and the wheel should begin to turn towards peace. (Sadat 1975, 619–20)

In 1977, Egypt's minister of foreign affairs, Ismail Fahmy, argues that Egypt "shoulders a great responsibility," a "pioneering role" in seeking peace (Fahmy 1977). In 1978, the Egyptian UN representative, Ahmed Esmat Abdel Meguid, argues that having "sacrificed itself for Arab rights," having faced four battles of war, Egypt now wanted to devote itself to the fifth battle, the "cause of peace" (Abdel Meguid 1978). In 1979, Egypt's minister of foreign affairs, Boutros Boutros-Ghali, in a speech at the United Nations, calls Egypt the "vanguard of the struggle for a better future of the Arab nation," whose "record in war is matched by its struggle for peace," arguing that "Egypt will pursue the peace process, issuing the challenge of peace to all parties, the rejectionists and the silent, Israelis and Arabs alike" (Boutros-Ghali 1979). Thus, Egypt increasingly portrays itself as a trendsetter for the other Arab states, a spearhead of peace in the region. From 1980–81, its new self-representation as the regional "spearhead of peace" is settled and not further justified anymore. In the same period, the representation of Israel changes substantially from representing Israel as a threat and aggressor to an intransigent violator of rights. The representation of the Palestinians also changes considerably as they are now seen as their own nation. Indeed, from 1976 on, Egypt shifts its responsibility onto the PLO as the political representative of the Palestinians and onto the United Nations, seeing the international community responsible for the economic and humanitarian situation of the Palestinians. In 1979, as Egypt signs a peace treaty that ignores the rights and needs of the Palestinians,[3] Boutros-Ghali states that "Egypt does not speak on behalf of the Palestinian people; it is not entitled to do so and never claimed to do so, for it is the Palestinian people alone who have the right to discuss their future and destiny or choose their own representative. . . . We hereby call upon both Israel and the PLO to recognize one another" (Boutros-Ghali 1979). Furthermore, after 1973, in the representation of the conflict the emphasis shifts from describing the source of the conflict toward its solution, that is, Israel's full withdrawal from the occupied territories and Palestinian right to self-determination and their own state (from 1976 onward). Regarding the role of the UN, after 1967, Egyptian minister of foreign affairs Mahmoud Riad sees the UN in a "cardinal responsibility" and "duty-bound to undertake effective measures to secure the implementation of the numerous resolutions," arguing that the UN has played a basic role in the creation of Israel and in all subsequent developments of the history of the Palestine question, thus making the UN an "essential party" to the question (Riad 1967). After 1967, Egypt still rejects bilateral negotiations with Israel and seeks to solve the conflict through the United Nations. From 1977 onward, however, Egypt downplays the role of the UN in negotiations, speaking first about bilateral, and then regional and international, diplomacy.

Saudi Arabia's role also changes after the 1967 war, when it becomes the "defender of the Palestinian cause" at the United Nations. In 1966–67, Israel is referred to as "an aggressive criminal gang," the "Zionist military machine" as ugly and bestial (Al-Sowayel 1967), and from 1968 onward again as an aggressor. The Palestinians are increasingly seen as their own actor with rights and responsibilities. In 1972, for example, the Saudi representative at the UN, Omar Sakkaf, states that "the Arab Governments are not responsible for what the Palestinians have undertaken to do" (Sakkaf 1972). After the 1973 war, Saudi Arabia begins to change its role representation from no role to mediator in an Arab framework. In 1974, Sakkaf refers to the

> unremitting efforts exerted by Arabs . . . to find a solution and to co-operate with friendly states in their search for a solution to the Palestinian question which would ultimately bring peace in the region based on equity, justice and self-determination in our region. . . . The position of Saudi Arabia is in conformity with that of other Arab and Moslem countries, as expressed at the Fourth Conference of Heads of State or Government of Non-Aligned Countries, held at Algiers, from 5 to 9 September 1973, and also at the Islamic Summit Conference in Lahore in 1974. (Sakkaf 1974)

Thus, as Egypt goes through a substantial role change, Saudi Arabia begins to assume a role on the Palestine question that it then consolidates in the 1980s.

The new Saudi role was connected to a regional shift in power from Egypt to Saudi Arabia, or from *thawra* (revolution) to *tharwa* (riches), as Mohamed Heikal (1978, 261–62) has termed it. The system of Arab states began to grow into what the Western literature has labeled a "normal," "standard," or "ordered" state system, dominated by sovereign states and the principle of noninterference, as initially intended by the founding document of the Arab League in 1945, that is, a system of Arab cooperation, but not integration. By and large Israel was now accepted by the two key Arab states as part of the regional state system with the conflict shifting—as Sayyid Yasin has argued—from a conflict over existence to a conflict over borders (Stein 2012, 90).

Initially, the 1967 war led to a process of reconciliation within the Arab world and to an increase in cooperation among its key states, Egypt, Syria, and Saudi Arabia (the so-called Arab triangle), which began to consult regularly on military and strategic issues. Saudi Arabia, in fact, began to turn into a driving force, increasingly placing its economic weight behind Egyptian and Syrian military capabilities (Bahgat 2009, 182). In their 1967 Khartoum Resolution, the Arab states agreed upon the "three nos": "no peace with Israel, no recognition of Israel, no negotiations with it, and insistence on the rights of the Palestinian people in their own country" (Arab League 1967). While Israel perceived the resolution as hostile, it actually represented a victory of the so-called Arab moderates who advocated diplomatic rather than military means. As Avi Shlaim has pointed out, "Arab spokesmen interpreted the Khartoum declarations to mean no formal peace treaty, but not a rejection of a state of peace; no direct negotiations, but not a refusal to talk through third parties; and no de jure recognition of Israel, but de facto acceptance of its existence as a state" (Shlaim 2014, 259). This consensus had been driven by Nasser and King Hussein of Jordan. Egypt and Jordan accepted United Nations Security Council Resolution 242, which contained what amounted to a de facto recognition of Israel along the 1949 armistice lines despite the fact that Resolution 242 did not acknowledge Palestinian collective rights.

Nasser also gave his consent to the Rogers Plan (named for US secretary of state William Rogers), which implied Egyptian readiness for a binding peace with Israel. As Ewan Stein has pointed out, in accepting the Rogers Plan, "Nasser indicated his willingness to come to terms with Israel" (Stein 2012, 100).[4] This was, indeed, a game changer; it "was the first time that an Egyptian government declared publicly its readiness to sign a peace treaty with Israel" (Shlaim 2014, 299–300). After Nasser's death, the new Egyptian president, Anwar el Sadat, continued on this line. While signals from Egypt were rather clear, including to the US, which Sadat tried to push into diplomacy to regain the Sinai, the US ignored them and Sadat tried to break through the diplomatic stalemate with a war that would draw the US deeper into the regional arena.

The 1973 war, while of limited military success, was a psychological success, and a sense of triumph emerged, but this triumph—as Beverly Milton-Edwards has pointed out—"was not associated with . . . pan-Arabism but with the economic strength of the oil-producing economies of the region" (Milton-Edwards 2011, 71). In fact, through the oil embargo, Saudi Arabia was catapulted into the international limelight and into a regional leadership position (Barnett 1998, 184).[5] Saudi Arabia now had to adopt a more direct role in the conflict.

Both Egypt and Saudi Arabia began to push for peacemaking. The Algiers meeting of the Arab League in November 1973 sanctioned the use of diplomacy and identified two key conditions for peacemaking, namely, the "evacuation by Israel of the occupied Arab territories and first of all Jerusalem" and "re-establishment of full national rights for the Palestinian people" (Arab League 1973). Another turning point was the Rabat meeting in 1974. It unanimously (and thus with the Jordanian vote) confirmed "the right of the Palestinian people to return to their homeland and to self-determination," and affirmed "the right of the Palestinian people to establish an independent national authority under the command of the Palestine Liberation Organization, the sole legitimate representative of the Palestinian people in any Palestinian territory that is liberated" (Arab League 1974). This had several intentions. First, it was meant to force Jordan to abandon its role of representing the Palestinians and its claims to the West Bank, therefore representing a step toward independent Palestinian statehood. This declaration, it should be noted, came in the same year as UNGA Resolution 3236, which also established the Palestinians' inalienable right to independence and national sovereignty (see chapter 6). Second, it took account of the independent role that the

PLO had assumed after the 1967 war.[6] Third, this in turn enabled the Arab states to rid themselves of this very responsibility and disassociate themselves from the PLO. As Avraham Sela has put it, it enabled the Arab states "to shift the form of the conflict with Israel from an international one between the Arab world and Israel . . . to a Palestinian struggle for national liberation spearheaded by the Palestinians themselves and only supported by the Arab world" (Sela 1997, 153). It so opened the door for Arab states to pursue more limited goals in terms of peacemaking. In 1976, the Arab League Council accepted Palestine, represented by the PLO, as a member of the Arab League.

But while the pre-1973 period had brought the Arab states together, peacemaking would now separate them—or, more concretely, bilateral instead of multilateral peacemaking. The latter approach as envisaged in the Geneva talks had failed for several reasons, chief among them Israel's rejection of the multilateral and comprehensive approach, signaling to Egypt that it could regain its territory only through bilateral negotiations. As in 1948, bilateral negotiations—the preferred option of both Israel and the US to break the Arab alliance and reduce their weight, a sort of divide-and-rule tactic for peace negotiations—was fatal for Arab cooperation and drove Arab states apart from each other. As Stephen Walt has pointed out, the "problem was how to preserve Arab solidarity while Syria, Jordan, and especially Egypt independently sought the best deal with Israel" (Walt 1990, 131).

In this situation, Egypt, having moved from the role of the spearhead of Arabism to the role of spearhead of "peace," changed the script of politics in the region in one of its key moments, as Egyptian president Anwar Sadat visited Israel in 1977. No longer the champion of the Arab world, Egypt had now moved into the limelight of international attention and applause. Sadat aimed for a "new sort of regional leadership based on mediating between the West and the Arab world" (Hinnebusch 2003, 153). He signed the Camp David Accords in 1978 and the Egyptian-Israeli peace treaty in 1979, and was heralded in the West as the champion of peace, fostering a close relationship between Cairo and Washington that lasts to this day.

The Camp David Accords changed the conflict and the order in the region at large. While the Arab triangle might have been able to pressure Israel into a withdrawal from all the territories it had occupied in 1967 (the Sinai, the Syrian Golan Heights, and the West Bank including East Jerusalem and the Gaza Strip), the separate "peace" of Egypt effectively ended this possibility. It meant that Sadat had not only given up on the Palestinians but also on the Syrians. "Together—and only together—they might have reached a comprehensive Middle East peace for, as Henry Kissinger remarked, the Arabs could not wage war without Egypt or make peace without Syria" (Hinnebusch 2003, 152). The separate peace between Egypt and Israel removed the need on the side of Israel to give up the Palestinian and Syrian territories it had occupied in 1967. The foundations for a new script on the conflict were thus laid. On the regional level, a new order came into being with the Camp David Accords. While the USSR was now sidelined, the US became the dominant power in the Middle East, at the center of a web of relations with Israel, Egypt, and Saudi Arabia, which is often referred to as the Camp David Order.

Indeed, while Egypt moved temporarily out of the Arab state system, it had nonetheless paved the way for Saudi Arabia to adopt and perform a role identity that would match the script of Camp David. Saudi Arabia represented itself as a regional "ringleader" (Bahgat 2003), a regional coordinator to keep the Arab world united, not divided. The Saudi strategy has focused on consensus building in the Arab world with the intention of reconciling domestic support for the Palestinian cause with the close Saudi relationship with the US as a key consumer of oil and provider of military equipment (Barnett 1998, 184). The role of a "regional coordinator among the various actors in the Middle East, including the United States" (Kostiner 2009, 417) enabled Saudi Arabia to strike a balance between both needs at least temporarily. The Saudi role identity has, therefore, been an outcome of what could be called omni-balancing (Nonneman 2007) on the identity level.

5.1.3. From 1979 until 2011

After 1979, Egypt's role representation is rather stable despite the assassination of Sadat and the Israeli invasion into Lebanon that followed the Egyptian-Israeli Peace Treaty. In 1983, for example, Egyptian president Hosni Mubarak states at the UNGA that Egypt's concern for the conflict "has been manifested in its various initiatives aimed at establishing a just and comprehensive peace in the Middle East" (Mubarak 1983). In the Oslo period, Egypt continues to perform its role as a spearhead of peace diplomacy in the region. In 1992, for example, Egyptian foreign minister Amr Moussa argues that Egypt's "view of a future Middle East within the context of new international relations, as well as the context of cultural affinity and the historical ties that bind all Arab States, together with Egypt's peaceful relations with Israel, enable Egypt to play an active role in the peace process and to provide some support for the negotiations" (Moussa 1992). Israel is presented as an advocator of peace until 1996, when it is again seen as an intransigent violator of international law. In this period, Egypt's prognostic framing of the conflict becomes rather detailed. It is a period in which the Arab states, as pointed out by Moussa, are defining their parameters "to coexistence with it [Israel] as a member of the family of the Middle East" (Moussa 1998). In the post-Oslo period—that is, the period in which the failure of US brokering efforts became most evident—Egypt even increases its support for the US brokering role. In 2001, Egypt's permanent representative to the United Nations, Ahmed Aboul-Gheit, argues, for example, that "Egypt supports the active role of the United States of America as the peace broker" (Gheit 2001).

The Saudi role representation, as already highlighted, initially remains stable in the form of a regional coordinator of peace initiatives. In this time period, Saudi Arabia's framing of Israel changes from aggressor toward violator of international law in the late 1980s. Together with this change, Saudi Arabia focuses more on the prognostic rather than the diagnostic side of the conflict. Its framing of a solution changes, focused on Israel's total withdrawal from the occupied territories including East Jerusalem and a right for the Palestinians to self-determination and their own state. This becomes specified in the eight-point plan for peace introduced at the UN in 1981 (and is repeated in the Saudi Peace Initiative presented to the UNGA in 2002).

Like Egypt, Saudi Arabia defines itself increasingly as a supporter of the US role as the key broker in the conflict. While in 1980 Saudi foreign minister Prince Saud al-Faisal complained at the UNGA that "Israel has been encouraged by the unconditional support that it receives from the United States," in 1991 he states that "the Government of the custodian of the two holy mosques offers its full support for the efforts of President George Bush" (Al-Faisal 1991), and, in 1993, the Saudi representative at the UNGA, Gaafar Allagany, expresses "the appreciation of the Government of the Custodian of the two holy mosques to President Clinton for his prudent initiative" (Allagany 1993).

In 1998, the Saudi UN representative, Nizar Obaid Madani, argues that Saudi Arabia has "supported the peace process from the very beginning" (Madani 1998). In the 2000s, Saudi Arabia scales up its role performance. In 2005, Crown Prince Sultan Bin Abdulaziz Al-Saud points out how Saudi Arabia is supported in its own peace initiative by the Arab states, stating that the "Arab countries have affirmed their commitment to a just peace by endorsing the initiative of the Custodian of the Two Holy Mosques, King Abdullah Bin Abdulaziz" (Al Saud 2005).

The Camp David script that emerged in 1978–79 has indeed been rather resilient over decades due to the stable role performances of both Egypt and Saudi Arabia. Even though it never led to peace or stability in the region, both continued their performances as coordinator for peace (Saudi Arabia) or spearhead of peace (Egypt) over decades. Both became increasingly open in supporting the role of the US as the key broker, and both focused almost exclusively on the prognostic side of the conflict—as all actors involved in the Camp David Order did—while sidelining questions about the roots of the conflict, international law, justice, and human rights. As a result of their performances, the US remained the dominant power in the region, despite the glaring fact that no peace or a Palestinian state has ever been established. Indeed, the Camp David script has given Saudi Arabia and Egypt the possibility to perform as "peacemakers" to their domestic audiences, without taking effective action regarding the ongoing Israel-Palestinian conflict.

In 1979, Saudi Arabia officially opposed the Camp David Accords not because it rejected peace with Israel, but because it rejected *bilateral* peace, preferring a comprehensive agreement that would prevent a fragmentation of and polarization in the Arab world by guaranteeing Palestinian rights, as opposed to Egyptian interests only (Bahgat 2009, 183). At the Arab League summit that expelled Egypt, Saudi Arabia lobbied for a resolution that eventually argued for a "just peace" based on "total Israeli withdrawal from the territories occupied in 1967 and the restoration of Palestinian national rights" (Sela 1997, 203). The Saudi position has also to be seen in the context of the revolution in Iran whose spread in the Arab world it sought to contain by all means. As the Arab world increasingly fragmented in the wake of the Camp David Accords as well as the eruption of the Iraq-Iran war, Saudi Arabia sought to identify the parameters of Israel's integration into the region. For Saudi Arabia, fragmentation of the region and Iranian penetration of it could only be prevented by the inclusion of Israel, which, however, never reacted very positively to such Saudi efforts.

In 1981, Saudi Arabia proposed the Fahd Plan, which represented "a fundamental departure from traditional Saudi policy" (Bahgat 2009, 184) as it implicitly recognized Israel in the 1967 borders by confirming the right of all states in the region to live in peace. The reaction in the Arab world was mixed; Jordan supported the plan, the Egyptians and the PLO were ambiguous about it, and Syria rejected it. At the Fez Summit of the Arab League in 1982, the plan was adopted in a changed version including the following key principles: full Israeli withdrawal from all Arab territories occupied in 1967, dismantling of the settlements, reaffirmation of the Palestinian people's right to self-determination and the exercise of its imprescriptible and inalienable national rights under the leadership of the PLO, placing the West Bank and Gaza Strip under the control of the UN for a transitory period not exceeding a few months, the establishment of an independent Palestinian state with Al Quds as its capital, and empowering the Security Council as a guarantor of peace among all states of the region including the independent Palestinian state (Arab League 1982). The borders of the Palestinian state were not explicitly named, but the Occupied Palestinian Territory was implied. While the European Community was supportive of the plan, the US and Israel rejected it, curtailing the Saudi role of mediator in the region (Abadi 2006, 65, 69). Nonetheless, the Saudi position remained firm: Israel would have to be included in the region—based on its withdrawal from the territories occupied in 1967.

In the 1980s, "Mubarak sought to position Egypt as the indispensable mediator between the United States, Israel and the Palestinians" (Stein 2012, 163). Egypt—having returned to the Arab League—came forward with a ten-point plan that would have provided for elections, but did not include the PLO in negotiations or speak about a Palestinian state or the 1967 borders. It was, nonetheless, rejected by Israel. US diplomacy now began to take over once again with a series of initiatives including the Baker Plan (1989), the Madrid talks (1991), the Oslo Accords (1993/1995), the Israel-Jordan peace treaty (1994), the Hebron agreement (1997), the Wye River memorandum (1998), the Camp David summit (2000), the Clinton parameters (2000) and Taba Summit (2001), the Road Map (2002), Sharm El Sheik Summit (2005), and the Annapolis conference (2007). As pointed out in more detail in the section on the US below, this script of the Middle East Peace Process (MEPP)—as it came to be called—has been characterized by (1) the negotiations paradigm and the sidelining of international law, (2) the dominance of the US as the chief broker in a system where the roles foreseen for other regional and global powers were supporters of the US—that is, a hierarchic system of roles, (3) the bilateral character of all talks (i.e., Israeli-Syrian, Israeli-Jordanian, Israel-PLO), and (4) the exclusion of the UN as a guarantor of peace; all of which sustains the hierarchic order, rather than an order based on multilateral and comprehensive coordination in the framework of international law. As a result, as will be seen further below, this script of US separate peacemaking did not lead to peace and was thus contrary to the interests of both Saudi Arabia and Egypt, which nonetheless continued to perform in their roles.

Specifically, after the conclusion of the Oslo Accords and the Israeli-Jordanian peace treaty, a system emerged whereby one part of the Arab neighbors of Israel (Egypt, Jordan, the PLO) established bilateral treaties with Israel (which never ended the occupation), while another part (Syria, Lebanon, Hamas) were excluded from it. As a reaction to the Israeli-Jordanian peace treaty, Riyadh and Cairo did seek to keep Syria in the Arab fold by signing the Alexandria Agreement with Damascus in 1994, which stated that no other bilateral peace agreement should be pursued with Israel without the consent of Syria, Egypt, and Saudi Arabia. This was, however, unsuccessful in face of the facts that had already been created by the bilateral peace treaties, and pushed Syria to intensify its relations with Iran and Russia. The Saudi Peace Initiative of 2002, reconfirmed in 2007, while comprehensive and getting indirect Iranian endorsement in 2007,[7] could not effectively change Syria's isolation, nor the ongoing occupation. The initiative demanded full Israeli withdrawal from all territories occupied since 1967, explicitly including the Syrian Golan Heights, the achievement of a just solution to the Palestine refugee question (a main step toward Israel as this framing does not demand the right of return), and the acceptance of the establishment of a sovereign independent Palestinian state on the Palestinian territory occupied since June 1967 with East Jerusalem as its capital. In exchange, the Arab states offered to consider the conflict ended, enter into a peace agreement with Israel, provide security for all states of the region, and establish normal relations with Israel in the context of such a comprehensive peace (Arab League 2002). This went much farther than the 1982 initiative as it offered full normalization of relations with Israel, and also sidelined the United Nations, which had been assigned a major role in the 1982, but not in the 2002, initiative.

But while this initiative was rather close to the script of the "peace process," it failed nonetheless, for several reasons. First, it is not clear how committed Saudi Arabia has really been in pushing this initiative; it may have mainly been meant as window dressing at home and toward the US. The Saudi regime came out with the initiative during the second Intifada, which raised resentment in the Arab world and was a source of opposition to Arab regimes and their good relations with the US. Saudi Arabia needed to show some activism. Furthermore, it was presented after the 9/11 attacks in which the Saudi role had been unclear, raising resentment in the US. Second, Israel had no incentive to respond to the initiative, as the "peace process," and the indirect alliance it implied between Israel, Egypt, and Saudi Arabia, has been more comfortable than territorial concessions or facing the Palestine refugee question.

5.1.4. From 2011 until Today

During the brief presidency of Mohamed Morsi, Egypt continues its role performance as peace broker, not only in Palestine but also with Syria. At the General Assembly, Morsi states in 2012 that he calls "for peace that will establish a sovereign Palestinian State," showed himself supportive of the Palestinian efforts at the United Nations and states that Egypt "is committed to continuing its sincere efforts to put an end to the catastrophe in Syria" (Morsi 2012). After the coup d'état, President Abdel Fatah Al Sisi states that Egypt "continues to pursue its best efforts to achieve peace in the region" and that "Egypt's inspiring and unique experience can in fact be replicated by solving the Palestinian problem" (Al Sisi 2016). Similar to Egypt, Saudi Arabia continues to represent itself as a mediator for peace. Despite the irrelevance of the Saudi peace initiative, Saudi representatives continue to mention it (Al-Jubeir 2017) while the main anchor point in their speeches is the perceived "Iranian threat."

How can this continuation of the Saudi and Egyptian role identity be explained in light of the hollowness of the peace process, which the Arab uprisings have also exposed? The Saudi peace initiative, as argued above, has partially served as window dressing for the Saudis—and this function has increased since the Arab uprisings as Saudi Arabia became one of the most counter-revolutionary powers in the region, moving against the local calls for democracy in the Gulf, the Arab world, and beyond. Increasingly, it has been transforming itself from a regional "ringleader" (Bahgat 2003) to what could be better termed a "gang leader" that uses criminal tactics toward dissidents, while seeking to bully nonconforming states such as Qatar into submission and normalizing its relations with Israel despite the ongoing occupation. In balancing its positioning toward Saudi citizens on one hand and the US on the other, it has clearly shifted course toward alignment with the latter by throwing its weight behind President Donald Trump's "ultimate deal of the century." Thus, Saudi Arabia's role performance is hollowing out. Although such a performance will ultimately undermine the script of the peace process, this does not mean that the web of relationships between the US, Saudi Arabia, Egypt, and Israel will not be sustained. Rather, the script—the roles assigned and the meaning that glues it together—might change, evolving increasingly around the "Iranian threat."

The case of Egypt is a bit different; it continues to perform as a supporter of peace, sustaining the script of the "peace process." While it does not contest current US and Saudi moves, it is not entirely comfortable with them. After the Arab uprisings, Egypt has continued its role performance, even during Morsi's short presidency. As Raymond Hinnebusch has pointed out, Morsi "assumed a Mubarak-like attempt to broker between Hamas and Israel" (Hinnebusch 2003, 283–84). This has been explained by Egypt's dependency on loans from international financial institutions, as well as fragile internal power balances in Egypt. At the same time, Morsi attempted to perform a different interpretation of this role, a more inclusive role of regional peace coordinator, specifically when it comes to the rupture with Iran and in Syria, as he sought to set up a contact group (including Iran) to settle the Syrian crisis. There have been continuities in this respect after the coup d'état. In 2016, President Al Sisi voted for two rival French- and Russian-sponsored UNSC resolutions on Syria, justifying this with the goal of ending the tragedy in Syria (MadaMasr 2016). In 2017, Egypt hosted reconciliation talks between Fatah and Hamas and drafted a press statement at the UNSC, together with Russia, that supported the reconciliation agreement, but was blocked by the US (Ministry of Foreign Affairs of the Russian Federation 2017). Following the move of the US embassy to Jerusalem, Egypt drafted a UN Security Council resolution (vetoed by the US) that affirmed the status of Jerusalem. Thus, Egypt is one of the few powers observed in this book that actually still performs—with its own interpretations—within the script of the "peace process."

5.2. Turkey and Iran

Turkey and Iran share some similarities that are important in the context of this research. They are key non-Arab powers in the Middle East that needed to define their own role in the regional system in terms of their relations with the Arab states and Israel, and in the global system where their role has—to an important degree—been determined by their regional role. During the initial period of the Cold War, neither Turkey nor Iran adopted a role in the conflict and both became "concerned bystanders" after the 1967 war. Iran went through a revolutionary change in 1979, which led to the establishment of the Islamic Republic; Turkey went through an electorally mediated change in the early 2000s when the Justice and Development Party (AKP) represented a model of a conservative democracy that takes Islam on board. As a result of these domestic changes, Iran changed its role radically after the 1979 revolution, while Turkey's role in the conflict intensified when the AKP entered power, but did not change substantially. Turkey over the whole period observed has been supportive of both US and Arab initiatives. Iran is the only actor that has played the role of opponent in the Camp David script and thus has, arguably, also been part of that play. In the first decades after the revolution, the Iranian role performance has been an unsettled one and in constant need of redefining itself in relation to the Camp David script. Beginning in the early 2000s, however, Iran began to define its role no longer in relation to that script, but rather in relation to its own script on the region, which stabilized specifically after the Arab uprisings and the nuclear deal. In this Iran poses a substantial challenge to the Camp David script.

Due to the different roads Iran and Turkey took, they are discussed together until the period of the 1967 war and after; following this, they are discussed separately.

5.2.1. Iran and Turkey up until the 1967 War and After

Until 1964 Turkey displays no role representation, and hardly refers to the conflict at all. Turkey is not even a concerned bystander. Just like Turkey,

Iran initially does not mention the conflict (except in 1956, the year of the Suez war) or foresee any role for itself in it.

From 1964 onward until the 1990s, Turkey becomes a "concerned observer" that voices sympathy for the Palestinian cause and supports peace initiatives, both from the US and the Arab world. Throughout the 1960s and 1970s, Israel is either not mentioned or mentioned without adjectives. Only in 1967 does Turkey refer to Israel as intransigent. The Palestinians are initially either not mentioned or mentioned as refugees. This changes after the 1973 war, when Turkey begins to express support for the PLO, and perceives the Palestinians as deprived of their rights, but rejects what it calls terrorism. The conflict is initially portrayed as a refugee issue, and after 1967 as an issue of occupation of the "Arab territories." As for the role of the UN, Turkey initially sees UN resolutions as central to the conflict, but from the 1970s onward it does not refer to the UN, but rather to US and Arab initiatives. In 1985, Turkish prime minister Turgut Özal is more outspoken at the UN, elaborating a specific view on the conflict without, however, foreseeing a role for Turkey that goes beyond supporter of any peace initiative. He argued that a

> Jewish State was created but the Palestinian people were not allowed to exercise their right to self-determination, and this injustice is still continuing. We recognize the right of every country in that area, including Israel, to live within secure and recognized borders, but we support the right to full self-determination of the valiant Palestinian people and maintain our view that Israel should withdraw from the territories it occupied in 1967. We commend the courageous initiative undertaken earlier this year by King Hussein and Chairman Arafat. We sustain the hope that if Israel refrains from further faits accomplis and seizes the recent peace initiative, a lasting and just solution of the Palestinian problem could still be within reach. (Özal 1985)

With the 1967 war, Iran—like Turkey—adopts the role of a concerned bystander, supportive of both US and Arab efforts. In the late 1960s and 1970s, Israel is portrayed as an adamant, negative, intransigent, and peace-refusing actor. The Palestinians are initially seen as victims and refugees, but from 1974 onward as actors in their own right. The conflict in the late 1960s and 1970s is represented as the Israeli occupation of Arab territories, and the refusal of Israel to return the lands and recognize Palestinian rights. The presented solution is the land for peace solution based on Resolution 242 and 338. Under the Shah the United Nations is not accorded a role, while Iran is supportive of the growing US role in the conflict. In 1968, for example, Iranian foreign minister Ardeshir Zahedi stated at the United Nations that "my country follows developments in that area with a sense of anxiety for the future and sympathy for the innocent people who are the first victims of war" (Zahedi 1968). In 1971, Iranian foreign minister Abbas Ali Khalatbary argues that the "situation in the Middle East continues to cause us profound concern and sorrow" (Khalatbary 1971), and in 1975 that Iran "praises the efforts made this year by the Secretary of State of the United States, Mr. Kissinger" (Khalatbary 1975).

In this initial period, the Turkish and Iranian role identities were rather similar, emerging in a similar regional context. After World War I, both Turkey[8] and Iran embarked on substantial secular reform processes that would reorient their domestic arenas toward the West. However, in stark contrast to each other, Turkey's reform process aimed at establishing a republic, Iran's at establishing an autocratic monarchy. Furthermore, while Turkey asserted its independence after World War I, Iran was not only occupied during World War II, but remained more intensely subject to Western dominance, as evident in the oil nationalization crisis and the subsequent CIA-orchestrated coup against elected prime minister Mohammad Mossadegh in 1952. After World War II, both Turkey and Iran did not see Israel, but the Soviet Union, as their key threat. Both shared borders with the USSR and moved into the emerging US alliance system in the Middle East.

In 1947, both Iran and Turkey favored the minority plan of the partition plan (federal state) and voted against the partition plan at the United Nations General Assembly in 1948. In 1949, Turkey abstained and Iran rejected Resolution 273, which admitted Israel to membership at the UN. In 1949 Turkey recognized Israel and in 1950 Iran recognized it de facto. Both countries began to develop rather good relations with Israel, specifically during the later 1950s in the context of the so-called Arab Cold War (Ramazani 2013, 415).

In 1955, the Baghdad Pact was formed by Iran, Turkey, Iraq, Pakistan, and the United Kingdom to contain the Soviet Union, as well as the rising power of Egypt. In 1958, Iraq went through a revolution and subsequently exited from the Baghdad Pact. In the same year, the United Arab Republic was established. As a reaction to both developments Iran signed a military and intelligence cooperation agreement with Israel in 1959 and expanded economic relations. In reaction to the same developments, Turkey entered into a secret "peripheral alliance" with Israel in 1958 (Bengio 2004). Nonetheless, both Iran and Turkey tried to keep some balance on the surface. Turkey, for example, withdrew its ambassador from Israel in 1956 in the wake of the Suez crisis. And Iran provided medical aid to Arab states in the 1967 war, as well as overflight rights to Soviet planes with military equipment for the Arab states in the 1973 war.

After the war, both Turkey and Iran became "concerned bystanders" in the conflict. But while Iran was increasingly enmeshed in domestic problems, Turkey began to drive a more balanced course that was directly related to problems it encountered in its relationship with the US related to the conflict in Cyprus. Turkey developed the role of contributing to "peace and security in the Middle East by reducing the friction with the Arab states that had prevailed in the 1950s" (Aykan 1993, 94). This role was meant to enable Turkey to have good relations with the West and the Arab world. Turkey became more supportive of the Palestinian cause, albeit always in the dominant international framework, whether that be UN Security Council Resolutions 242 or 338 or the two-state solution today. In the UNGA, Turkey voted for resolutions that included the right of the people of Palestine to national independence and sovereignty, as well as for the ones that confirmed the PLO as the representative of the Palestinians. At the same time, Turkey did not maintain close relations with the PLO until 1979 when the PLO was allowed to open an office in Ankara. This Turkish approach remained contingent throughout the 1980s during which not much variance in the Turkish role representation could be found and the discussion of which will, therefore, focus on Turkey's role from the 1990s until today, following the case of Iran after the revolution in 1979, which will be discussed next.

5.2.2. Iran after the Revolution in 1979 and up until Today

In 1979, Iran's role identity changed radically, initially being unsettled and continuously subject to change, in stark contrast to the rather stable role identities of Turkey, Saudi Arabia, and Egypt in the same time period.

In 1979, the Iranian interim minister of foreign affairs, Ibrahim Yazdi, noted at the UN that this is

> the first time since the coup engineered in Iran by the Central Intelligence Agency in 1953 that the Iranian delegation to the United Nations has represented the true preference of the Iranian people. . . . While the Iranians felt a deep sense of solidarity with the people of Palestine and their sole and legitimate representative, the PLO, the Iranian delegation voted with the Zionists, whose repression of the Palestinians and the Lebanese has become comparable to Nazi criminal acts. (Yazdi 1979)

Iran now begins to represent itself as the anti-Zionist spearhead, the spearhead of resistance, and the revolutionary center of the Islamic world. In 1982, for example, the Iranian foreign minister, Ali Akbar Velayati, states at the UNGA that the new foundations of Iran's foreign policy are

> resistance to oppression and tyranny, support for the oppressed nations and the tyrannized masses in the developing countries, non-reliance on foreign Powers, rejection of all forms of domination and being dominated, respect for other countries' sovereignty, independence and territorial integrity, and non-interference in the internal affairs of other countries, on a basis of reciprocity. (Velayati 1982)

In this new role, the Palestine question becomes central:

> We believe that the root solution to the Palestine problem and to the whole Middle East crisis can be found only by placing emphasis on the fact that the problem is an Islamic one and through an endeavor to create a unity of views among Moslem forces. For that reason, the Islamic Republic of Iran has always tried to emphasize the Islamic dimension of the problem, and the proposal made by Iran for the formation of a united Islamic front against Zionism and imperialism is in fact nothing but a way of emphasizing the Islamic nature of the Palestinian issue. (Velayati 1982)

This role performance, however, begins to change again in 1986, when Iran starts to frame its role in relation to the dominant international and regional framework of peace. In 1986, Velayati states in relation to the Fez plan that Iran opposes "any peace plan that includes direct or indirect recognition of the Zionist entity" (Velayati 1986). This role as an *opponent of peace* moves to *opponent of "unjust peace"* in 1993, and finally to *promoter of just and lasting peace* in the later 1990s. In 1993, referring to the Oslo Accords, Velayati seeks to highlight the hollowness of the Middle East Peace Process script—calling it out as a "fanfare"—by stating that

> historical realities, the recent accord, notwithstanding the international fanfare, does not present a realistic solution to the root causes of the conflict, does not promise restoration of Palestinian rights, and thus cannot establish justice, which is the only foundation of a lasting peace. And no one can cede Palestine on behalf of the Palestinian people or Al-Quds Al-Sharif on behalf of the Muslims. (Velayati 1993)

In 1997, the Iranian minister of foreign affairs, Kamal Kharrazi, states that "I reiterate once again that the Islamic Republic of Iran also seeks peace and stability in the Middle East—a just and lasting peace that would receive regional consensus and that would cure this chronic crisis once and for all" (Kharrazi 1997). Such a comprehensive peace is further developed in President Mohammad Khatami's proposal for a "Dialogue among Civilizations," based on dialogue and understanding (Khatami 1998).

President Mahmoud Ahmadinejad portrays Iran as an actor of peace and stability. In 2005 he states that because

> of its key importance and influence in the important and strategic Middle East region, the Islamic Republic of Iran is committed to contributing actively to the promotion of peace and stability in that region. . . . In Palestine, a sustainable peace will be possible through justice, an end to discrimination, an end to the occupation of Palestinian land, the return of all Palestinian refugees and the establishment of a democratic Palestinian State with Al-Quds Al-Sharif as its capital. (Ahmadinejad 2005)

What is notable in the speeches of Ahmadinejad is that rather than representing roles for Iran, he focuses on the framing of Israel. Before turning to that issue, however, it should be noted that Iran strengthened its role representation as an actor committed to stability and justice after the Arab uprisings and with the nuclear deal. In 2013, President Hassan Rouhani states that "Iran is an anchor of stability in an ocean of regional instabilities" (Rouhani 2013). In 2017, he employs the term "moderation," which "is the path of peace. But a just and inclusive peace, not peace for one nation, and war and turmoil for others" (Rouhani 2017). Thus, while Iran's role performance has been subject to change until the 2000s, from the early 2000s onward and following the Arab uprisings specifically, it becomes comparatively settled, focused on its role as a regional power working toward stability and peace.

As for Israel, from 1979 onward, Iranian representatives describe it as a tool of imperialism, criminal and brutal, at times equated with the Nazis (Yazdi 1979; Velayati 1983) or called a "cancer" (Velayati 1984). This changes in the mid-1980s when it is described mainly as imperialist, criminal, expansionist, aggressive, barbaric, brutal, and ruthless. In the early 1990s and until 2007, this representation of Israel moves tendentiously toward intransigent violator of human rights and international law. In 1996, for example, Velayati states that "Israel has neither regard for international law nor any commitment to peace" (Velayati 1996). This framing, however, breaks down again during the presidency of Ahmadinejad.

In 2011, several delegations, including the entire EU delegation, leave the General Assembly during Ahmadinejad's speech when he states that

> if some European countries still use the Holocaust—after six decades—as an excuse to pay ransom to the Zionists, should it not be an obligation of the slave masters and colonial Powers to pay reparations to the affected nations? . . . By using their imperialistic media network, which is under the influence of colonialism, they threaten anyone who questions the Holocaust and the event of 11 September with sanctions and military action. (Ahmadinejad 2011)

This changes again with President Rouhani when Israel is mainly portrayed as an impediment to a nuclear-weapon free zone, but also as aggressive and brutal (Rouhani 2013), or as a "rogue and racist regime" that "tramples upon the most basic rights of the Palestinians" (Rouhani 2017).

As for the Palestinians, from 1979 onward, they are represented as the "Muslim people of Palestine" (Velayati 1982), so sidelining other religious groups present in the area, and Palestine as "the holy land of the divine prophets" (Velayati 1984). Thus, they are placed in a Muslim, rather than an Arab, framework. From the 1990s onward, the Palestinians are mainly represented in terms of their inalienable rights. From 1997 onward, Iran speaks of the "indigenous Palestinian people," a category that now includes Muslims, Christians, and Jews.

The diagnostic representation of the conflict remains rather stable in the observed time period, focusing mainly on occupation, oppression, and exploitation, the destruction of Palestinian resources, systematic violation of human rights, expulsions and settlements. In contrast to the representation of the conflict, which remains rather stable, the proposed solutions do change substantially. In the 1980s, the represented solution is to "expel and annihilate the usurpers and destroy the basis and foundation of the Israeli regime, which is Zionist racism" (Velayati 1982), or the "expulsion of Israel from Palestine and all Arab lands and the return of Palestinians to their homeland to establish an independent State therein" (Velayati 1986). This changes in the 1990s to ending "the occupation of the Palestinian land and the establishment of an independent Palestinian State in the entire land of Palestine" (Velayati 1991) and the "full realization of all the rights of the people of Palestine, including the return of all Palestinian refugees to their own land, enabling them to exercise their inalienable right to self-determination, and the liberation of all occupied territories" (Velayati 1994). In 2000, this framing increasingly approximates the script of the UNGA (see chapter 6) as Iran speaks of an "end to the occupation of all Arab and Muslim territories, including the Golan Heights, the restoration of the rights of Palestinian people, including their right to return to their homeland, the exercise of their inalienable right to self-determination through democratic means and the establishment of their independent State with Al-Quds al-Sharif as its capital" (Kharrazi 2000). This somewhat changes again with Ahmadinejad, when the framing is more about apartheid and a one-state solution. In 2005, Ahmadinejad states that "in Palestine, a sustainable peace will be possible through justice, an end to discrimination, an end to the occupation of Palestinian land, the return of all Palestinian refugees and the establishment of a democratic Palestinian State with Al-Quds Al-Sharif as its capital" (Ahmadinejad

2005). In 2008, Ahmadinejad speaks again about the "entire Palestinian lands" where a "free referendum in Palestine to determine and establish the type of State" (Ahmadinejad 2008) should be held. Rouhani focuses more on the diagnostic rather than the prognostic part, speaking about Israeli apartheid (Rouhani 2016).

Regarding the United Nations, in the early years after the revolution, Iran argues that the "Zionist regime" should be expelled from the UN. In 1983, for example, Velayati states that "under Article 6 the Zionist regime should be expelled from the United Nations for persistent violation of the principles of the Charter" (Velayati 1983). In the 1990s and 2000s, Iran mainly points out that the UNSC "has repeatedly fallen prey to the interests of a permanent member" (Velayati 1996). It does not explicitly foresee a role for the UN in its solution for the conflict. Regarding the Palestinian statehood bid at the UNGA, Iran, while voting affirmatively on it, has been skeptical of this Palestinian Authority (PA) move.[9]

Homeira Moshirzadeh (2007) has pointed out that there are three meta discourses that constitute the identity of the Islamic Republic of Iran: the discourses of independence, justice, and resistance. All three relate to the Palestine question. The discourse of independence was already evolving and used in Iran's role conception before 1979, dominated by the idea of being an "independent country" (Holsti 1970). After the revolution, this discourse became institutionalized in the constitution, which rejects oppression, colonialization, and foreign control (Moshirzadeh 2007, 530–31). The second meta discourse is related to the central role justice plays in Islam and in Shiism in particular. It has translated into support for liberation movements, thus giving it a transnational dimension, as well. Finally, the discourse of resistance stems directly from the revolution and, as Moshirzadeh has pointed out, some "of the elements of the discourse of resistance were absorbed into the official discourse of the Islamic Republic," even though over the course of time, "most of these elements of the movement discourse were substituted by elements of a state discourse in which the legitimacy of international institutions such as international law, international organizations, diplomacy, etc. was recognized" (Moshirzadeh 2007, 535), specifically during the Akbar Hashemi Rafsanjani and Khatami presidencies, which sought to normalize Iran's relations with the society of states.

While in the early 1980s, Iran's identity has been described as "messianic" (Ehteshami 2014, 268), after the Iran-Iraq war and toward the end of the Cold War, Iran went through a "transition to pragmatism and the establishment of the pragmatist line in Iran's foreign policy" (Ehteshami 2009, 332). After Khomeini died in 1989, Ayatollah Ali Khamenei—considered as part of the conservative camp—became supreme leader. While Khamenei has the last word on foreign policy matters and sets a general course for it in the framework of Iran's Islamic role understanding, since 1989 the president is the key agenda setter in this context. While the presidents have not represented the whole spectrum of political forces in Iran, variances in their role representations do show how the Islamic revolution—as Arshin Adib-Moghaddam has pointed out—"continues to be constructed and reinvented" (Adib-Moghaddam 2017, 126–27).

President Rafsanjani (in office from 1989 to 1997) sought to break Iran's isolation through an economic opening. This agenda was intensified by President Khatami who had campaigned on a program framed as "Islamic democracy" for Iran, for which he rallied the votes of women and youth (Behrooz 2012, 382), while internationally his key initiative became the "dialogue of civilizations" oriented toward a world society in which rights are respected and realized.[10] In 2005, the neoconservative Mahmoud Ahmadinejad won on a populist agenda. In 2009, he was reelected under allegations of substantial vote rigging, which triggered the Green Movement's protests in 2009. Since 2013, the reformist Hassan Rouhani has been president of Iran, presiding over the negotiation, signing, and implementation of the Joint Comprehensive Plan of Action on Iran's nuclear file in 2015.

In the 1990s, Iran's position toward the "peace process" has also to be seen in the context of Iran's relationship to the US and its role in the region. With the US's first Iraq invasion in 1990, Washington not only moved its troops into the Gulf, but under President Clinton's dual containment policy it also dropped diplomacy in the Gulf at a time when it was heavily investing in diplomacy in the Levant. This, as Anoushiravan Ehteshami has pointed out, was a minefield for Iran as it not only "threaten[ed] to subsume its ally, Syria, in a Western-oriented peace agreement with Israel but it also took Iran dangerously close to being frozen out of the unfolding regional order following the first Iraq war. Teheran was rather concerned that the emergence of new agendas from Israel, the Arab states, and the Palestinians had left no room for

Iranian involvement, bar opposition to the whole process" (Ehteshami 2009, 333). As Rafsanjani attempted to lower tensions with the US, he was rebuffed by the Clinton administration, which—as Trita Parsi has pointed out—was a critical strategic mistake, as it gave Iran an incentive to oppose the peace process to defeat the dual containment policy (Parsi 2019).

Iran's threat perceptions, however, skyrocketed as the Bush junior administration entered office and placed Iran in the so-called "axis of evil" that would be subject to US regime change policies. The US intervention first in Afghanistan and then in Iraq heightened fears of a pincer movement aimed at regime change in Iran, and Iranian public opinion became extremely hostile toward the US (Gause 2013, 295). In 2005, neoconservative and staunchly anti-Western President Ahmadinejad was elected, and he abandoned the integrationist approach of his predecessor. As the wars evolved, however, threat perceptions declined, since

> Iranian ruling circles quickly realized that the United States was stuck, not in one quagmire, but two. They also realized that Iran was a key player in both of these theatres and that it would be extremely difficult for the United States to disengage from either Iraq or Afghanistan in the absence of Iran's cooperation or at least consent. . . . Iran was indispensable to the construction of a stable and legitimate security structure in the Persian Gulf and beyond. (Ayoob 2014, 408)

President Barack Obama understood this dynamic, "recognizing that Iran's prolonged isolation was neither possible nor necessarily helpful" (Parsi 2019) and—together with China, France, Russia, the United Kingdom, and Germany—negotiated the Joint and Comprehensive Plan of Action with Iran. Obama's approach was also enabled by the election of President Rouhani who had returned to the integrationist approach.

Iran's power in the region has increased in the wake of the US-led Iraq invasion and with the Arab uprisings, which Iran has framed as an "Islamic awakening" (Ehteshami and Mohammadi 2017; Mohseni 2013) and a countermove to the US-led order in the region. At the same time, with its crackdown on the Green Movement in 2009 and its political and military involvement in the civil war in Syria, Iran has also appeared as a counterrevolutionary actor itself. In light of this, its rhetoric of resistance to Israel might be even more crucial for maintaining its identity, fostered not least by Israel and the Trump administration, which seeks to tear down the Joint and Comprehensive Plan of Action and has reinstalled Bush's confrontational policy toward Iran.

As opposed to the early 2000s, however, Iran today is a regional powerhouse that has forged an alliance of those actors that have been excluded by the web of relations in the Camp David Order; the "axis" or "chain" of resistance is also an effect of this exclusionary order, which is often referred to as the "US Project." As opposed to the early days of the revolution when Iran arguably just played its distinct role as an opposer in the Camp David script, today Iran performs a role that provides a substantial external challenge to that script through its own stable web of relations, which it coordinates but does not dominate, and the meaning that ties this web together, such as freedom for self-determination and independence, freedom from foreign interference, oppression, colonialism, and occupation (Saad-Ghorayeb 2011; Huber 2021).

5.2.3. Turkey after the End of the Cold War until Today

As opposed to its role as a concerned bystander that supports US and Arab initiatives since the 1967 war up until the 1980s (see section 2.1), in the early 1990s, Turkey begins to display a more active role identity on the conflict. In 1993, the Turkish minister of foreign affairs, Hikmet Cetin, states that as "a country that neighbors the Middle East, has a record of constructive involvement in the region's affairs and good traditional ties with all the parties to this dispute, Turkey hails with the utmost satisfaction this momentous shift from enmity towards reconciliation. . . . We are committed to assisting their endeavours in every way" (Cetin 1993). In 1996, Deputy Prime Minister Tansu Ciller frames Turkey as a "devoted supporter" (Ciller 1996) and Foreign Minister Ismail Cem as an active supporter of lasting peace and security in the Middle East in 1999. This role understanding continues into the AKP government. In 2003, Deputy Prime Minister Abdullah Gül states that "Turkey has close ties with both Israelis and Palestinians. We remain ready to contribute to the implementation of the road map, to which we believe there is no alternative. We are also willing to contribute to the improvement of the security environment as needed, and to the alleviation of the harsh living conditions of Palestinians" (Gül 2003). In 2007, Prime Minister Recep Tayyip Erdogan states that "we stand ready to support in every way possible the parties in the efforts to revive the peace process" (Erdogan 2007) and in 2009 that "Turkey has made every possible effort to contribute to the peace process in the Middle East. The indirect negotiations between Syria and Israel, which we hosted in 2008, are a case in point. Depending on the mutual desire of both parties, we are ready to resume our active role in the future" (Erdogan 2009).

In 2011, this role representation continues, even though Turkish-Israeli relations enter into troubled waters as evident in Erdogan's long elaboration on the theme at the United Nations General Assembly:

> Turkey's support for the recognition of the State of Palestine is unconditional. Turkey will continue to work actively in the Middle East to ensure peace. . . . This commitment is a natural extension of our vision for regional peace and stability and our commitment to international law and justice. . . . Turkey has never pursued hostile and confrontational policies against any State. Our foreign policy is based on the principles of friendship and cooperation. Our policy towards Israel is no exception to these principles. . . . Let me also emphasize from this rostrum that we do not have a problem with the people of Israel. Our problem arises from the aggressive policies of the current Israeli Government. (Erdogan 2011)

From 2012 onward, Turkey mainly frames itself as a committed supporter of the Palestinian cause, but never outside dominant international and regional solutions to the conflict.

As regards the representation of Israel, in the first half of the 1980s with Israel's invasion in Lebanon, Israel is for the first time portrayed as intransigent, defiant, provocative, aggressive, arrogant, violent, scrupulous, and stubborn. This changes in the second half of the 1980s, when Turkey calls it intransigent and that it should be more conciliatory. In the early 1990s, the portrayal goes back to Israel without adjectives, and in 1996–97—during the first Benjamin Netanyahu period—to intransigent. From 1998 to 2003, Israel is called a "friend." From 2009 onward (the onset of the Netanyahu government) Israel is called aggressive, defiant, and an obstacle to peace. Regarding the Palestinians, from 1998 onward, Turkey refers to them as friends. From 2004 until 2009, Turkey—in line with the US and EU—focuses on a reform of the Palestinian Authority, but after 2007 also highlights how problematic the political rift between Fatah and Hamas is.

Regarding the representation of the conflict, from the mid-1980s until the mid-2000s, Turkey hardly focuses on identifying what the conflict is about, but follows the general trend to focus on its solution. In this respect, Turkey first highlights the withdrawal of Israel and the legitimate rights of the Palestinians and their right to a state, supports the land for peace formula, and from 2002 onward the two-state solution, calling for an "independent and geographically unified Palestinian State" (Erdogan 2017). From 2010 onward, Turkey begins again to define what the conflict is about, focusing mainly on the occupation and settlement expansion. Also from 2010 onward, Turkey begins to stress the role of the UN again, in terms of how the UN should become more effective, send a fact-finding mission, and accept Palestine as a member state.

In the 1980s, Turkey continued with its role as a "concerned bystander" in a balanced way (Aykan 1993, 103), seeking to neither alienate the Arab world nor the US and Europe. While Ankara was initially supportive of Sadat going to Jerusalem, it then opposed the actual deal on grounds of its failure to solve the Palestinian question. In 1979, the PLO was allowed to establish an office in Ankara, but—again as part of Turkey's balancing strategy—at the level of chargé d'affaires like its Israeli counterpart. At about the same time as relations with Israel started to become denser again, Turkey recognized the 1988 Palestinian Declaration of Independence. In 1991, both sides reached ambassadorial level.

With the end of the Cold War, Turkey had to reconfigure its role in the region and the world. Not only was the future of NATO and Turkey's place in it uncertain, but its immediate security environment deteriorated. New conflicts emerged in the Balkans, the Caucasus, and in Iraq, while the conflict with the Kurdistan Workers' Party (PKK) flared up and Turkey increasingly perceived the Middle East as the number-one source of security threats to Turkey (Altunişik 2004). Domestically, in this period, Turkey went through a period of governmental instability with ten different coalition governments being formed within ten years. The National Security Council benefited from a lack of political consensus and unity in the coalition governments (Gözen 2004, 44), and the 1990s represented the "age of the military's involvement in domestic and foreign policy" (Canan 2009, 56). With this domestic background, Turkey's foreign relations with its neighbors (Syria, Iran, and Greece specifically) became highly securitized. At the same time, relations with Israel intensified as did relations with the US. "Under the strong personal influence of President Ozal . . . it has followed a course of intimate cooperation with the United States to ensure stability in the region, which is reminiscent of the 1950s" (Aykan 1993, 106).

Turkey also developed a role identity as a mediator in the 1990s in response to the Balkan wars. This policy further strengthened under Foreign Minister Ismail Cem (in office 1997–2002) who initiated dialogues with Syria and Greece and changed Turkey's foreign policy toward the Middle East, focusing on historical and cultural aspects of Turkey's relationship with the region, Turkey's multicultural identity, its role as a model for the region, and the improvement of relations and reconciliation with the Middle East (Terzi 2010, 42). As the Justice and Development Party entered power in Turkey, this approach grew and was substantiated, and was also applied to Israel and Palestine as the peace process broke down and violence escalated.

The role of the Turkish military in politics started to decline, leading to political rather than securitized approaches to Turkey's interests in the region. The AKP government developed its "zero problems with neighbours" policy, in the framework of which Turkey came to terms with Syria and Iran, and started viewing American interventionism and the deterioration of the Israel-Palestinian conflict as the main source of instability in the region. Israel, in contrast, increasingly focused on Iran as the main danger. Thus, foreign policy objectives between Turkey and Israel began to diverge substantially. But while no longer a privileged partner under the first years of AKP rule, Israel remained one of Turkey's "neighbours" with whom to seek "zero problems." The AKP also inherited Turkey's role as a regional interlocutor. It acted as a mediator between Israel and Syria, as well as between Israel and Hamas. Turkish troops also participated in the United Nations Interim Force in Lebanon (UNIFIL) after the 2006 July War between Israel and Hezbollah. Thus, the change in government in Turkey from secular parties to political Islam meant that Turkey intensified its role as a mediator through active involvement in diplomacy. This mediating role, however, was not accepted by Israel from 2009 onward.

Just before the uprisings, Turkey was engaged in mediation between Israel and Syria, which broke down with the Israeli war on Gaza in

December 2008/January 2009, perceived by Turkey as an Israeli rebuffing of its mediating role and an improper act of aggression, a perception that was heightened by the 2010 Gaza Flotilla raid. With general elections approaching in 2011, the AKP's outspoken opposition to the war on Gaza and the Flotilla incident increased. Ankara requested an apology from Israel, which chose to express regret instead. In September 2011, after the leaking of the UN Palmer Report, Ankara downgraded diplomatic relations with Israel. Turkey has thrown its weight behind the uprisings and against counter-revolutionary forces such as Saudi Arabia or Egypt in the region. As opposed to any other actor observed in this book, it has been supportive of all the revolutions, even though democracy in Turkey itself has been deteriorating (Aydın-Düzgit 2019). Initially, the AKP styled itself as a model for political Islam in countries such as Egypt or Tunisia. It also took the side of the Syrian opposition in 2011, abandoning its newly found friendship with Bashar al-Assad. This approach, however, increasingly put Turkey on a confrontation course with after-coup-Egypt and Saudi Arabia, on the one hand, and with Syria, Iran, and Russia, on the other. Turkey has recently tried to solve this problematic situation through a more pragmatic foreign policy approach that implied normalization of relations with Israel, Egypt, and Russia. Since 2016, Turkey has militarily intervened in Syria; together with Russia and Iran, it is part of the Astana talks. While Turkey has not departed from the Middle East Peace Process, it increasingly does represent alternatives to it. This is specifically crystalizing as the Trump administration is tearing down the script of the "peace process" from within. Turkey has contested the Trump administration's policies on the Palestine/Israel question, rejecting its embassy move to Jerusalem, withdrawal from the United Nations Relief and Works Agency (UNRWA) (to which Turkey increased its funding), as well as its recognition of Israel's annexation of the Syrian Golan Heights in contravention to international law. President Erdogan has stated that the US has "chosen to be part of the problem, not a solution, and lost its mediator role in the Middle East peace process" (Oliphant 2018). Turkey, as opposed to any other actor performing within the script of the "peace process," has consistently called for an end to the Israeli blockade on Gaza where it also engages in humanitarian aid and reconstruction. Turkey, which has close relations to Hamas as well as the Muslim Brotherhood, is however prevented by both Israel and Egypt from becoming a mediator regarding Gaza or a reconciliation between Hamas and Fatah.

5.3. EC/EU, USSR/Russia, and the United States

Europe, the USSR/Russia, and the US are discussed together, as all three have been global powers involved in the conflict. Historically speaking, these three powers had different levels of involvement with the region. While European states have been colonial and imperial powers in the region—and the UK in Palestine specifically—the same does not apply to the US and Russia, even though Russia had long-standing societal relations with the region and its internal policies had also affected Palestine specifically. It was the pogroms in anti-Semitic Czarist Russia that contributed to the waves of immigration to Israel. Czarist Russia was, in fact, in favor of founding a Jewish state. As Sergei Witte, Russian minister of finance under Tsar Nicolas II, stated, "the Jews are being given encouragement to emigrate—kicks for example" (Kreutz 2007, 46). The persecution of Jews in Europe and Russia triggered waves of immigration to Palestine (Hollis 2012).[11] A special responsibility is also held here by Germany, which annihilated more than six million Jews in the Holocaust and caused an immense refugee crisis.

Different from both Europe and Russia, when the US entered the stage of world politics in the early twentieth century, it had no comparable historical relations with the region, and—most importantly—no colonial history there. The US was also not part of the League of Nations (even though it did accept the Palestine mandate in a convention with the UK). It was, therefore, initially seen as a source of hope for the region. Similarly, the USSR after the 1917 Bolshevik Revolution diverged from the Russian Empire by seeing itself as the spearhead in a global proletarian revolution against Western capitalism and its colonial/imperial rule. Indeed, when looking at both the US and the USSR—as Odd Arne Westad has pointed out—it is the great tragedy of the Cold War "that two historical projects that were genuinely anticolonial in their origins, became part of a much older pattern of domination because of the intensity of their conflict, the stakes they believed were involved, and the almost apocalyptic fear of the consequences if the opponent won" (Westad 2007, 397).

5.3.1. Up until 1967

Initially, neither the USSR nor European states present at the UN represent any roles for themselves in the conflict at the United Nations. When they mention the conflict, European states see it in terms of a refugee and humanitarian issue. In contrast to this, the United States does present a role for itself prior to 1967, namely as a supporter of action under a UN umbrella. While it hardly mentions Israel, it also sees the Palestinians mainly as refugees and the conflict as a refugee and humanitarian problem. Corresponding to this vision, it sees the repatriation of refugees "who wish to live in peace," as well as economic aid and financial assistance, as the main solutions, perceiving the UN in the driving seat in this respect.

In light of the enormous European responsibility in the Israel-Palestinian conflict, the framing of the conflict by European states in the United Nations in the postwar years as a "refugee issue" cannot be read as anything else than a monumental denial of the disastrous role Europe had played in causing the conflict, specifically the UK, which not only laid the basis for the conflict in the mandate period but also dropped the issue on the United Nations in 1947, unwilling to engage in the necessary efforts to bring the mandate for Palestine to its political conclusion, namely the self-determination of the people in Palestine. Furthermore, in the postwar years, France and the UK still behaved as imperial powers in the region. France did not only become Israel's main weapons supplier, but France and the UK cooperated with Israel in the tripartite invasion in Egypt in 1956, which, however, resulted in the shattering of their power, and the US moving into the subsequent power vacuum with the Eisenhower Doctrine in 1957. Europe's denial of its own legacy in the conflict is a clear example of what Michelle Pace and Roberto Roccu have referred to as "Amnesiac Power Europe" (Pace and Roccu 2020).

The USSR was initially quite supportive of Israel.[12] In 1947, it abandoned its previous support for a one-state solution for Arabs and Jews, and instead supported the partition plan, provided Israel with military aid in the 1948 war through Czechoslovakia, and was the first state to officially recognize Israel in 1948, allowing Jews from the Soviet sphere of influence to emigrate. This Soviet position has been explained by several factors, including the perception that Israel was fighting against pro-British forces such as the Transjordanian Arab Legion and that the "USSR had come to view Zionism as a potentially progressive force in an Arab world dominated by reactionary regimes" (Stein 2012, 42). The USSR was also deeply influenced by the Holocaust, as well as the support the USSR had received from Jews in World War II.[13] As Andrei Gromyko, then permanent representative of the USSR at the United Nations, pointed out at the General Assembly meeting in 1947,

> the Jewish people has been closely linked with Palestine for a considerable period in history. Apart from that, . . . we must also not overlook the position in which the Jewish people found themselves as a result of the recent world war. . . . The solution of the Palestine problem based on a partition of Palestine into two separate states will be of profound historical significance, because this decision will meet the legitimate demands of the Jewish people. (Gromyko 1947)

While the Soviets might have feared that a binational state "would be Arab-dominated and, therefore, pro-British" (Golan 1990, 36), the Soviet Union did support an Arab state on the basis of the partition plan. After the 1948 war, however, the Soviets dropped the discourse on the Palestinians' right to national self-determination, framing Palestinians mainly as refugees—and putting the blame for the Palestine refugee question on the British (Golan 1990, 42). Moscow mainly focused on opposing the annexation of the West Bank by Jordan and supported the internationalization of Jerusalem so that East Jerusalem would not fall under Jordanian control (Golan 1990, 42). In the early 1950s, however, relations with Israel begun to enter troubled waters as the latter began to back the US more clearly in the emerging Cold War. This did not lead to an improvement in Soviet relations with the Arab world, which took place only after Joseph Stalin's death in 1953. Stalin had not only considered the Arabs as backward, but the USSR also moved toward the Global South where the US-USSR competition was increasingly pursued (Golan 1990, 10). In response to the Baghdad Pact (1955), Moscow began to back the so-called radicals and relations intensified specifically under Nikita Khrushchev and after the 1956 Suez crisis, and even more so under Leonid Brezhnev (Freedman 2012, 326). Egypt became the pillar of the Soviet alliance system in the Middle East and it was, in fact, the time of USSR-Egyptian cooperation that characterized the heyday of Moscow in the Middle East.

Along with the USSR, the US had initially been supportive of a one-state solution in which Muslims, Jews, and Christians would live together (Radosh and Radosh 2009). However, and again similar to the USSR, the

US changed course in 1947 and not only supported the partition plan but actively lobbied other countries to do so as well, ensuring a majority in the UNGA for Resolution 181. As with the USSR, the American public weighed most heavily the Holocaust and the humanitarian needs of Jewish refugees in the displaced person camps for which a Jewish state represented a solution that would relieve Washington of immigration pressure. American political institutions were split on the issue of partition. As Steven Spiegel has pointed out, the "public and Congress were generally more sympathetic toward the Zionist movement. The government, especially the national security bureaucracy (National Security Council, Defense and State departments, and the intelligence community), on the whole saw the nascent dispute in the context of American policy toward the Arabs and even the Muslim world" (Spiegel 2012, 295). Against the opposition of the State Department—both Secretary of State George Marshall and George Kennan believed that the recognition of the State of Israel would negatively affect key US interests in the region as it would not only anger US ally Saudi Arabia but also give rise to extremism in the Arab world, enabling the USSR to gain a foothold there (Radosh and Radosh 2009)—President Harry Truman de facto recognized Israel immediately, while official recognition followed after Israeli elections in January 1949. Both US and Soviet support were therefore crucial for the establishment of Israel, even though the US, initially, sought to keep a more neutral stance to prevent opposition in the Arab world to the US in an intensifying Cold War. The French weapons supply to Israel was, therefore, useful to the US at the time, as it guaranteed Israel's military edge over its neighbors without the US being directly involved in supplying it.

How different the US stance was in the early Cold War years to today is best exemplified by its reaction to the Suez invasion of the tripartite alliance of France, the UK, and Israel, when President Dwight Eisenhower intervened not only to stop their military campaign (freezing public aid to Israel), but in its aftermath forced Israel to withdraw from Sinai by threatening to also freeze private aid (the Lyndon Johnson administration reacted very differently to the 1967 war; see below). At the same time, the Eisenhower Doctrine (1957) gave Israel the opportunity to intensify relations with the US. A more substantive change in that direction, however, emerged under the administration of John F. Kennedy, which sold Hawk antiaircraft missiles to Israel in response to Soviet military aid to Cairo (Bass 2004). "In terms of the American–Israeli relationship," as Spiegel has pointed out, "this assistance was a critical step in forging a new policy that broke with the earlier taboo about providing military assistance to Israel" (Spiegel 2012, 298), a trend that intensified under President Johnson.

5.3.2. From 1967 until 1979

After the 1967 war, the conflict became a vehicle for the US and USSR to build role identities at the international and regional level, and for projecting influence on the whole Middle East due to the immense presence of the conflict to now not only the regional but also to the international public. In the immediate aftermath of the war, the US stuck to its previous role, but then developed its role as a key broker in the conflict. The USSR and Europe also began to represent roles for themselves in the conflict. While most European nations supported Israel in 1967, French president Charles de Gaulle had declared an arms embargo on Israel a few days before the war. France, indeed, presents itself as an active mover on the conflict in the UN system now, with the other European states as supporters of peace efforts in the UN arena and beyond. In 1976, for example, Max van der Stoel, the representative of the Netherlands, at the time rotating president of the EC's Council of Ministers and therefore representing the EC at the UNGA, states that "the countries of the European Community are prepared to assist, to the best of their ability and to the extent desired by the parties, in the achievement of a settlement, and, as soon as the settlement is approved by all parties, to help in making it a reality" (van der Stoel 1976).

Israel is framed by European states mainly in terms of its right to existence, to security, and peace, and—from 1973 onward—increasingly also as an occupying power. The framing of the Palestinians evolves from refugees to people with legitimate rights until 1975, from 1976 onward identifying the need for a homeland, and from 1979 stressing the necessity to include the PLO in negotiations and the Palestinian right to self-determination in the framework of a peace settlement. The European states also begin to detail what the conflict is about—namely, a question of refugees and from 1973 onward increasingly an occupation, with repressive measures and settlements being built in contravention to international law, constituting an obstacle to peace. Responding to this, the EU highlights the inadmissibility of the acquisition of territory by force, the need to end the occupation, respect for sovereignty and peace, as well as the legitimate rights of the Palestinians and the applicability of the Geneva Convention. As for the role of the UN, the European states see the UNSC in a pivotal role until 1973, when preferences begin to shift to direct peace talks with UNSC Resolutions 242 and 338 as reference points and the UN in a peacekeeping role only.

From 1967 until 1980, the USSR represents itself as a concerned and principled supporter of peace and of the Arab states. In 1971, for example, Soviet foreign minister Andrei Gromyko states that the Soviet Union "wants to see peace in the Middle East. It will continue to support the Arab States which have suffered aggression and their efforts to liberate their territories" (Gromyko 1971). In the war and interwar years, Israel is presented as an aggressive, expansionist actor obstructive to peace, while the USSR, however, is always explicit about Israel's right to existence. After 1975, the USSR refers to Israel without adjectives (except for during the Lebanon invasion when Israel is named aggressive). The representation of the Palestinians changes from Arab refugees to Arab people of Palestine with inalienable rights (1973) and a right to a state (1974), with the PLO as the only legitimate representative (1975). The conflict is portrayed mainly in terms of Israel's occupation, even though the USSR is also explicit about rejecting what it calls Palestinian acts of terrorism. Its solution is security for all states and a Palestinian state. The UN is seen as the key platform for a solution, with UNSC resolutions as a basis and the UNSC as a guarantor of a solution. The Soviet Union explicitly rejects bilateral peacemaking. In 1979, Gromyko discards the Camp David Treaty, stating that

> like all peace-loving peoples, the Soviet people are gravely concerned over the state of affairs in the Middle East. . . . The Soviet policy with respect to the Middle East problem is one of principle. . . . A just settlement and the establishment of lasting peace in the Middle East require that Israel should end its occupation of all the Arab lands it seized in 1967; that the legitimate rights of the Arab people of Palestine, including the right to establish their own state, be safeguarded; and that the right of all States in the Middle East, including Israel, to independent existence under conditions of peace be effectively guaranteed. The separate deal between Egypt and Israel resolves nothing. (Gromyko 1979)

In contrast to the USSR and Europe, the US does not immediately change its role in 1967 and initially remains a supporter of action under a UN umbrella until 1970 when its brokering role takes off. It begins to represent itself as a broker at the request of the conflict parties and, specifically since 1978, describes itself as a successful broker. In 1970, for example, US representative Charles Woodruff Yost states that "the United States has made major diplomatic efforts in recent months and weeks to help bring about peace at long last in the Middle East. . . . In this spirit, my Government is prepared to contribute to renewed efforts toward peace in the Middle East" (Yost 1970). In 1973, Henry Kissinger speaks of the US "special obligation" to assist in the search for solutions (Kissinger 1973), and states in the year after that during "the past year my country has made a major effort to promote peace in the Middle East. President Ford has asked me to reaffirm today that we are determined to press forward with these efforts" (Kissinger 1974). In 1976 he argues that "at the request of the parties, the United States has been actively engaged in the search for peace in the Middle East" (Kissinger 1976). Israel is portrayed in its right to live in peace and security, and from the President Jimmy Carter period onward, also in terms of its shared values with the US and the US's unquestionable commitment to Israel's security. In 1977, President Carter states at the General Assembly that the "commitment of the United States to Israel's security is unquestionable. . . . One of the things that binds the American people to Israel is our shared respect for human rights and the courage with which Israel has defended such rights" (Carter 1977). The Palestinians are either not represented at all or are mentioned in terms of legitimate interests and rights, which are not further specified. The conflict as such is not described, while its solution is framed varyingly in terms of economic development, justice for the refugees, mutual respect for independence and territorial integrity, curbing the arms race, lasting arrangements through binding treaties, and diplomatic relations. In the run-up to the Camp David Accords, the issues of an end to the occupation and self-governing authority for the Palestinians are added to this. As for the role of the UN, the US mainly refers to UNSC Resolutions 242 and 338 as reference points that need to be substantiated through negotiations, arguing that no settlement can be imposed from the outside.

The 1967 war had opened the region's door to superpower penetration and an increased military dependency of regional states on the US and the USSR (Hinnebusch 2003, 31). Indeed, the defeat of Egypt in 1967 also meant a major blow to Soviet standing in the region and the world. Thus, after the 1967 war, the USSR provided economic and military aid to the so-called confrontation states (Egypt and Syria), just as the US lifted its relations with Israel to a whole new level. Mohammed Heikal (1978) argued that raising the conflict to the global level was an intended strategy of Egyptian president Nasser, as the regional balance of power was dominated by the Israelis. The strategy, however, opened the door to a diplomacy that would enshrine this balance of power in an order sustained by bilateral "peace treaties" instead of a comprehensive peace, which would have guaranteed stability in the region.

President Johnson, in stark contrast to Eisenhower in 1956–57, did not attempt to force Israel to withdraw from the territories it had occupied in 1967 in line with the principle of the inadmissibility of the acquisition of territory by war. Rather, his administration adopted the Israeli position that withdrawal from conquered territory would come only in exchange for a peace agreement. In the run-up to Resolution 242, the "Arabs, on the one hand, insisted on full Israeli withdrawal from newly occupied territory prior to the end of belligerency. Israel, on the other hand, held out for direct negotiations and a 'package settlement' in which withdrawal would occur only after the conclusion of a peace agreement" (Quandt 2005, 46). Johnson was largely supportive of the Israeli version and "American policy shifted from its long-standing emphasis on maintaining the territorial integrity of each state to . . . emphasizing negotiated settlement" (Quandt 2005, 44). The *negotiations paradigm* (K. Makdisi 2018, 7) was born.

This shift can also be seen in the 1969 Rogers Plan, devised by US secretary of state William Rogers after the UN's Jarring Mission (named after its leader, Gunnar Jarring) had failed to implement Resolution 242. Even though this plan represented an attempt to balance the Israeli and Egyptian (and US-Soviet) positions, it was doomed to fail, as it was internally opposed by National Security Adviser Henry Kissinger, who found the plan "too demanding of the administration's friends, too generous to its opponents, and insufficiently attentive to the Soviet threat in the region" (Eisenberg 2012, 86). Where Rogers prioritized diplomacy to tackle the conflict as such, Kissinger saw this conflict in a Cold War framework and prioritized the strengthening of Israel in line with the Nixon Doctrine whereby allies would be supported with economic and military aid and weapons, thus preserving a certain regional balance in favor of the US. US Middle East policy began to look as "little more than open support for Israel" (Walt 1990, 119), and Israel received a tenfold increase in aid in the Kissinger period (Quandt 2005, 104). The idea that was presented to justify this was that the subsequent military edge of Israel over its neighbours would constitute a deterrent that ensured that no further war would break out. In line with this reasoning, Kissinger ignored Sadat's attempt to push the US into diplomacy to regain the Sinai. As a result of boosting military support to Israel while dropping diplomacy, Kissinger triggered an arms race in the Middle East and drove some Arab states further into the hands of the USSR. How much both Israel and the US were fooled by deterrence-without-diplomacy is best shown by their utmost surprise when Egypt and Syria launched the 1973 war—a war that would even raise the specter of great power confrontation as the USSR threatened to intervene militarily. Like in 1967, in 1973 both great powers worked together in passing Resolution 338 with both sides promising to pressure their "clients" into acceptance.[14]

Until today, the military edge is portrayed as ensuring stability and Israel's security in the region while it could not prevent war in 1973. Rather, it has been the so-called peace process with the US at its head that provided for a structure that successfully prevented further war, but which—as this book also shows—has also prevented the unfolding of peace. Kissinger, in fact, immediately understood his error in 1973. Israel's military edge alone had not prevented war in the Middle East, and the war had proven highly dangerous on a global scale in a Cold War context, threatening US key interests such as the free flow of oil. Kissinger, therefore, moved to the diplomatic front, but in a different way than Rogers had. Rather than involving all actors, including the USSR, in diplomacy, Kissinger first sidelined them, and then got them out of it altogether. He came forward with a script that in its essence has remained valid until today.

Rather than seeking to balance between both sides, the US continued its support of Israel. This, as Walt has pointed out, was driven by two considerations of Kissinger. First, as opposed to Eisenhower in 1956, he claimed only complete confidence in US support would move Israel toward concessions; and, second, a strong relation with Israel would make the US the key power in the region as the Arab states would need to take it into the equation when seeking to regain occupied territories. Beyond this deterrence strategy, Kissinger also laid the basis for the script for the four decades-long US-led "peace process." This process has been characterized by the following two "paradigms."

First, a divide and rule paradigm: the US has sidelined the UN out of the talks and pursued bilateral talks at the expense of comprehensive talks.

As Raymond Hinnebusch has pointed out, while "the Arabs as a bloc may have had the leverage to extract a comprehensive settlement if no one of them settled for less, Kissinger's step by step diplomacy had divided them and henceforth forced them to individually play weakened hands in negotiations with Israel" (Hinnebusch 2003, 201). Step by step, the US has bound individual states and actors through bilateral treaties (Egypt, the Palestinian Authority, Jordan) in its alliance system with Israel and Saudi Arabia in the region, while excluding those it calls the "radicals" (Syria, Iran, Hezbollah, Hamas). This has cemented cracks in the region, rather than seeking to bridge them. Thus, this approach has *split the region*.

Second, a negotiations paradigm: there is a clear tendency to *focus on process instead of peace* by having the parties talk and pursuing step-by-step diplomacy, which has "remained a tactic for buying more time, . . . cut off from a larger political concept of peace in the Middle East" (Quandt 2005, 156). The preconditions of Israel have been structurally incorporated into the "peace process," while Palestinian rights, which are anchored in international law, have been rejected and made subject to negotiations. For the US, the Israeli right to security is not negotiable, while the Palestinian right to self-determination is—so there is neither a right to a state nor a right to return unless negotiated with Israel. This gives the occupying power a de facto veto over these rights. As Valentina Azarova has pointed out, under the law of occupation, to "protect a people's right to self-determination, the resolution of any 'final status' issues . . . is deferred until the end of occupation. Relegating this process to the end of the occupation is meant to prevent the occupier from coercing local authorities into ceding territorial or other sovereign rights while under the gun" (Azarova 2017, 3).

The position of the USSR on these issues had in this period been decisively different. It advocated talks under a UN umbrella and of a multilateral nature. In the Soviet peace plan presented by Yevgeny Primakov in *Pravda* in 1970, Moscow advocated a negotiated settlement prior to a two-phased withdrawal (Golan 1990, 75), making the 1949 armistice lines the accepted international border (as opposed to the one of the partition plan, which had hitherto been the only border accepted in a UN resolution). After the 1973 war, the Soviets insisted on a comprehensive settlement, rather than a step-by-step approach, whereby borders would be guaranteed by the USSR and the US. Again, the USSR insisted on a complete withdrawal from all the territories occupied in 1967. Regarding Palestinian rights, while Moscow had ignored them since

1949, it began to increase its interest in the issue after the 1967 war (in 1968 Arafat visited Moscow as part of an Egyptian delegation), and relations intensified after 1973 specifically, as Egypt began to move out of the Soviet alliance system. Palestinian nationhood and the right to self-determination were publicly mentioned for the first time in 1974 and became an official position in 1978 when Camp David was nearing its successful completion and when Soviet leader Leonid Brezhnev declared that "there is only one road [to a real settlement] full liberation of all Arab lands occupied by Israel in 1967, of full and unambiguous respect for the lawful rights of the Arab people of Palestine, including the right to create their own independent state" (Kreutz 2007, 60). This Soviet position was crucial for the Palestinians in the international arena and helped them to reach observer status at the UN in 1974. At the same time, Moscow always condemned what it referred to as terrorism,[15] and even though it canceled diplomatic relations with Israel in 1967, it always considered the existence of Israel a legitimate fact.

President Carter initially sought to move away from both Kissinger's step-by-step diplomacy and from bilateral talks back to a comprehensive approach that would include the USSR. As Avi Shlaim has pointed out, when Israeli prime minister Yitzhak Rabin arrived in Washington, "he discovered that the new president had firmly made up his mind in favor of three things: reconvening the Geneva conference; Israeli withdrawal, with only minor modifications, to the borders of 4 June 1967; and recognition of Palestinian rights" (Shlaim 2014, 239)—all three anathema to the Israelis. It was the Egyptians who forced Carter out of his first idea (reconvening Geneva), and who eventually accepted the sidelining of his second and third conditions.

In 1977, Carter came forward with five principles for a Geneva conference convened with the Soviets, including comprehensive peace as the goal of negotiations, Security Council Resolutions 242 and 338 as the basis of negotiations, an end to belligerency and the establishment of the relations of peace, mutually agreed borders and withdrawal in phases, and a provision for a demilitarized Palestinian entity with open relations with Israel and means to permit self-determination by the Palestinians in deciding on their future status (US National Security Council 1977). Specifically, the last point was rejected by the Israelis. Sadat did not like the idea of comprehensive negotiations, either, as he feared these would block talks and put him into a "straitjacket" (Quandt 2005, 188). He commented that "we kicked the Russians out of the door and now

Mr Carter is bringing them back through the window" (Shlaim 2014, 359); undermining Carter, he leapt forward on the bilateral front, with his historic visit to Israel in 1977 setting the road toward the Camp David talks. The eventual Israeli-Egyptian peace treaty consisted of two documents, the Framework for the Conclusion of a Peace Treaty between Egypt and Israel, which provided for Israel's withdrawal from Sinai and normal diplomatic relations between the countries, on one hand, and the more comprehensive Framework for Peace in the Middle East, on the other. The latter, however, was not only a mere paper tiger but also ignored the Syrian Golan Heights as occupied territory. Regarding the OPT, it even adopted the Israeli distinction between Palestinian land and people, as it aimed at establishing an autonomous self-governing authority in the OPT that would replace the Israeli military government without speaking about the Palestinian people's right to a homeland or statehood. It also did not mention East Jerusalem or the right of return. Egypt had, therefore, agreed to an accord that even undermined hitherto existing American positions. Egypt was now firmly bound into the US alliance system—the Camp David Accords foresaw enormous American economic and military aid to Egypt, as well.

For the Europeans, the 1970s was a period in which the European Community began to form its identity, also through an emerging common foreign policy, and the Palestine/Israel question played a key role in this. The European Community can, in fact, be seen a vehicle for European powers—above all Germany, but also France and the UK—to change their identity, and reappear on the world stage in a more legitimate form. Europe's past, as Waever (1996) has pointed out, was represented as the "other" from which Europeans were now departing. The Palestine/Israel question played a key role in defining this departure, specifically after 1970 when the European Political Cooperation was formed, but—as already pointed out before—in an "amnesiac" way, erasing the European legacy in the conflict. In wake of the 1973 war, the nine foreign ministers of the European Community began to explore "common foreign policy values" in a shared document (European Council 1973) and in their first common declaration pointed out that

> they consider that a peace agreement should be based particularly on the following points: (1) The inadmissibility of the acquisition of territory by force. (2) The need for Israel to end the territorial occupation which it has maintained since

> the conflict of 1967. (3) Respect for the sovereignty, territorial integrity and independence of every state in the area and their right to live in peace within secure and recognized boundaries. (4) Recognition that in the establishment of a just and lasting peace account must be taken of the legitimate rights of the Palestinians. (European Council 1973)

It is important to mention here, first, that before 1973, there is no mention of Palestinians in any EC documents; only Arabs are mentioned, and the 1971 Schuman document is indicative of this as it does not mention Palestinians anywhere (Persson 2014, 74) (it refers to the "Arab refugees"). Only in 1973 did the EC begin to refer to Palestinians. Second, this EU position differed remarkably from the US, which, as Stephen Walt has pointed out, indeed sought to shunt "aside the EEC [European Economic Community] from the peacemaking efforts in the region, just as it did the Soviet Union, giving Washington the power of a sole broker" (Walt 1990, 172). The EC, however, continued on its path. In 1977, the EC reconfirmed these principles, and added that "a solution to the conflict will be possible only if the legitimate rights of the Palestinian people to give effective expression to its national identity is translated into fact. This would take into account the need for a homeland for the Palestinian people" and that Palestinian representatives must be included in negotiations (Simonet 1977). Most pathbreaking, however, was the 1980 Venice declaration of the nine foreign ministers, which—happening just after the US-brokered Egyptian-Israeli peace treaty—was a European contestation of the US brokering role and an expression of European discontent with a treaty that had not solved the Palestine question. The nine recognized the Palestinian right to self-determination, demanded the inclusion of the PLO in negotiations, stressed "the need for Israel to put an end to the territorial occupation which it has maintained since the conflict of 1967, as it has done for part of Sinai," and pointed out that "the Israeli settlements constitute a serious obstacle to the peace process in the Middle East" and that they "consider that these settlements, as well as modifications in population and property in the occupied Arab territories, are illegal under international law" (European Council 1980). While the Venice declaration was pathbreaking, it nonetheless did not confirm a Palestinian right to a state and was thus still a far cry away from the position of the United Nations General Assembly, which in the same year determined the Palestinians' right to a state.

5.3.3. From 1979 until 2011

As already mentioned before, in the 1980s, the EC begins to perform a more unique role as an active promoter of peace, which is also evident in its representation at the United Nations. In 1981, as the UK held the rotating presidency of the Council, the UK representative at the UNGA, Lord Peter Alexander Rupert Carrington, stated that the

> European Community believes that it has a *distinctive role to play* in the search for a negotiated, comprehensive settlement, which must be both just and lasting. . . . The members of the Community will pursue their efforts to promote a peace settlement energetically. . . . One of Europe's main aims is to facilitate such negotiations, complementing the efforts of others towards the same objective. (Carrington 1981)

The framing of Israel and the Palestinians remains similar to the 1970s, as does its description of the Palestine/Israel question.

This changes in the 1990s, when the EU does not see a unique role for itself anymore in the peace process; it now performs as an active supporter of peace but mainly in an economic function. In 1994, for example, as Germany held the rotating presidency, Deputy Federal Chancellor Klaus Kinkel argued at the UN that from "the outset the European Union actively supported the Middle East peace process, playing a leading role in international assistance for the development of the Palestinian economy and society" (Kinkel 1994). In the 2000s, the EU is absorbed into the Quartet and its role representation shifts from an active, independent supporter of the peace process to being a member of the Quartet (a development similar to Russia; see below). This role, however, further waned as the Quartet became irrelevant. In this period also the EU representation of the conflict shifts to the prognostic side, concretely to the two-state solution, while calling on Israel to end the occupation, settlement activity, and the isolation of Gaza, and on the Palestinians "to stop violence." It also does not foresee an important role for the UN any longer, seeing negotiations as the main way to find a solution, which the "international community" should back.

As for the USSR, after 1979, the representation of Israel, the Palestinians, the conflict, and its solution does not change substantially, and Moscow continues to point out its conviction that separate deals aggravate the conflict. From 1982 onward, the USSR does not represent a role for itself anymore in the conflict. This changes in the 1990s, when it is increasingly absorbed into the US "peace process" and represents itself as a cosponsoring contributor to peace. In 1996, for example, Russian foreign minister Primakov frames Russia as "one of the sponsors of the peace process" that appreciates "the peacemaking efforts of the United States of America, the European Union, France, Egypt and other members of the international community and we support an even closer partnership in peacemaking" (Primakov 1996). In the early 2000s, Russia does not perform a role and hardly refers to the conflict. This changes in 2007, when Russia again begins to portray itself as a supporter of peace initiatives (by the US or the Arab League) and as an active member of the Quartet, advocating the two-state solution. In 2007, Russian foreign minister Sergei Lavrov supports the "solution of the Palestine problem based on the two-state concept," arguing that

> we consider the United States initiative to convene in November a multiparty meeting on a Middle East settlement as a step in that direction. We appreciate the preliminary considerations voiced by the United States side regarding the agenda and composition of that event. We reaffirm the importance of involving the Quartet of international mediators and the Arab League in the preparations. (Lavrov 2007)

In 2009 Russian president Dmitry Medvedev highlights the constructive role that Russia "as a member of the Quartet of international mediators on the Middle East settlement" plays in the region (Medvedev 2009).

The US in the 1980s continues to portray itself as a "committed and engaged" broker (Shultz 1985). In 1983, President Ronald Reagan repeats his peace initiative at the United Nations, arguing that its approach was "realistic and workable" (Reagan 1983), while he sees the United Nations as an "inversion of morality" (Reagan 1985). In the early 1990s, the US portrays itself again as a broker. President Clinton, for example, states that the "United States occupies a unique position in world affairs today: we recognize that and we welcome it. . . . The United States intends to remain engaged and to lead. We cannot solve every problem, but we must and will serve as a fulcrum for change and a pivot point for peace" (Clinton 1993). Israelis and Palestinians are called brave (Clinton 1994), while the Palestine/Israel question as such remains undefined. The solution presented is the protection of Israel's security and giving Palestinians "control over their daily lives" (Christopher 1995). As the peace process breaks down, the US stops speaking about the conflict, as well as its role in it. This changes in the early 2000s from which time onward the US is again represented as a committed broker. In 2001, President George W. Bush states that the "American Government also stands by its commitment to a just peace in the Middle East" (G. W. Bush 2001). Bush adopts the two-state solution, but conditions it on negotiations and "democratic reform" of the Palestinian Authority, arguing that "commitment to democratic reform is essential to resolving the Arab-Israeli conflict. Peace will not be achieved by Palestinian rulers who intimidate opposition, tolerate corruption and maintain ties to terrorist groups" (G. W. Bush 2004). Upon taking office in 2009, President Barack Obama states at the UNGA that "America has worked steadily and aggressively to advance the cause of two States—Israel and Palestine—in which peace and security take root and the rights of both Israelis and Palestinians are respected." He focused less on democracy than Bush and hardened the tone on the settlements, arguing that "America does not accept the legitimacy of continued Israeli settlements" (Obama 2009). It should be noted here that the concept of legitimacy evades the notion of *illegality* of settlements under international law.

What can be concluded from this overview of representations at the UNGA is that while the US role was still somewhat challenged on the global level by the EC and the USSR in the 1980s, this changed in the 1990s and especially in the 2000s, when both the EU and Russia abandoned their independent roles and began to perform their roles within the US-led Middle East Peace Process.

In the 1980s, the EC heightened its activism. Following its paradigmatic 1980 Venice declaration, as Joel Peters has highlighted, the European Community "issued a stream of statements on the Israeli Palestinian conflict reaffirming the principles outlined in the Venice Declaration. . . . Although differences between European states remained, at the margin, over the best strategy to adopt, Europe in the 1980s developed a greater sense of unity on the Palestinian issue than on any other foreign policy issue" (Peters 2010, 514). In the 1980s, the EC used terminology that its successor, the EU, would not use today, including speaking of an Israeli "policy of colonizing the occupied territories" and calling on Israel to "abandon its policy of gradual annexation" (Persson 2018). It should be noted, however, that the EC still did not recognize a Palestinian right to a state. Since 1982, the EC spoke of "the right to self-determination for the Palestinians with all that implies" a formula that—as Jean Salmon (1989) has pointed out—means that "the Palestinian people could exercise their right to self-determination by creating a state but are taking care not to recognize that such a state actually exists now." Thus, while it has often been argued that with the Venice declaration the EC did set normative parameters on the conflict (Aoun 2003), and influenced the US position (Persson 2017), it should also be pointed out that the EC with its approach to Palestinian statehood actually positioned itself quite close to the US position, and far from the one of the UNGA.

Moscow's role in the 1980s in the region began to wane. Indeed, with Egypt's move into the US alliance system formalized in the Camp David Accords, the heyday of Soviet presence in the Middle East was gone, which became maybe most evident in 1982 during Israel's invasion of Lebanon to which Moscow failed to react. Brezhnev did come forward with the Brezhnev plan on September 15, 1982 (in response to the Reagan plan issued two weeks earlier), which proposed a Palestinian state in the West Bank including East Jerusalem and Gaza. Starting one day later, from September 16 to 18, the massacre in Sabra and Shatila was pursued by the Christian Lebanese Phalange with the help of the Israeli army; both plans faltered. In 1984, the Soviets presented another plan, proposing to convene a conference in the form of working groups on specific issues (even bilateral ones) plus plenary meetings to endorse the outcomes of these groups (Golan 1990, 108), a different version of which became the template of the Madrid talks (see below).

Moscow's interest in the region, however, increasingly declined. In the 1980s, even Russian-Syrian relations began to cool down, specifically when Mikhail Gorbachev came to power in 1985 and retreated from the Soviet role identity as a revolutionary actor in world politics, seeking to project a new image of the USSR in the world. With Gorbachev's "new thinking" having important inroads into foreign policy, Moscow became what was termed as more "pragmatist." In the Middle East, it was the Gorbachev period that oversaw the beginning of the end of the USSR's active role and the beginning of a tacit acceptance of US predominance in the region. In the late 1980s and under US pressure, the Soviet Union opened the doors for a substantial wave of Jewish emigration to Israel, perceived as a major blow by the Arab world. The USSR was also reluctant to recognize the Palestinian statehood declaration in 1988 in stark deviation from previous Soviet foreign policy.

For the US, in the 1980s, the gaze shifted from the Levant to the Gulf. With Egypt the US had added a pillar to its alliance system in the Middle East just as another one was falling. In the year of the peace accords, the Iranian Revolution brought down the shah—and, as the US feared, potentially also the second pillar in its alliance system, the Saudi royal family. Thus, with the Camp David Accords and the Iranian Revolution, the focus of the US now began to move toward the Persian Gulf and the Arabian Peninsula where the US used the emerging Iranian-Iraqi war "and the wider security crisis in the Gulf as an opportunity to extend its reach and consolidate its partnerships with several Gulf Arab states" (Ehteshami 2003, 118). Thus, just as the US had consolidated its role in the Levant, it also began to do so in the Gulf, with both arenas being deeply interconnected as evident, for example, in the Iran-Contra Affair—the secret arms deals with Iran whereby Israel delivered the weapons and the US used the proceeding to fund the Nicaraguan Contras against the prohibitions of Congress.[16] With its shift to the Gulf as well as the increasing focus on the issue of "terrorism" in US foreign policy, the Reagan administration "produced little in the way of tangible progress toward Arab-Israeli peace" (Quandt 2005, 286). The 1980s were indeed a period of stagnation in the "peace process." In 1982, President Reagan did come forward with the Reagan plan, which rejected the idea of a formation of an independent Palestinian state as well as Israeli sovereignty or permanent control over the OPT and instead proposed self-government by the Palestinians in association with Jordan. As Quandt has pointed out, all "administrations have opposed the creation of a fully independent Palestinian state, preferring, at least until the mid-1990s, some form of association of the West Bank and Gaza with Jordan" (Quandt 2005, 6). Reagan's plan, however, sank to irrelevance with the prolonged Israeli invasion of and war on Lebanon, and no significant US initiative came forward until the initiative of Secretary of State George Shultz in 1988. Like the Reagan plan, this initiative followed in the footsteps of the Camp David Accords in calling for Palestinian self-rule over Palestinian people, but not Palestinian land. Shultz did not support the idea of Palestinian self-determination in terms of a right to statehood, stating that "the Palestinians, as far as we are concerned, have the right to pursue an independent state through negotiations" (Quandt 2005, 283). At the same time, Shultz played with the idea of bringing the UN back in, to convene an international conference with all parties of the conflict and with the five veto powers of the UNSC proposing a nonbinding solution before the onset of negotiations. No one was enthusiastic about this approach, however: "Whereas [Israeli prime minister Yitzhak] Shamir professed fears that the conference would become authoritative and would work to undermine the Israeli position, the Soviet concern was just the opposite. The international conference, as envisaged by the Americans, appeared to the Soviets to be only symbolic" (Quandt 2005, 276). What did remain from the Shultz initiative was that he spelled out the conditions for the US to negotiate with the PLO, which contributed to empowering factions within the PLO that were trying to steer the internal debate in a direction that would eventually lead to the Algiers Declaration/the Palestinian Declaration of Independence in 1988, which recognized all relevant UN resolutions since 1947. In a speech at the UN in the same year, Yasser Arafat explicitly recognized Israel's right to exist and the PLO's readiness to enter into negotiations (Arafat 1988).

With the end of the Cold War and the Bush senior administration intensifying its role in the Gulf, it had to do the same in the Israel-Palestinian conflict. Secretary of State James Baker came forward with a new initiative. In a rare moment of US diplomacy and a clear deviation from the typical US script, at a speech to the American Israel Public Affairs Committee Baker argued that

> for Israel, now is the time to lay aside, once and for all, the unrealistic vision of greater Israel. Israeli interests in the West Bank and Gaza—security and otherwise—can be accommodated in a settlement based on Resolution 242. Forswear annexation. Stop settlement activity. Allow schools to reopen. Reach out to the Palestinians as neighbors who deserve political rights. (Baker 1989)

Baker came forward with a five-point plan, including Palestinian participation (but excluding the PLO) in talks, which was, however, rejected by Prime Minister Shamir. As the first US invasion in Iraq ended, the US saw a window of opportunity in light of its apogee of power in the region, and set out to create a "new order" (G. H. W. Bush 1991) in the Middle East. In the run-up to the Madrid talks, the Bush administration was maybe the only US administration that has ever really confronted the Israeli government on the settlements. In 1991, during testimony at the

House Foreign Affairs Subcommittee on Foreign Operations, Baker stated that "nothing has made my job of trying to find Arab and Palestinian partners for Israel more difficult than being greeted by a new settlement every time I arrive. . . . I don't think that there is any bigger obstacle to peace than the settlement activity that continues not only unabated but at an enhanced pace" (Friedman 1991). In a showdown with the Israeli government the US administration pressed the former into a settlement freeze by withholding loan guarantees. The road to the Madrid talks was open. While the Madrid talks per se failed, its bilateral and multilateral set-up situated the conflict in larger security issues of the region, while excluding Iran. It also paved the way for the Israeli-Jordanian and Israel-Palestinian bilateral talks. More than anything, however, it may have demonstrated the now almost uncontested power of the US in the region.

After the fall of the Berlin Wall and the disintegration of the USSR, Moscow's own role in the region had collapsed. It became part of the so-called Middle East Peace Process, which was, however, entirely dominated by the US in terms of substance and participation. Moscow became an actor in a play dominated by the US; it adopted a "purely nominal role" (Kreutz 2007, 55) and did not even influence the Syrian-Israeli track, which had constituted its classic area of influence. Thus, initially, Moscow retreated to a position that amounted to nothing less than a "passive acceptance of the US-Israeli position" (Kreutz 2007, 53). This began to change when Primakov became first foreign minister and then prime minister, and when the very beginnings of a new Russian role identity developed. Russia condemned settlement policies in the Occupied Palestinian Territory and Primakov issued a twelve-point plan named "Code of Peace and Security in the Middle East." The aim was, as Primakov pointed out, not to become "an alternative player in the Middle East, but *rather an equal partner in the 'conflict resolution club'* " (Kreutz 2007, 77; italics added). The plan addressed key issues that were neglected by the US at the time, such as that the "security for some cannot be based on impairing the security of others," that the "security of the parties to the conflict cannot be viewed in isolation: the Islamic Republic of Iran, Turkey, northern Africa and the Arab countries of the Persian Gulf, including Iraq, must be involved in a 'Middle East zone of peace,'" and that "international law is the basis for security and stability" (Primakov 1997). This reflected a quite concise understanding of what the US "peace process" script in the Levant, coupled with its abandonment of diplomacy in the Gulf, would lead to.

The Clinton administration oversaw, in fact, an immense setback for diplomacy in the Gulf with the dual containment policy aimed at Iraq and Iran, while diplomacy in the Levant was accelerating. In the Israel-Palestinian theater President Clinton let Israel set the pace, acting more as a facilitator than a mediator (Quandt 2005, 340) without a comprehensive vision for a security architecture for the whole region. In contrast to the more comprehensive Madrid talks of the Bush administration, two bilateral peace treaties were signed by Israel with Jordan and the PLO. The agreement with the PLO was inherently flawed. The PLO—isolated internationally and regionally due to its standpoint in the Iraq war as well as increasingly also among the Palestinians as a new grassroots leadership had evolved during the first Intifada—had a strong interest in regaining its position among the Palestinians and in the Arab world, which made it an inherently weak negotiating partner (Brynen 2000). The new Israeli government—Labor led under Prime Minister Yitzhak Rabin—had an interest in relieving Israel of the burden that the occupation and the control of the Palestinian population was posing financially as well as in terms of Israel's international standing, while holding on to overall control over the Palestinian territory, and specifically over those areas that could be annexed to Israel without posing a "demographic threat" to it. Rather than solving the conflict, the Oslo Accords cemented Israeli power over the OPT (and Area C specifically), while giving the false impression that the Palestinians were now governed by the Palestinian Authority, rather than the Israeli military regime (Gordon 2008; Azoulay and Ophir 2012). The accords did not even mention Palestinian statehood.

President Clinton, in fact, did not support the creation of a Palestinian state if it was not created as an outcome of bilateral negotiations. Only toward the end of his second presidency, at the Camp David negotiations and in the Clinton parameters, was the goal of statehood explicitly spelled out, thus finally giving "legitimacy to the idea that peace would eventually involve the creation of a Palestinian state" (Quandt 2005, 377). However, that never meant a real departure from the US negotiations script, since it did not imply a *right* to statehood. On the larger, regional level, as talks on the Israeli-Syrian front failed, Syria—just like Iran—remained excluded.

The EU in the 1990s still somewhat contested the role of the US as the forefront broker (Peters 1998). As the US was mainly invested in facilitating bilateral talks, the EU came out with the Barcelona Process (later Euro-Mediterranean Partnership), which was based on a more comprehensive approach to the conflict. In essence, the EU approach has, however, sustained the US-led Middle East Peace Process. As Mouin Rabbani has pointed out, in the 1990s, the EU was seen "as a donor promoting development in the southern and eastern Mediterranean, and facilitator of Arab-Israeli normalization in the context of the Middle East peace process" (Rabbani 2017). The Barcelona Process was, in fact, conceived of in a way that would undermine the non-normalization policy of the Arab states without ending the Israeli occupation of the Palestinian territory. The Barcelona Process broke down with the collapse of the Oslo talks, but the EU's role as a donor remained, committed to state building but without recognizing a Palestinian state, so continuing to assume the financial burden of the occupation from the occupying power. Pursuing a policy of "normalization without peace," or of building a Palestinian state without recognizing a Palestinian state,[17] the EU has been "effectively paying for Israel's occupation" (Azhar and Pinfari 2017). The Europeans, as Anne Le More has argued, "were made to underwrite the American-Israeli dominated diplomatic process financially" (More 2008), and its development aid was securitized alongside Israeli parameters (Tartir 2018).

Paying for state building but being excluded by the US from diplomacy, the EU now began to push the issue of statehood, which had not been explicitly incorporated into the Oslo Accords. While the European Community had previously spoken vaguely of a "homeland to the Palestinian people" and the "legitimate right of the Palestinian people to express a national identity and to self-determination," in 1998 it called on Israel "to recognize the right of the Palestinians to exercise self-determination, *without excluding the option of a State*" (European Council 1998), and stated in the 1999 Berlin Declaration that

> the European Union reaffirms the continuing and unqualified Palestinian right to self-determination *including the option of a state* and looks forward to the early fulfilment of this right. It appeals to the parties to strive in good faith *for a negotiated solution* on the basis of the existing agreements, without prejudice to this right, *which is not subject to any veto*. The European Union is convinced that the creation of a democratic, viable and peaceful sovereign Palestinian State on the basis of existing agreements and through negotiations would be the best guarantee of Israel's security and Israel's acceptance as an equal partner in the region. The European Union declares its readiness to consider the recognition of a Palestinian State in

due course in accordance with the basic principles referred to above. (European Council 1999)

This statement was highly ambiguous as it affirmed on one hand the right to Palestinian self-determination not subject to any veto, but called a state just an option whose realization depends on negotiations, thus according Israel as the occupying power a de-facto veto over it. Thus, the EU continues to deny the Palestinians a *right* to national independence and sovereignty. It should be noted here that EU member states are split on the issue of statehood as evident during the 2012 UNGA vote that accorded Palestine nonmember observer state status in the United Nations as fourteen member states voted in favor,[18] twelve abstained,[19] and one voted against.[20] The current lowest common denominator is represented in a 2014 motion of the European Parliament, in which recognition of a Palestinian state has been made conditional on peace talks, arguing for the "recognition of Palestinian statehood and the two state solution, and believes these should go hand in hand with the development of peace talks, which should be advanced" (Barbiere 2014).

It has been often argued in the academic literature (Persson 2017) that by adopting the Berlin Declaration, the EU has acted as a normative power as the US adopted the two-state solution shortly afterward. At the same time, Clinton moved toward this position already in the late 1990s. Thus, it is rather the case that the EU, which had a strong independent position on the conflict in the 1980s, has watered down its position, approximating its own position to the US one in terms of equating the settlements and terrorism issue,[21] and denying the Palestinian people a right to statehood.

As the second Intifada was accelerating, President George W. Bush initially backed up Israeli policies. As Quandt has pointed out, rarely "had any president gone so far in subcontracting American policy to an Israeli leader" (Quandt 2005, 408). This approach, however, changed with 9/11 when the administration began to develop its approach to tackle what is singled out as the root causes of terrorism, namely the lack of freedom in the region, but also the Israel-Palestinian conflict. In November 2001, Bush spoke for the first time of a Palestinian state, and began to bring in the EU, US, and UN (not in the form of the Secretary-General) into the MEPP through the formation the Middle East Quartet. The Quartet, however, as Nathalie Tocci (2013) has pointed out, was multilateral only in name, and unilateral in practice. The EU now lent legitimacy to a forum that has sidelined international law (Tocci 2013, 38) and in the framework of which the EU watered down its own language (for example, signing statements that question the legitimacy instead of the legality of the settlements—see Huber 2018), while Russia did at times deviate from Quartet (or US) positions. It has, for example, not adhered to the no-contact policy of the Quartet toward Hamas and has recognized Palestinian statehood.

The Quartet—like the US-led Middle East Peace Process since its beginnings—focuses almost exclusively on state security rather than human security. It does not address underlying power asymmetries and instead invests in building state capacities and improving socioeconomic conditions, thus managing, rather than solving, the conflict through what Pogodda et al. (2014) have termed "liberal peacebuilding." The imaginary of the two-state solution that the Quartet upholds through financial and political support to the Palestinian Authority glosses over the "one-state condition" that has existed since 1967. The OPT is treated as a separate, outside entity while Israel has effectively exercised control over the whole historic area of Mandatory Palestine (plus the occupied Syrian Golan Heights) by applying diverse legal regimes within it in the past fifty years (Huber 2018). The MEPP has thus been a key factor in the normalization of the occupation, and the EU through its inclusion in the US-led peace process has lent this normalization legitimacy. Besides its donor role, in 2005, it also engaged in so-called crisis management practices through the European Union Police Mission for the Palestinian Territories, based since 2005 in the West Bank to train PA security services, and the European Union Border Assistance Mission Rafah, established in 2005 to monitor the border crossing between the Gaza Strip and Egypt, which was suspended in 2007 when Hamas took over control of the Gaza Strip. The EU has so become part of the security management of the occupation (Bouris 2014; Tartir 2018).

While the US with the Quartet continued its focus on diplomacy in the Israel-Palestinian conflict, it intensified its coercive policies in the Gulf. There, President Bush's freedom agenda served as a justification for the second US-led invasion of Iraq, which continued to put the US at the head of a security structure that was guaranteed by US military power, not by a security architecture. The "axis of evil" rhetoric increased threat perceptions in Iran, Syria, and other states of an imminent, coercive US regime change. The US thus further cemented a deep split in the region, which became ever more evident with the implosion of Iraq and the security problems this posed to states in its neighborhood, leading regional powers to adopt more independent foreign policies on their own.

The latter trend, notably, also applied to Russia. Since coming to power, Russian president Vladimir Putin had begun to form a new role for Russia in the world with a focus on "pragmatism" and "Russian interests" that initially did not directly challenge US dominance, at least in the Middle East. However, the acceptance of US unipolar domination of the Middle East, and its policies toward Iraq and Iran in particular, soon created a series of problems for Russia. Russian politicians have frequently referred to the Middle East as a "soft underbelly" to which Russia connects not only through societal ties, but where developments have direct consequences for the country. Russia is home to a substantial native Islamic community and has perceived the import of Islamic fundamentalism to Russia and its direct neighborhood as a threat, seeing the Israel-Palestinian conflict as a fueling factor in this respect. At the same time, due to Israel's large Russian community, it also has direct societal ties to Israel that are reflected in ever increasing trade relations, including with the settlements.[22] With the US invasion of Iraq, Russia saw its "soft belly" disintegrating—a development that it has perceived as problematic for its own interests in the region (Dannreuther 2015). It is from that period onward that Moscow began to drive a more independent policy in the Middle East, initially, however, still in the framework of good relations with the West. It also sought to reengage and rebuild ties with the Arab world. Speaking repeatedly at Arab League meetings, Putin has stressed the need for a comprehensive approach. At the 2002 Beirut meeting where the Arab Peace Initiative was adopted, for example, Putin stated that

> peace can be achieved in the Middle East only by ending the occupation of the Arab territories, the realization of the national rights of the people of Palestine, including their right to self-determination and the creation of their own independent state, and also the equal and reliable security of all the countries and nations of the region, both the Arabs and the Israelis. (Kreutz 2007, 73)

In 2004, at the Arab Summit Meeting in Tunisia, Putin pointed out that "no comprehensive agreement in the Middle East can be reached without returning the Golan Heights to Syria and without settling the disputes between Israel and Lebanon" (Kreutz 2007, 302). This has to be seen in a context where the UNSC, driven by the US and France, was moving toward Resolution 1559 (2004), which called for the removal of Syrian forces from Lebanon and, according to Moscow, "covered just one aspect of the Middle East situation while other issues in a comprehensive regional settlement are left out'" (Kreutz 2007, 37). In fact, as the US began to intensify pressure in Syria and Lebanon (specifically following the assassination of Rafik Hariri in 2005), Russia began to scale up its role in Syria. Enabled by a strengthening Russian economy, Moscow forgave the Syrian debt accumulated during the Cold War.

With the Obama administration, the US role as the key broker did not change substantially, even though Obama abandoned the Clinton-Bush template of diplomacy in the Levant and coercion in the Gulf. President Obama not only began to disengage from Iraq, but—together with the Europeans—also succeeded in striking a nuclear deal with Iran against virulent opposition from Israeli prime minister Benjamin Netanyahu who even sought to marshal the US Congress against the president. Obama initially also tried to force Israel into a settlement freeze, from which he eventually backed down, even vetoing a UN resolution that called settlements illegal in 2011.

5.3.4. From 2011 until Today

The Russian role performance remains rather constant after the Arab uprisings, as initially does the US one. The European performance becomes increasingly unpronounced on the Palestine/Israel question—EU representatives at the UN define its identity through other issues.

Russia continues to see itself in a supporting role to the Quartet. As Russian foreign minister Lavrov pointed out in 2017 at the General Assembly, "Russia is ready to assist in any way possible was the resumption of direct talks between Israel and Palestine, and cooperate with Quartet partners and Arab League for this purpose" (Lavrov 2017). In 2018, Lavrov suggested that the "long-standing Palestinian question" must not be forgotten, warning against "unilateral approaches . . . or attempts to monopolize the peace process," arguing for talks on "the basis of the relevant United Nations resolutions and the Arab Peace Initiative," and that "Russia will continue to do its utmost to facilitate the process, including within the Middle East Quartet and in cooperation with the League of Arab States and the Organization of Islamic Cooperation. Mutually acceptable agreements must ensure the peaceful and safe coexistence of the two States of Israel and Palestine" (Lavrov 2018). Thus, Russia performed within the MEPP even as the US abandons it.

The representatives of the EU, in contrast, hardly mention the conflict anymore at the annual UNGA meetings, focusing on other topics, which might indicate that the EU increasingly does not define itself through its position on the Palestine/Israel question at the international level. In 2016, Donald Tusk focuses on refugees and terrorism (Tusk 2016); in 2017, on refugees, terrorism, and the Paris agreement (Tusk 2017). While EU representatives do not seem to define its role through the conflict any longer, EU member states in council conclusions or statements at the UN continue to insist on internationally established parameters (European Council 2016a; Permanent Mission of France to the UN in New York 2019).

Regarding the US, following the Arab uprisings, Obama, like his predecessors, highlights the deep friendship and unshakable US commitment to Israel's security (Obama 2011), and portrays the Palestinians as friends with the legitimate right to live in security and dignity in their own sovereign state (Obama 2013) without mentioning a right to such a state. While the conflict remains undefined, the US continues to focus on negotiations as a basis for a Palestinian state rather than a right to statehood. The UN is seen mainly in terms of its supporting role for US-led negotiations and Obama insists on these negotiations, arguing that peace can be realized only through them, not through statements or UN resolutions (Obama 2011). President Trump decisively departs from this position—from a negotiations paradigm toward a coercive imposition paradigm. First, unlike Obama, he focuses more on Israel's conflict with Iran rather than on Israel in the context of the Palestine/Israel question. This is, for example, evident in his first speech at the UNGA (Trump 2017). In 2018, he defines Israel as "proudly celebrating its seventieth anniversary as a thriving democracy in the holy land" and speaks about the "significant step" the US took in moving the US embassy to Jerusalem. The US is portrayed as being "committed to a future of peace and stability," but not to be "held hostage to old dogmas, discredited ideologies and so-called experts who have been proven wrong over the years" (Trump 2018). This speech, indeed, reflects well how Trump departs from the "peace process" script, which he calls an "old dogma."

In the period since the Arab uprisings, the US, Russia, and EU initially continued on their course despite the hollowness of the peace process being increasingly exposed. Thus, the Arab uprisings and the enormous power shifts in the Middle East did not trigger a role change immediately. The EU has maintained its support for the US brokering role. In 2013, it introduced a special "Privileged Partnership" to Israel as an "instrument of support for the US attempts led by [US Secretary of State] John Kerry to engage Israelis and Palestinians in direct negotiations" (Nikolov 2017, 233), and withheld the publication of its labeling guidelines until 2015 for the same purpose. Thus, the EU has continued to play a supporting role in terms of diplomacy where it did not assume an active role for itself. This has also been maintained when the Trump administration enters power in the US. While, as Martin Konecny (2018) has argued, "Europe's role has rarely been as important and its responsibility rarely as big as they are now," instead of moving proactively to affirm international parameters, the EU has adopted a wait and see approach. When the US president moved the US embassy to Jerusalem, a strong Council Declaration on Jerusalem was blocked by Hungary,[23] Romania, and the Czech Republic; indeed as Neve Gordon and Sharon Pardo have shown, EU cohesiveness and coherence is increasingly undermined by third parties lobbying single member states—the Visegrad Group particularly—to block certain positions (Pardo and Gordon 2018; Dyduch 2018; Asseburg and Goren 2019). The EU even sent the EU Special Representative for the Middle East Peace Process to the Manama workshop (see below) in contrast to Russia, which abstained from that meeting.

Furthermore, while downgrading its own role, on the bilateral level the EU is simply continuing its deep entanglement with Israel as a result of which it has potentially violated its third party obligations under international law. Continuing EU trade with the settlements, for example, makes the latter a viable and sustainable enterprise, thereby contributing to their permanence and even growth (Tonutti 2013; International Federation for Human Rights 2012). This has not only violated long-standing EU policy positions such as that settlements are illegal under international law, but also violates the EUs own obligations under the Lisbon Treaty,[24] and its member states' duties as high contracting parties to the Fourth Geneva Convention.[25] Mandated by the Council in a series of conclusions (European Council 2012a, 2012b, 2015, 2016b), the EU came forward with its differentiation policy, which has been translated in practice in terms of trade through the Rules of Origin issue (whereby goods from settlements are not allowed to enter the EU market under the preferential conditions staked out in the Israeli-EU Association Agreement which allows Israeli products to enter the European market with reduced customs); the Labelling Guidelines (framed as a consumer protection issue, which gives European consumers a choice to boycott settlement products); Business Advisories; and the Funding Guidelines (which exclude Israeli entities based in and activities/operations taking place in the occupied territories from EU grants, prizes, and financial instruments, most importantly the research and development program, Horizon 2020). The differentiation policy, however, does not address the root of the problem, which only a strict nonrecognition policy, as applied in the case of Crimea, could. What the differentiation policy does is an artificial creation of two separate economies: the Israeli economy and the settler economy. While this does not respond to reality, because the settler economy is deeply integrated into the Israeli economy, the EU nonetheless singles out one as legitimate (the Israeli one) and shames and delegitimizes the other (the settler one). Gordon and Pardo are skeptical about the differentiation policy, arguing that it could also be seen as a way to "legitimize EU research co-operation and trade ties with Israel, thus allowing Israel to continue the occupation as if business was usual" (Gordon and Pardo 2015b, 417). Furthermore, this EU policy has also found its way into UNSC Resolution 2334, which not only declares settlements as illegal but also calls upon all states "to distinguish, in their relevant dealings, between the territory of the State of Israel and the territories occupied since 1967" (UNSC 2016).

While Russia's role in the Middle East grew before 2011, it was in response to the Arab uprisings that Russia has reassumed an activist role in the region comparable to the pre-Gorbachev era; this has, however, not translated into a more active role in the Israel-Palestinian conflict. As Robert Freedman has pointed out, one needs to keep in mind that "while its regional policy under Putin had major anti-Israeli components, such as its diplomatic and military support for Israel's enemies Iran and Syria and the diplomatic legitimization of Hamas, unlike the situation through most of the Soviet period, Russian-Israeli relations on a bilateral basis are now quite warm" (Freedman 2012, 334). Russia has, in fact, remained committed to the Middle East Peace Process until today. On the larger regional level, Russia did not perceive the Arab uprisings as a threat to its foreign policy interests and initially even abstained on UNSC Resolution 1973, which authorized the establishment of a no-fly zone in the Libyan civil war and all necessary measures to protect civilians;

Russia later argued that NATO subsequently exceeded the resolution's limits on military action. Russia accused the West of having pursued a regime change, which was now leading to the same chaos and instability as Western intervention in Iraq (Dannreuther 2015, 81). Armed with the Libyan precedent, Russia argued that in order to prevent a similar development in Syria, it directly had to intervene in the civil war,[26] while seeking to maintain Israeli security interests in Syria (Suchkov 2018). Russia remains committed to the negotiations paradigm and has not participated in the Manama conference (see below).

After the Arab uprisings, the US continued in its role, even though the US image as a broker had already become broken. While in the 1970s there was a short period when US prestige was on the rise in some parts of the Arab world (Quandt 2005, 143), first cracks in that image appeared already at Camp David. Today, half a century after 1967 and after almost forty years of US-led "peace processes" without peace, Israel's occupation of the Palestinian territory and military regime over the Palestinian population is so deeply entrenched and the Palestinian territory so fragmented, that even the Quartet came to the conclusion that the viability of the two-state solution is "imperiled" (Middle East Quartet 2016). President Trump, when entering office, had already declared his will to depart from the two-states solution/negotiations paradigm. While the previous US approach sidelined the UN in terms of diplomacy (though still making use of some UN instruments deemed useful), Trump is now seeking to tear down central multilateral instruments and institutions, including the United Nations Relief and Works Agency for which the US has stopped its funding as a direct attack on the rights of the Palestine refugees, or the International Criminal Court (ICC), which it has threatened with sanctions. Furthermore, while the US previously made issues on which international law exists (the status of Jerusalem and the Palestinian refugees) final status issues in negotiations,[27] the Trump administration is attempting instead to take them off the negotiating table even in outright violation of international law. The US has also closed the mission of the PLO to the US. This approach is not only an onslaught on Palestinian rights; it is an "onslaught against the international community and the international system."[28] In 2019, at the Manama workshop in Bahrain, the US presented an economic plan that, as Tareq Baconi has pointed out, asks Palestinians to "dream of funding amounts that dwarf what has been slashed" (Baconi 2019) by the US in exchange for accepting a total surrender to a Greater Israel. The document does not mention the

Israeli occupation and settlements, nor a Palestinian state, the Palestine refugee question, or Jerusalem. Thus, the performance of the Trump administration almost amounts to what could be called a hyperbolic performance of the "peace process" script—it performs it so exaggeratedly that its double standards become clearly exposed; its performance is so radical that is displaces the script.

Epilogue

In conclusion, four periods can be identified: two periods dominated by diverse scripts and two periods of transition. The first period up until the 1967 war is characterized by two rather stable scripts: a regional one spearheaded by Egypt, and a global one set in the context of the United Nations. In the first period, Egypt developed its role as the spearhead of the Arab cause in the early 1950s, at a time when Saudi Arabia did not represent a role for itself in the conflict. Thus, on the Palestine question, Saudi Arabia indirectly acknowledged the leadership of Egypt in writing and performing a script. In this period, Turkey and Iran, as well as European states and the USSR, did not display any role in the conflict. Only the US represented itself as a supporter of governing the conflict through the United Nations, seeing it mainly as a refugee and humanitarian issue. Thus, in this first period, there was a regional system headed by Egypt and glued together by the script of pan-Arabism, and what appeared as a rather disinterested global system whereby the script was one of refugees, managed through the United Nations.

The second period is a phase of transition that begins with the 1967 war and ends with the Egyptian-Israeli peace treaty in 1979. The 1967 war represented a watershed that unraveled all role identities, changing relationships and the framing of the Palestine/Israel question. Egypt entered into a period of struggling with its role performance that took almost a decade. Initially, it did not refer to the role of the self anymore and then slowly began to present itself as the vanguard of peace in the region. Saudi Arabia's role changed to mediator in an Arab framework after the 1973 war. Both Egypt and Saudi Arabia began to work toward a de-facto acceptance of Israel in the pre-1967 borders in the Arab regional system, while insisting in line with international law on Israeli withdrawal from all the territories it had occupied in the 1967 war and from the mid-1970s onward on the Palestinian right to national independence and sovereignty. Turkey and Iran both performed roles of concerned bystanders in this period. The other big change took place on the global level where the conflict became a vehicle for both the US and USSR (later on also for the EC) to project an international and regional role. The USSR now represented itself as a principled supporter of peace through the UN and the land for peace principle, while the US developed its role performance as the key broker in the conflict. The European Community also began to represent a role for itself in this time period, while the US still sought to exclude both the USSR and the EC. In this period, the script of the peace process is developed, whereby the preconditions of Israel have been structurally incorporated into the "peace process," in terms of process (bilateral negotiations outside the UN, which would split the Arab world) and in terms of substance (Palestinian rights have been made subject to negotiations). Initially, both the EC and the USSR rejected parts of the script (EC) or the script at large (USSR), which, however, changed over time, as they were both absorbed as players into it.

In the third phase, all role identities stabilize into one regional-global system, whereby all powers observed increasingly perform their role in the script of the "peace process" with the US at its head. The performances and thus the script have proven highly resilient even in the face of region-shaking events such as Israel's Lebanon invasion and two US-led invasions of Iraq. The US has principally performed as the lead broker, while at the regional level, Egyptian and Saudi role identities have remained stable (even during Egypt's short Muslim Brotherhood rule) whereby Egypt's role has been more oriented toward being the US's "indispensable regional interlocutor" on specific issues such as Gaza, while the Saudi role has tended more toward being the core in a regional web of diplomacy that has ultimately backed up US diplomacy. Turkey, which began to develop a more active role identity in the 1990s with an increasing tendency when the AKP entered power, has represented itself as a contributor to the peace process just like the EU. The EC in the 1980s increasingly saw a distinctive role for itself in the peace process, but in the 1990s it became a payer backing up the peace process, and was then absorbed into the role of a member of the Quartet in the early 2000s, as a result of which the EU has hardly voiced any independent role anymore. The USSR dropped its own role in the 1980s, but from the 1990s onward began to perform as a cosponsoring contributor to peace and then in the 2000s as an active member of the Quartet, a role performance that has remained stable after the Arab uprisings and the onset of the Syrian civil war. Within this script, the UN has been sidelined and the framing of the Palestine/Israel question has shifted focus from the diagnostic to the prognostic part.

Within this script, ideas have traveled forth and back in a certain framework. Carter's national security advisor, Zbigniew Brzezinski, for example, came forward with ideas of interlocking circles of parties to negotiations, a model that was picked up in a different format in the early 1980s by the Soviets, and then traveled back into the Madrid talks. Similarly, the two-state solution—often seen in the literature as an EU idea—has its origins in the solution proposed by Saudi Arabia and the Arab League in the 1980s based on the 1967 borders. It traveled from the Arab world into the transatlantic one, even though in a different form.[29] The two-state solution, which became dominant in the late 1990s and early 2000s, has seen some variance whereby the Arab states have focused on full Israeli withdrawal and the establishment of a Palestinian state in the pre-1967 borders, which has also been supported by Russia, while the EU and the US have focused on the negotiations paradigm, that is, that negotiations, rather than rights, should determine a Palestinian state.

The only outlier in this picture has been Iran, whose role identity changed radically in 1979, after which it appeared as deeply unsettled, in stark contrast to, for example, the role of Saudi Arabia or Egypt in that time period. Initially, Iran began to represent itself as the anti-Zionist spearhead, the spearhead of resistance, and revolutionary center of the Islamic world, referring to Israel as a "cancer" and calling for its "erasure" at the UN. Indeed, one could argue that Iran thus played its own role in that "play," namely what the other key players would refer to as the "villain." The Iranian role representation began to change in the mid-1980s, when Tehran started to frame its role identity in relation to the dominant international and regional framework of the peace process, namely as an opponent of peace and then as an opponent of unjust peace in the early 1990s. In the later 1990s, Iran began to represent itself as a promoter of a just and lasting peace. As with all role identities oriented toward "peace," the Iranian one was performed in a framework where Iran challenged the US's prognostic framing of the conflict with a one-state solution, while also identifying the diagnostic framing (occupation, oppression, and exploitation of the Palestinians).

Thus, the evolution of the Iranian role performance still has to be seen in the context of the script of the "peace process" in relation to which Iran has continuously sought to (re)define itself. The US has thus not only partially set the terms of the self-understanding (Barnett and Duvall 2005, 46) of the powers within its script but arguably also of the one power outside of it, which makes it a rather prominent example of what Jutta Weldes and Diana Saco have called an "asymmetric capacity to define or be defined. One of the generally overlooked capabilities of great powers, then, is precisely their ability to define identities, both their own and those of other states" (Weldes and Saco 1996, 372).

This picture has, however, changed rather substantially since the Arab uprisings. Iran, from the early 2000s onward and specifically with the Arab uprisings, has defined itself mainly as a regional stabilizer, an identity that seems rather settled and which does not perform in relation to the script of the "peace process." Iran does not play the role assigned to it any longer, but has built a web of relations tied together with its own meaning that deeply challenges the script from the outside (in a way similar to the first period, when pan-Arabism glued a regional web of relations together). Egypt and Russia remain rather committed to the MEPP, as do—to a less vocal extent—the EU and Turkey. The latter two also do represent alternatives, which they have not yet driven forward forcefully, however. Turkey, with its strong position on the humanitarian crisis in Gaza, and the European Union, with the differentiation policy, do go back in the direction of international humanitarian and human rights law. Finally, the US—the gravitational power of the Camp David Order—has begun to engage in a hyperbolic performance of its own script, similar to Saudi Arabia. What does this amount to? It means that the script is losing its players who are displacing the very parameters that enabled the performance of the script in the first place. In this period of "interregnum," in which redefinitions of role identities and meaning are possible, agency will make the difference.

6

The Authoritative International Normative Framing of the Conflict

The previous chapter has identified four periods of continuities and ruptures regarding the performance of the seven key powers in the context of which the role of the UN was first crucial, then contested, and finally marginalized. This chapter now explores in more detail how these powers viewed and used the United Nations as an instrument to govern the conflict in these four time periods, but also which alternative scripts emerged within bodies of the United Nations. Thus, it shows how the dominant normative international framing of the conflict developed from 1948 to today.

Almost from its very beginning, the Palestine/Israel question has indeed been defined in the United Nations arena where discursive struggles over the root of the conflict, its solution, and the role of the United Nations have been conducted. Such dominant framings have not only meant to define the situation and its solution, but also to justify specific actions (or no action) toward the conflict through the United Nations. These discursive battles and their outcomes—UN resolutions—have constructed knowledge about it. There is almost no book on the conflict that does not refer to milestone resolutions such as UNGA Resolutions 181 and 194 or UNSC Resolutions 242 and 338. These resolutions constitute politically authoritative parameters of the conflict.

Resolutions of the Security Council and the General Assembly are formal expressions of the opinion or will of these UN organs whereby the preamble outlines the basis on which action is taken and the operative part the opinion or the action to be taken (UNSC 2017). Resolutions can include decisions, recommendations, and declarations whereby decisions have binding effects, while recommendations and declarations are nonbinding. The decisional powers of the UNGA are "restricted to 'organizational' matters internal to the UN legal order (including semi-external matters such as the budget, or admission, suspension and expulsion of members)," while the Security Council "also possesses decisional powers in the 'operational' realm of international peace and security" (Öberg 2005, 883).[1] Resolution 273, for example, which accepted Israel to membership in the UN, is legally binding, while UNGA resolutions outside of these organizational matters are considered as nonbinding "recommendations." The International Court of Justice has, however, also attributed to them an impact on general international customary law (Öberg 2005, 903). UNSC resolutions under Chapter VII of the UN Charter are considered binding, while resolutions under Chapter VI have no enforcement mechanisms and are generally considered nonbinding. However, it should be noted that many of the nonbinding resolutions invoke international treaties such as the UN Charter or the Fourth Geneva Convention—to which all powers covered in this book are party, as is Israel, while the PLO has sought to become a party. Furthermore, these resolutions should also be seen in the context of national law where such resolutions can be legalized. UNGA Resolution 181 (Partition Plan) is an example in this respect. Whereas the Arab states argued that Resolution 181 violated the rights of the Palestine Arabs, Israel's minister of foreign affairs, Moshe Sharett, argued that it conferred statehood to Israel (Quigley 2005, 62). Israel invoked Resolution 181 in its Declaration of the Establishment of the State of Israel in 1948.

However, rather than the legally binding nature of such resolutions, what is important in the framework of this research is that UNGA and UNSC resolutions reflect politically authoritative, normative representations of the conflict. Inis Claude has described the UN as a body bestowing "collective legitimization . . . as a dispenser of politically significant approval and disapproval of the claims, policies, and actions of states" (Claude 1966, 367). While the majority of UNGA and UNSC resolutions on the Palestine/Israel question have only been declaratory, they shape the perception of the conflict and the parameters of its solutions. They justify and enable (or delegitimize and block) certain UN actions on the conflict.

In terms of actions, the Israel-Palestinian conflict has been called a "laboratory" for UN innovation with many UN instruments being developed by the UN toward it, including "the first subsidiary organ (UNSCOP), the first specialized agency (UNRWA), the first mediator (Count Folke Bernadotte), the first observer mission (UNTSO), the first peacekeeping mission (UNEF), the first integrated mission (UNSCO), and the first instance of investigatory challenge to a member state (Detlev Mehlis)" (Bruce 2010, 322). Thus, the Palestine question—as Karim Makdisi has pointed out—actually "helped produce the UN" (K. Makdisi 2019, 9). The UN's standard repertoire of today includes the following:

- Mediation: sending mediators such as Count Folke Bernadotte and convening peace conferences such as the Lausanne or Geneva conferences;

- Monitoring: sending international monitors or fact finding missions such as UNSCOP or the UN Fact Finding Mission on Gaza, as well as more long-lasting committees, such as the Committee on the Exercise of the Inalienable Rights of the Palestinian People (1975), which became a special division within the UN Secretariat in 1979—the Division for Palestinian Rights, the Committee to Investigate Israeli Practices Affecting the Human Rights of the Population of the Occupied Territories;

- Peacekeeping: establishing peacekeeping missions such as UNTSO, UNEF, UNDOF, or UNIFIL;

- Humanitarian action: setting up specialized agencies such as UNRWA;

- International Court of Justice: the UNSC and the UNGA can request an advisory opinion of the International Court of Justice (which is not legally binding, because only states can submit legal disputes to the ICJ);

- UN membership: upon recommendation of the UNSC and with a two-thirds majority, the UNGA can grant states UN membership and thus bestow them with international legiti-

> macy. The UNSC can also impose sanctions on a state, or it can delegitimize a state by recommending that the UNGA exclude it from UN membership.

The following sections examine the evolution of the dominant international normative framing of the conflict in the form of UNSC and UNGA resolutions—that is, the resolutions of the UN's two key decision-making bodies—in light of internal power dynamics on this framing in both bodies. It shows that until 1967, the definition of the conflict was focused on the regional level, while the local level was mainly framed as a refugee issue. In this period, the UNGA and the UNSC were the key arenas where the conflict was managed by the superpowers, which made use of all the instruments available—indeed, developing these instruments to manage the conflict through the UN.

Between 1967 and 1979, the definition of the conflict broadened out in both the UNGA and the UNSC, and during this period the foundation for today's international normative framing of the conflict was laid. The UNGA was no longer dominated by the US as a result of decolonialization, while the UNSC remained a key forum for both the US and the USSR to deal with security issues that arose from the conflict and posed substantial threats in a Cold War context.

After 1979, however, the UNSC has been sunk into irrelevance in the conflict by the US, except for its peacekeeping functions, which were still deemed useful by Washington. The mediation role was now monopolized by the US up until the early 2000s, when the US reintroduced the UNSC—not, however, in an independent function, but rather in a very confined and limited manner to back up its own mediation role and its framing for a solution of the conflict in terms of a two-state solution conditioned on direct and bilateral negotiations. Through UNSC resolutions, the US has tried to legitimize an approach that silences Palestinian rights. Relations between the UNGA and the UNSC in this period also eased, partially a result of the Non-Aligned Movement losing its focus on the issue of self-determination. Since the Arab uprisings, two actors—the PLO and the EU—are hesitantly bringing the UN and international law back into the picture. Before turning to the role of the United Nations, however, it is important to briefly discuss how the League of Nations was instrumentalized by European powers to dominate the Middle East, laying the foundation for the conflict.

6.1. The League of Nations as a Tool of Domination

As the Ottoman Empire dissolved after World War I, the League of Nations was founded in 1920 at the Paris Peace Conference and used by the victorious Allied Powers—France and Britain first and foremost—as an instrument to convey legitimacy to their artificial division of the "Middle East" into "nation-states" and to control these states through the mandate system. As John Quigley has pointed out, the "mandate system was a compromise between the nineteenth century and the twentieth," between colonialism and self-determination (Quigley 2005, 237). The British mandate for Palestine, formalized by the League of Nations in 1923, included the Balfour Declaration in which, in 1917, the UK's foreign secretary, Arthur Balfour, promised the establishment of a "national home for the Jewish people" while not even mentioning the local Arab-Palestinian majority by name, referring to them as "existing non-Jewish communities in Palestine" whose civil and political rights should not be "prejudiced" (UK Foreign Office 1917). Based on such a premise, the British mandatory power failed to achieve what the ICJ in its Namibia decision later highlighted as the objective of such a mandate, namely "the self-determination and independence of the peoples concerned" (Quigley 2005, 15). Under British rule tensions increased between the local population and the Yishuv, turning violent in 1921–22, in 1929, and in 1936–39 when two important documents were produced by the British: the report of the Peel Commission (1937) and the White Paper (1939). The Peel Commission was the first to recommend partition as a solution to the conflict into a Jewish and an Arab state (which would become part of Transjordan). The White Paper, in contrast, rejected the idea of a Jewish state and of partition. During World War II, the situation increasingly deteriorated, and in 1947, the UK, unwilling to deal with mounting tensions and violence, referred the question of Palestine to the newly established United Nations, supported in this by both the US and the USSR. Thus, with its very foundation in the wake of World War II in 1945, the United Nations became the key arena in which the Palestine question was "managed" by extraregional powers. Rather "than see the establishment of an independent Arab Palestinian state, the League of Nations, and later the United Nations oversaw the dispossession and displacement of the Palestinian people" (Erekat 2016, 96).

6.2. 1947–1967: The United Nations as the Superpower's Conflict Management Tool

In the first period, the global and local systems were divided. On the global level, the US actively and the USSR passively embraced the idea of managing the conflict through the United Nations. None of them, as pointed out by Urquhart (1995, 574), "wanted to be directly involved in the solution of the Palestine problem"—that is to say, they were involved, but through the instrument of the United Nations. As opposed to this global framework, the Arab regional system—spearheaded by Egypt—was skeptical of this superpower instrumentalization of the UN on the Palestine question. At the same time, Egypt and Saudi Arabia used the UN as the main forum where they confronted Israel (Sela 1997, 50). While these states claimed to represent the Palestinians at the UN—each with its "own considerations and calculations" (Rashid Khalidi 2007, 125)—the Palestinians themselves in this decisive period first had no locally rooted and internationally recognized representative and, after 1948, "were a spent force, dispersed, leaderless, many living as dependent refugees, and without a territorial base" (Caplan 2011, 131).[2]

As the Palestine question was referred to the UN, the five Arab states (Egypt, Iraq, Lebanon, Saudi Arabia, Syria) represented at the UN at the time asked the General Assembly to treat the issue in terms of "the termination of the Mandate over Palestine and the declaration of its independence" (Quigley 2005, 32), but this approach was rejected by the UNGA, which instead created the United Nations Special Committee on Palestine (UNSCOP), the first UN fact-finding mission to Palestine. While the Jewish Agency actively sought to influence the composition and agenda of the committee, the Arab Higher Committee refused to work with UNSCOP, arguing that the Arab right to the land was self-evident and that the issue should be decided by an international court. Seeking the advisory opinion of the International Court of Justice on the issue of self-determination of the Palestine population was discussed during the debate on the Partition Plan, but it was dropped. UNSCOP came forward with the partition plan as outlined in the majority report favored by UNSCOP members Canada, Czechoslovakia, Guatemala, the Netherlands, Peru, Sweden, and Uruguay, while UNSCOP members India, Iran, and Yugoslavia favored the minority report that suggested a federal state. The Arab states represented at the UNGA rejected the partition plan but supported a plan close to the minority report. With the US pressuring particularly South American states to bring their votes in line with the US position (Quigley 2005, 36), the UNGA voted in favor of the majority report in United Nations General Assembly Resolution 181, which, as Phyllis Bennis has pointed out, "bestowed international legitimacy on the nascent, borderless and still-expanding state of Israel, while postulating an abstract Palestinian state and protected international status for Jerusalem, neither of which were ever allowed to come into existence" (Bennis 1997, 47).

Following the approval of Resolution 181 by the UNGA in November 1947, clashes erupted in different areas of Palestine: they were the prelude to the outbreak of the Arab-Israeli-Palestinian war of May 1948. A draft proposal for the establishment of a UN force that would enforce the partition plan was rejected by the US (Bruce 2010, 301), and the former mandate power was unwilling to assume responsibility for implementing the partition plan. As David Ben-Gurion declared the establishment of the State of Israel in May 1948, military units from Egypt, Syria, Lebanon, Transjordan, and Iraq crossed mainly into the areas that the UNGA had assigned to the Arab state (Quigley 2005, 78). The Arab forces hardly cooperated as each followed its own, often conflicting, aims and logic, which was specifically evident for the Transjordanian Arab Legion, the strongest Arab army, which primarily sought to expand the territory of Transjordan.

In UNGA Resolution 196, Swedish diplomat Folke Bernadotte was appointed United Nations mediator in Palestine to help bring about a cease-fire. The United Nations Security Council in Resolution 50 called for a truce to be supervised by Bernadotte with the assistance of the United Nations Truce Supervision Organization (UNSC 1948a)—UNTSO, the first precursor to a peacekeeping operation ever established by the United Nations—but despite a four-week truce fighting continued. The UNSC then passed a resolution under Chapter VII of the UN Charter, UNSC Resolution 54, which determined that the situation in Palestine constituted a threat to peace, allowing the UNSC to take action to "restore international peace and security," and ordering a cease-fire (UNSC 1948b). Passing a resolution under Chapter VII had an immediate impact, with a truce coming into effect shortly afterward, in July 1948. In September, Bernadotte was assassinated by the Lehi group (a Zionist paramilitary organization). He was replaced by US diplomat Ralph Bunche, and a month afterward, fighting resumed. The UNSC established a new instrument in

UNSC Resolution 61, a committee of seven UNSC members to advise "on further measures it would be appropriate to take under Chapter VII of the Charter" should either party violate the truce (UNSC 1948c). In Resolution 62, the UNSC called for an armistice, and under Bunche's supervision the armistice agreements were signed under UN auspices (UNSC 1948d). As Bruce Jones has pointed out, this "protracted episode laid the foundations for Security Council diplomacy and more broadly for UN peace-making and peacekeeping, not only in the Middle East" (Jones 2010, 303).

The armistice agreements were negotiated bilaterally, thus in line with Israel's request to split the Arab states rather than negotiating with all Arab delegations at once in the framework of the Palestine Conciliation Commission (Shlaim 2014, 42, 51, 57).[3] The UNSC called for the UNTSO observers to supervise the armistice agreements in Resolution 73 (UNSC 1949b). With the armistice lines over time becoming the internationally accepted borders of Israel, it thus achieved an area much larger than originally allotted to it in the partition plan (with about 50 percent more territory). The UN took over another key function as it conferred legitimacy to the newly founded State of Israel when it was admitted as a member to the United Nations in UNGA Resolution 273(III)[4]—as recommended by the UNSC in Resolution 69 (UNSC 1949a)[5]—conditioned on Israel's acceptance and implementation of UNGA Resolutions 181 and 194 (UNGA 1949a); it's a conditionality that has never been implemented.

A Palestinian state was not realized. Jordan annexed the West Bank and Egypt administered the Gaza Strip. Thus, while Israel became a member of the UN, the issue of Palestinian statehood vanished from the UN agenda, and the Palestine question was mainly treated by the superpowers as a humanitarian issue, as Israel's mass expulsions in 1948, such as in the case of the "Lydda and Ramle exodus" (July 1948), made 750,000 Palestinians refugees (Grandi 2016, 319).[6] In 1948, the UNGA passed Resolution 194, which recognized the Palestine refugees' right to return, called for the demilitarization and internationalization of Jerusalem, and provided for the establishment of the UN Conciliation Commission for Palestine, focused on territories, refugees, and Jerusalem (UNGA 1948). Resolution 194 has been annually reasserted by the UNGA. It also served as a basis for Resolution 302 (UNGA 1949b), which has established the key UN humanitarian agency for the conflict: the United

Nations Relief and Works Agency (UNRWA), in 1949, whose mandate is annually renewed. For the Palestinians, as Karim Makdisi has pointed out, "UNRWA has from its inception embodied the international community's responsibility and commitment to implement the right of return" (K. Makdisi 2018, 16). For the next two decades, in "the international arena the 'Palestine question' receded almost totally from the agenda and was replaced by a relief and humanitarian issue known as 'the Arab refugees.' At the General Assembly, the debates on UNRWA's annual reports and the votes allocating new funding for its refugee relief and educational budgets served as the main platform for considering Palestinian issues" (Caplan 2011, 132). The other issue related to the Palestine question that remained "alive" was the issue of Jerusalem, which was also addressed in repeated UNGA resolutions.

To recap, in this first period, the UN was used by the emerging superpowers to bring into being one state, but not another. Washington and Moscow at the time worked more in concert than in opposition to each other on the issue, and so did the UNSC and the UNGA (while the UK tended to abstain on votes and the rotating Arab member of the UNSC had no veto). Furthermore, the UN developed mediation and peacekeeping instruments. The Security Council was, however, as a Security Council report (2007) points out, mainly responsive rather than preventive in this period. It did not set up an arms embargo or an international military force that would implement the partition plan, and so indirectly supported the side that was militarily stronger. It failed to employ what is now considered a standard toolkit toward other conflicts, relied mainly on chapter VI resolutions, and moved toward Chapter VII only rather late when facts on the ground had already been implemented.

The only time in this period where the UNSC/UNGA acted decisively, creatively, and fast was in 1956, notably despite two veto powers—France and the UK—being involved in a military aggression. The US, supported by the USSR, came forward with a procedural resolution that called for a UNGA emergency session that could not be vetoed by the UK and France. At that session, seven resolutions were adopted by the UNGA, which called for an immediate cease-fire and a full withdrawal of British and French forces. It also established the United Nations Emergency Force (UNEF), the UN's first major peacekeeping force with over six thousand troops from ten nations deployed within forty-eight hours to Sinai to oversee the Israeli, French, and British withdrawal (Bruce 2010, 305). It "was a milestone in the development of the United Nations and signaled the birth of UN peace-keeping" (Urquhart 1995, 575).

6.3. 1967–1979: Sidelining the United Nations

After 1967, as seen in the previous chapter, the US increasingly began to represent itself as the forefront broker in the Kissinger and Carter periods, while the USSR represented itself as a supporter of peace initiatives taken at the UN or Arab League level. On the regional level, Egypt switched from spearhead of the Arab cause to spearhead of peace. Saudi Arabia, responding to this new role by Egypt, responded by first framing its role as a defender of the Palestinian cause, and then later on as a mediator for peace. The three non-Arab regional powers, Europe, Turkey, and Iran, all changed from no role to the role of supporter/willing contributor to regional or global peace initiatives. Thus, all role identities aligned toward "peace-making," but differed on the role the UN should play in this. While in the period 1967–73 all agreed on the central role of the UNSC, this focus declined after 1973. The US now began to downplay the role of the UN, as did Egypt. Only Saudi Arabia began to advocate a more active UN role from 1973 onward, and the USSR saw a pivotal role for the UN in the whole period, while the three bystanders (Iran, Turkey, Europe) all insisted on UNSC Resolutions 242 and 338 but remained rather silent on an independent role for the UN as such. For the involvement of the UN in the conflict, Egypt's switch toward bilateral negotiations has been the game changer. Sadat, as highlighted in chapter 5, explicitly sought to get the UN and the USSR out of peacemaking and so crowned the US the key broker and enabled the marginalization of the UN. In effect this meant that with the Egyptian-Israeli peace treaty, the so-called Camp David system was ushered in, built on bilateral peace treaties guaranteed by the US at the top of this system instead of a comprehensive security architecture for the whole region guaranteed by the UN.

As will be seen below, initially after 1967, UNSC and UNGA activity on the conflict accelerated. The UNSC was used by the superpowers in this period to end war, even though it became increasingly evident that it would not similarly be used to make "peace," a role that the US now sought for itself. Even though the UN was sidelined from diplomacy, the

UNSC and the UNGA both continued to define the conflict in respective resolutions, but in divergent ways, as the UNSC increasingly became subjected to US vetoes, while the UNGA, as result of decolonialization, became more independent and concerned with the issue of the Palestinian right to self-determination, thus beginning to play a key role in defining the Palestine/Israel question.

6.3.1. The Immediate Reaction to the 1967 and 1973 Wars, Resolutions 242 and 338

In direct response to the 1967 war, several draft resolutions circulated. The "three power draft" by India, Mali, and Nigeria stated that the "occupation or acquisition of territory by military conquest is inadmissible under the Charter of the United Nations and consequently Israel's armed forces should withdraw *from all the territories* occupied as a result of the recent conflict" (UNSC 2007). In stark contrast to this draft, the one presented by the US called for the "withdrawal of armed forces *from occupied territories*." A last-minute Soviet draft called for a withdrawal to *the lines preceding the outbreak of hostilities*. The UK then produced a draft that tried to bridge these differences and became the basis of Resolution 242, the land for peace resolution adopted under Chapter VI of the UN Charter, which asserts "the inadmissibility of the acquisition of territory by war" and calls for the withdrawal of Israeli armed forces *from territories* ("the territories" in the French version) occupied in recent conflict, and respect for the sovereignty, territorial integrity, and political independence of every state in the area and the right to live in peace within secure and recognized boundaries (UNSC 1967b). The resolution was not an unconditional call for withdrawal, but conditioned it on the recognition of Israel by the Arab states. It also implicitly made the 1949 armistice agreements borders Israel's borders. While Resolution 242 was notable as it, for the first time, laid down principles of peacemaking (Bruce 2010, 309), it also simply cemented existing realities in the region, as it only spoke of the rights of states. The Palestinians and their right to self-determination were not even mentioned in the resolution, which only spoke of them indirectly and solely in terms of a just settlement of the Palestine refugee question. The human rights of the Palestinians under occupation were dealt with in UNSC Resolution 237, which called for respect for the Fourth Geneva Convention (UNSC 1967a). Resolution 242 also made no reference to

Jerusalem, which was covered in Resolution 252, which considered that "all legislative and administrative measures and actions taken by Israel, including expropriation of land and properties thereon, which tend to change the legal status of Jerusalem are invalid and cannot change that status" (UNSC 1968). Swedish diplomat Gunnar Jarring was tasked by the UN Secretary-General to make Resolution 242 operational and shuttled between Israel and the Arab states, but his efforts ultimately failed over differing interpretations of Resolution 242. As Avi Shlaim has pointed out, "Egypt and Jordan agreed to peace but insisted that the first step be complete Israeli withdrawal. Israel would not return to prewar borders and declared that before it would withdraw from any part of the territories, there must be direct negotiations leading to a contractual peace agreement that incorporated secure and recognized boundaries" (Shlaim 2014, 260). Resolution 242 failed to prevent another war.

Even more than in 1967, the end of the 1973 war "was dictated by the realities of the US-Soviet relationship" (Bruce 2010, 310). Washington and Moscow agreed on Resolution 338 (UNSC 1973a), focused on the termination of hostilities and the recognition of Resolution 242. It also included an important third, binding paragraph on negotiations under "appropriate auspices." Under UN auspices and joint USSR-US chairmanship, the Geneva conference was convened in December 1973, attended by Egypt, Israel, and Jordan, but not by Syria. The PLO was not invited. No agreement was reached at the conference, and it was the last of its kind: since 1973, UN auspices have no longer served as the key negotiation forum. "Starting in the early 1970s, the US became critical and circumspect of the UN and its multilateral diplomacy" (Sarsar 2004, 459); it now saw itself in the driving seat in this respect.

Furthermore, Council activity on the conflict was now frequently blocked mainly by US vetoes (see figure 6.2) except for resolutions that involved the UN's peacekeeping role. Two peacekeeping forces were established: the second United Nations Emergency Force (UNEF II) in 1973 to supervise the cease-fire between Egypt and Israel (and later the disengagement of forces, UNEF II ended with Camp David), and the United Nations Disengagement Observer Force (UNDOF) in 1974 to supervise the disengagement of Israeli and Syrian forces in the Golan, which remains stationed there until today. In 1978, the Security Council established the United Nations Interim Force in Lebanon (UNIFIL) to confirm the Israeli withdrawal from South Lebanon and to assist the Lebanese government to restore its authority in the area. But while the UN has kept—even intensified—its peacekeeping role, from 1973 on it has been "denied a role as a significant player in Middle East diplomacy" (Bennis 1997, 48), a role increasingly monopolized by the US. However, both the UNSC and the UNGA retained important roles in defining the conflict at the international level, which will be examined next.

6.3.2. The Normative Framing of the Conflict at the UNSC

The dominant normative framing of the Palestine/Israel question—with the analysis focused only on the local, and not the interstate, dimension—differed decisively between the UNSC and the UNGA. Figure 6.1 shows all UNSC resolutions passed on this question. What is notable is that before 1967, the Council is not concerned with the local dimension, apart from its admission of Israel to the United Nations. The Palestinian refugees are never dealt with and only mentioned once in a side note in Resolution 89 in 1950. In Resolution 101, on the Quibya massacre in 1953,[7] the Palestinians who were killed by the Israeli army are not even mentioned and the resolution focuses only on Israeli-Jordanian security cooperation.

After the 1967 war, the UNSC begins to deal with the local dimension. Resolution 242 is mainly focused on the interstate dimension as it concentrates on the rights of established states and mentions Palestinians only as refugees.

In 1968, UNSC begins to deal with *Jerusalem* and passes one of its first resolutions (Resolution 252), which states that "all legislative and administrative measures and actions taken by Israel, including expropriation of land and properties thereon, which tend to change the legal status of Jerusalem are invalid and cannot change that status" (UNSC 1968)—which is invoked repeatedly in UNSC Resolutions 267 (1969), 298 (1971), 452 (1979), 465 (1980), 476 (1980), 178 (1980), 672 (1990), and 2334 (2016). *The Palestinian territory (West Bank including Jerusalem and Gaza) under Israeli military occupation since 1967* was dealt with in an array of resolutions starting with Resolution 259 in 1968. In 1969, Resolution 271 confirms the Geneva Conventions as applicable to the OPT, sustained in an array of resolutions including resolutions passed under the hawkish Reagan and Clinton administrations. There is, however, some variance: whereas in 1979–80 the Geneva Convention is mentioned in relation to the illegality of settlements (i.e., applied to Palestinian land and people), in the 1980s and 1990s, it is only applied to the protection of the Palestinian people against deportations, human rights violations, abductions, or mass violence (i.e., applied to Palestinian people but not Palestinian land).

1949	***Res 69* Admission of Israel to the UN**
1950	*Res 89* Mentions the Palestinian refugees: "expulsion of thousands of Palestine Arabs"
1953	*Res 101* (Quibya massacre) focuses on Israeli-Jordanian security cooperation
1967	*Res 237* recommends to the Governments concerned the scrupulous respect of the humanitarian principles . . . contained in the **Geneva Conventions** *Res 242* inadmissibility of the acquisition of territory by war, withdrawal of Israel armed forces from territories occupied in the recent conflict, termination of all claims or states of belligerency and respect for and acknowledgment of **the sovereignty, territorial integrity and political independence of every State in the area** and their right to live in peace within secure and recognized boundaries free from threats or acts of force, achieving a **just settlement of the refugee problem**
1968	*Res 250* Israel to refrain from holding military parade in **Jerusalem** *Res 251* deplores holding by Israel of military parade in **Jerusalem** *Res 252* all legislative and administrative measures and actions taken by Israel, including expropriation of land and properties thereon, which tend to change the legal status of **Jerusalem** are invalid and cannot change that status. *Rest 259* dispatch a Special Representative to the Arab **territories under military occupation** by Israel
1969	*Res 267* all legislative and administrative measures and actions taken by Israel which purport to alter the status of **Jerusalem**, including expropriation of land and properties thereon, are invalid and cannot change that status *Res 271* (Arson attack on Al Aqsa) Israel to observe the provision of the **Geneva Conventions**
1971	*Res 298* all legislative and administrative actions taken by Israel to change the status of the City of **Jerusalem**, including expropriation of land and properties, transfer of populations and legislation aimed at the incorporation of the occupied section, are totally invalid and cannot change that status
1979	*Res 446* affirming applicability of Geneva convention, Israeli **settlements** in the Palestinian and other Arab territories occupied since 1967 have no legal validity and constitute a serious obstruction to achieving a comprehensive, just and lasting peace in the Middle East, establishes commission to examine the situation *Res 452* the policy of Israel in establishing **settlements** in the occupied Arab territories including Jerusalem has no legal validity and constitutes a violation of the Fourth Geneva Convention

Figure 6.1. United Nations Security Council Resolutions on the Palestine/Israel question.

1980	*Res 465* all measures taken by Israel to change the physical character, demographic composition, institutional structure or status of the Palestinian and other Arab territories occupied since 1967, including Jerusalem, or any part thereof, have no legal validity and that **Israel's policy and practices of settling parts of its population and new immigrants in those territories constitute a flagrant violation of the Fourth Geneva Convention** relative to the Protection of Civilian Persons in Time of War and also constitute a serious obstruction to achieving a comprehensive, just and lasting peace in the Middle East. **Calls upon all States not to provide Israel with any assistance to be used specifically in connection with settlements in the occupied territories.** *Res 468* (expulsion of mayors) **Geneva Convention relative to the Protection of Civilian Persons** *Res 469* (expulsion of mayors) **Geneva Convention relative to the Protection of Civilian Persons** *Res 471* (assassination attempts against mayors) **Geneva Convention relative to the Protection of Civilian Persons** *Res 476* Reaffirms the **overriding necessity to end the prolonged occupation** of Arab territories occupied by Israel since 1967, all legislative and administrative measures and actions taken by Israel, the occupying Power, which purport to alter the **character and status of the Holy City of Jerusalem** have no legal validity and constitute a flagrant violation of the Fourth Geneva Convention relative to the Protection of Civilian Persons in Time of War and also constitute a serious obstruction to achieving a comprehensive, just and lasting peace in the Middle East; *Res 478* all legislative and administrative measures and actions taken by Israel, the occupying Power, which have altered or purport to alter the character and status of the Holy City of **Jerusalem**, and in particular the recent "basic law" on Jerusalem, are null and void and must be rescinded forthwith *Res 484* (expulsion of mayors) applicability of **Geneva Convention relative to the Protection of Civilian Persons**
1986	*Res 592* (release students) **Geneva Convention relative to the Protection of Civilian Persons**
1987	*Res 605* (violation of human rights of Palestinians) **Geneva Convention relative to the Protection of Civilian Persons**
1988	*Res 607* (deportations) **Geneva Convention relative to the Protection of Civilian Persons** *Res 608* (deportations) **Geneva Convention relative to the Protection of Civilian Persons**

continued on next page

1989	*Res 636* (abduction) **Geneva Convention relative to the Protection of Civilian Persons** *Res 638* (deportations) **Geneva Convention relative to the Protection of Civilian Persons** *Res 641* (deportations) **Geneva Convention relative to the Protection of Civilian Persons**
1990	*Res 672* (violence in Jerusalem) **Geneva convention, mission to the region** *Res 673* refusal of the Israeli Government to receive **the mission of the Secretary-General** to the region *Res 681* **urges Israel to accept de jure applicability of the Geneva Convention** and **calls upon the High Contracting Parties to the said Convention to ensure respect by Israel**, the occupying Power, for its obligations under the Convention
1991	*Res 694* (deportations) **Geneva Convention relative to the Protection of Civilian Persons**
1992	*Res 726* (deportations) **Geneva Convention relative to the Protection of Civilian Persons** *Res 799* (deportations) **Geneva Convention relative to the Protection of Civilian Persons**
1994	*Res 904* (Hebron massacre) measures to be taken to guarantee the safety and **protection of the Palestinian civilians** throughout the occupied territory
1996	*Res 1703* cessation of violence, resumption of negotiations
2000	*Res 1322* (Sharon visit Al-Haram Al-Sharif) Calls upon Israel, the occupying Power, to abide scrupulously by its legal obligations and its responsibilities under the **Fourth Geneva Convention**
2001	
2002	*Res 1397* **two state solution:** vision of a region where two States, Israel and Palestine, live side by side within secure and recognized borders *Res 1402* call for ceasefire *Res 1403* call for ceasefire *Res 1405* (Jenin) call for humanitarian access *Res 1435* cessation of violence
2003	*Res 1515* **two state solution** / endorsement of Road Map
2004	*Res 1544* (demolition of Palestinian homes Gaza) **Fourth Geneva Convention**
2008	*Res 1850* **two state solution** / support for Annapolis
2009	*Res 1860* (call for ceasefire) **Gaza Strip constitutes an integral part** of the territory occupied in 1967 and will be a part of the Palestinian state
2016	*Res 2334* Israel's **settlements** have no legal validity, constitute flagrant violation of international law, **calls upon all States . . . to distinguish, in their relevant dealings, between the territory of the State of Israel and the territories occupied since 1967**

Source: UNSC (2017)

Figure 6.1. *Continued.*

The one veto power that has determined this normative framing of the conflict at the United Nations Security Council since the early 1970s has been the United States, which has assured that only resolutions that were in line with the US's own vision were passed. Noam Chomsky has argued that the US "systematically blocked a peaceful resolution in terms of the international consensus" (Chomsky 1997, 218). Figure 6.2 shows all vetoes at the UNSC by the five permanent members of the United Nations Security Council from 1946 until 2015. It highlights how the Council was blocked by Soviet vetoes in the first period of the Cold War, and by US vetoes in its second part.[8]

The US has used its veto power mostly on the Palestine/Israel question. From 1946 through 2016, the US has wielded its veto eighty-four times, half of which were on this question. The US veto was most used during the 1970–89 period with the exception of the Carter presidency. After the Cold War, this ratio still increased, with more than 80 percent (fifteen out of eighteen vetoes) of the US vetoes concerning the Palestine/Israel question.

Regarding the US vetoes on resolutions concerning the Occupied Palestinian Territory, the US exercised its first veto in 1973. During the Kissinger period, as well as in the first Reagan presidency, all resolutions in relation to the OPT were blocked. During the second Reagan presidency, the US blocked all but two resolutions, while Presidents Clinton and Obama vetoed all but one. In contrast to this, the administrations of

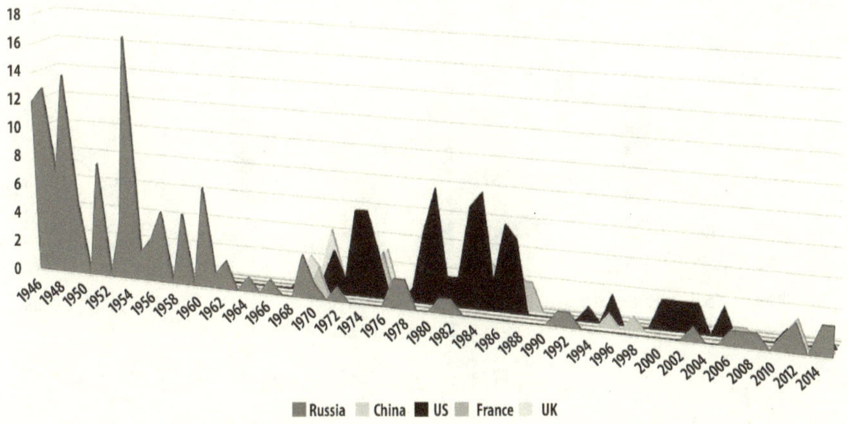

Figure 6.2. Numbers of UNSC vetoes 1946–2015. Source: United Nations Dag Hammarskjöld Library (2017).

Presidents Carter and George H. W. Bush voted for more resolutions than they blocked (see figure 6.3).

The one issue that all US presidents have blocked consistently has been the issue of *Palestinian statehood.* Any resolution that raised the unconditional right of the Palestinian people to statehood was vetoed also under Presidents Carter, Bush senior, and Obama. In 1976, the Ford administration vetoed the first such resolution, which called for the Israeli withdrawal from all the territories occupied in 1967 and affirmed the right to establish an independent state in Palestine in accordance with the Charter of the United Nations (UNSC 1976). In 1980, Carter vetoed a resolution that affirmed the Palestinian right to self-determination, including the right to establish an independent state (UNSC 1980a).

Related to *settlements*, in 1973 the US vetoed a first UNSC resolution that declared that in the OPT "no changes which may obstruct a peaceful and final settlement or which may adversely affect the political and other fundamental rights of all the inhabitants in these territories should be introduced or recognized" (UNSC 1973b). The Carter administration did not veto a series of resolutions that condemned settlements as illegal: Resolution 446 and 452 in 1979, and 465 in 1980 (UNSC 1979a;

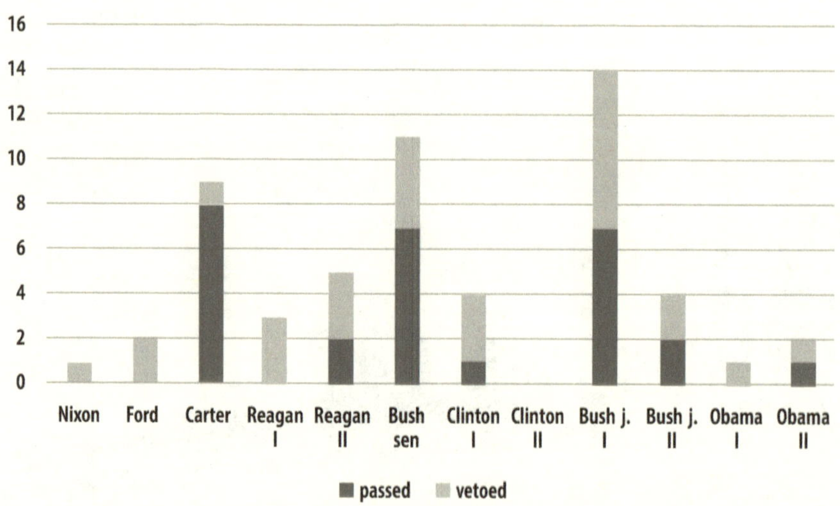

Figure 6.3. US vetoes on resolutions on the Occupied Palestinian Territory by president. Source: United Nations Dag Hammarskjöld Library (2017).

1979b; 1980b), which determined that the policy and practices of Israel in establishing settlements have no legal validity and constitute a serious obstruction to peace, and established a commission to examine the issue. Resolution 465 also invokes for the first time *third party responsibilities* as it calls upon all states "not to provide Israel with any assistance to be used specifically in connection with settlements in the occupied territories" (UNSC 1980b). On Jerusalem, specifically, Resolution 476 confirmed that all Israeli actions to alter the character and status of Jerusalem have no legal validity and constitute a flagrant violation of the Geneva Convention (UNSC 1980c), and Resolution 478 affirmed that the enactment of the "basic law" (on Jerusalem) by Israel constitutes a violation of international law and does not affect the continued application of the Geneva Convention (UNSC 1980d). Resolution 476 has in many respects been the strongest UNSC resolution passed so far on the conflict; it called for an end of occupation without conditions in its operational part.

Regarding the *issues of armed struggle versus terrorism*, the Council was rather deadlocked and—as a Security Council report frames it—"unable to condemn either the terrorist acts or the counter-terrorism measures taken in response" (Security Council Report 2007). An example is the veto by the US representative to the UN, George H. W. Bush, over a resolution in response to the killing of eleven Israeli Olympic athletes by the Black September group in 1972. In 1985, in Resolution 579 the Council passed a general resolution, condemning "unequivocally all acts of hostage-taking and abduction" and affirming the obligation of states to prevent, prosecute, and punish such acts "as manifestations of international terrorism" (Security Council Report 2007). In contrast to the UNSC, the UNGA in Resolution 3236 affirmed "the right of the Palestinian people to regain its rights *by all means*" (UNGA 1974a). Later, and more explicitly, in 1982 Resolution 37/43 affirmed the "legitimacy of the struggle of peoples against foreign occupation by all available means, *including armed struggle*" (UNGA 1982a). The UNGA passed three antiterrorism conventions between 1969 and 1973.

6.3.3. The Normative Framing of the Conflict at the UNGA

The dominant international normative framing of the conflict at the UNGA has evolved significantly since the 1967 war. Two key developments in the General Assembly were crucial in this respect. First, the composition of the UNGA changed. As Joshua Muravchik has pointed out, in

> its early decades, the UN was dominated by the Cold War competition between East and West, but between 1952 and 1968 these two blocs became outnumbered by a third, as the UN's rolls increased from eighty-two to one hundred and twenty-six member states. Most of the new members were former colonies that had recently won their independence, and they formed what became the leading bloc at the UN, the Non-Aligned Movement. (Muravchik 2013, 35)

Thanks to the Non-Aligned Movement, the issue of "self-determination from colonial control became a preeminent global value" (Graubart and Jimenez-Bacardi 2016, 30). Second, after the 1967 war, the PLO—previously dominated by Egyptian president Nasser—became a more independent actor. As Graubart and Jimenez-Bacardi (2016, 31) have pointed out, the Palestinians succeeded in linking "statehood to the broader norm of self-determination from colonial control and the second by framing Israel's occupation as a violation of territorial integrity." The Non-Aligned Movement backed the Palestinian call for self-determination, resulting in supermajorities in the UNGA that exposed the US as internationally isolated with its position. This became increasingly problematic for the US, as its European allies also began to shift their position in the wake of the 1973 war. As outlined in the previous chapter, Turkey, Iran, and the USSR all acknowledged the PLO as a legitimate actor in 1973–74, and the European Community began to acknowledge PLO agency in 1975 and the Palestinian right to self-determination in 1979. Furthermore, the Israeli occupation and practices of the occupying power were increasingly singled out as the root of the problem and the major obstacle to peace not only by the Arab states and the USSR but increasingly by the European Community.

Of the more than 750 UNGA resolutions on issues related to the conflict passed between 1947 until today, figure 6.4 shows the issues that were covered in UNGA resolutions on the Palestine/Israel question over the years. As the graph highlights, it was in the late 1960s and the 1970s that the normative framing in terms of its key issues broadened out.

Although until 1967 the rights of the Palestinian people were mainly regarded as individual rights (refugee rights), after the war they "re-emerged as the collective rights of a people" (Salmon 1989, 52). In 1969, UNGA Resolution 2535 highlighted "the denial of their [the Palestine refugees] inalienable rights under the Charter of the United Nations and the Universal Declaration of Human Rights" (UNGA 1969) and mentioned for the first

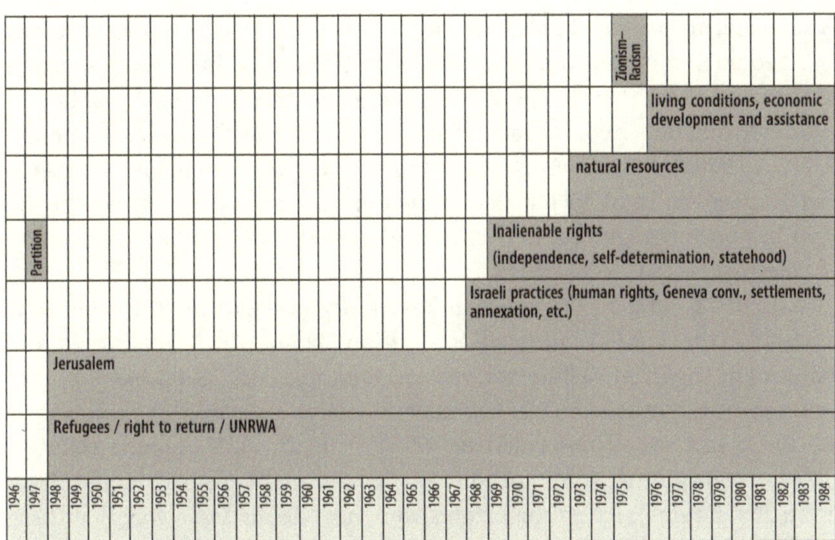

Figure 6.4. Issues covered by UNGA resolutions on Israel/Palestine between 1946 and 2015. General Source: UNISPAL (2017) (Part 1).

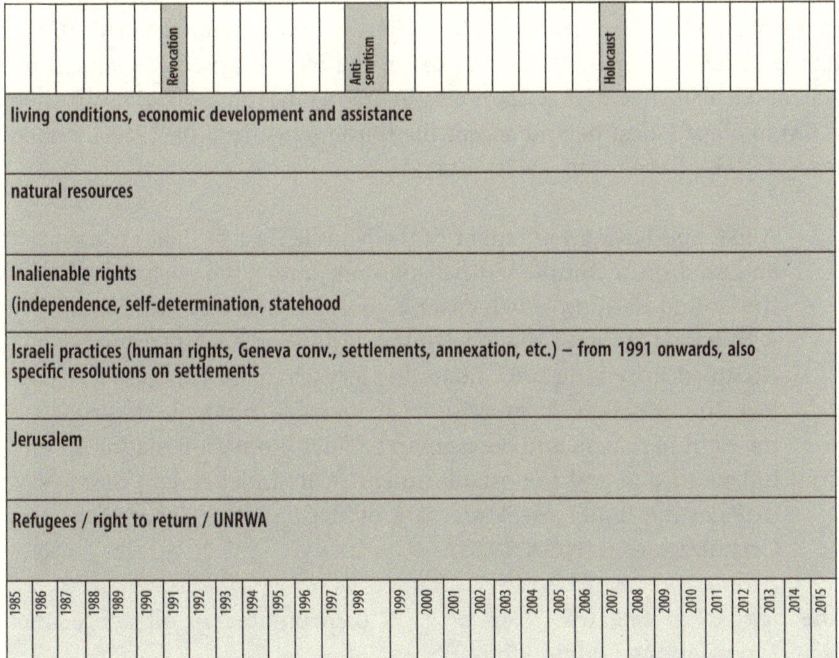

Figure 6.4. Issues covered by UNGA resolutions on Israel Palestine between 1946 and 2015 (Part 2).

time the term "people of Palestine"; from now on, it referred to Palestinians as a people and began to affirm their collective rights. In 1970, Resolution 2672 stated that "the people of Palestine are entitled to equal rights and self-determination in accordance with the Charter of the United Nations" (UNGA 1970a). Resolution 2649 in the same year condemned governments that "refuse the right to self-determination to those people in whom the right has been recognized, in particular the peoples of Southern Africa and of Palestine" (UNGA 1970b).

In 1974, after PLO chairman Yasser Arafat's address to the General Assembly, the UNGA adopted Resolution 3236, which reaffirmed the Palestinian *right to self-determination and national independence and sovereignty*, requested the UN Secretary-General to establish contacts with the PLO, and added the Palestine question to the UN Agenda (UNGA 1974a) (eighty-nine votes for the resolution, eight against, and thirty-seven abstentions). Palestinian rights were now defined in a way that these meant an independent state. Resolution 3237 granted observer status to the PLO (UNGA 1974b). In 1975, Resolution 3376 set up a Committee on the Exercise of the Inalienable Rights of the Palestinian People and a Special Unit on Palestinian Rights in the UN Secretariat (later upgraded to a division of the secretariat) to assist the committee (UNGA 1975a). At the same time, getting the support of the Non-Aligned Movement for statehood also meant that the Palestinians would have to give up their claim to all of Palestine and accept the borders before June 1967 for their state. UNGA Resolution 35/207 stated:

> A just and lasting settlement of the Middle East problem must be based on a comprehensive solution, under the auspices of the United Nations, which ensures complete and unconditional withdrawal from all the Palestinian and other Arab territories occupied since June 1967, including Jerusalem, and enables the Palestinian people to exercise its inalienable rights, including the right of return, and the right to self-determination, national independence and the establishment of its independent State in Palestine under the leadership of the Palestine Liberation Organization. (UNGA 1980)

The right to a state was from now on incorporated in all subsequent UNGA resolutions (Salmon 1989).

Apart from the question of statehood, after the 1967 war the UNGA also addressed the issue of the rights of the Palestinian people under occupation. In 1968, it created the Special Committee to Investigate Israeli Practices Affecting the Human Rights of the Palestinian People and Other Arabs of the Occupied Territories (UNGA 1968), which, however, was denied access by Israel. An array of resolutions began to be passed annually and until today, focused on Israeli practices affecting the human rights of the population under occupation, the obligations and responsibilities of the occupying power, compliance with the Fourth Geneva Convention, Israeli exploitation of human and natural resources, and reassertion of Palestinian permanent sovereignty over national resources in the occupied territory. From 1971 onward, the UNGA called upon Israel to stop policies and practices such as annexation; the establishment of settlements and transfer of parts of its civilian population into the occupied territory; the destruction and demolition of villages and the confiscation and expropriation of property; the evacuation, transfer, deportation, and expulsion of the inhabitants of the OPT; the denial of the rights of the refugees and displaced persons to return to their homes; the ill-treatment and torture of prisoners; and collective punishment (UNGA 1971). From 1976 onward, the UNGA raised third party responsibilities in Resolution 31/106, demanding all states "not to recognize any changes carried out by Israel in the occupied territories and to avoid actions, including those in the field of aid, which might be used by Israel in its pursuit of the policies of annexation and colonization" (UNGA 1976). The UNGA also intensified its efforts on the socioeconomic and living conditions of the Palestinians in the occupied territories. In 1978, it called upon the United Nations Development Program to establish a program of assistance to the Palestinian people and has dealt with their socioeconomic conditions in annual resolutions.

As the UNGA became more assertive on the national rights of the Palestinians and the Palestine question, it also brought the "Israel question" back to the agenda. In 1974, when South Africa was suspended from the UNGA (but not expelled as this was vetoed in the UNSC), the UNGA also increased pressure on Israel. However, the UNGA was less united in this respect, and Egypt proved a crucial partner for Israel. Sadat argued that "Israel must be present at the United Nations if it is expected to comply with its resolutions" (Muravchik 2013, 37). In 1975, the UNGA passed Resolution 3379, which equated Zionism with racism, but did not call for the suspension of Israel's UN membership (UNGA 1975b). The UNGA also called for economic sanctions and an arms embargo on Israel in the mid-1970s to early 1980s period, noting that "Israel's record and action establish conclusively that it is not a peace loving Member State and that it has not carried out its obligations under the Charter" (UNGA 1982b).

6.4. 1979–2011: The Peace Process Script and Making the United Nations Irrelevant

In the 1980s, the US continued to see itself as the key actor in the conflict but outside of the UN, while the USSR, specifically since the mid-1980s, was increasingly overwhelmed by domestic issues. Only Saudi Arabia and the EC sought to boost their roles as mediator or contributor to peace, while Turkey remained a concerned bystander. Iran represented itself as the spearhead of the anti-Zionist cause, but was deeply embroiled in the long war with Iraq. The only support for an explicit role for the UN in this period came from Saudi Arabia and to a lesser extent from the EC. Saudi Arabia foresaw a rather substantial role for the UN in guaranteeing the implementation of its eight-point plan and advocated a comprehensive UNSC resolution as a framework for a comprehensive and just solution to the conflict. The European Community proposed a comprehensive peace conference under UN auspices in the late 1980s. Nonetheless, in the 1980s, the United Nations were almost entirely blocked by the Reagan administration on the Palestine/Israel question as is evident in the rise of US vetoes in figures 6.1 and 6.2.

This continued into the 1990s. As Jones has pointed out, unlike "the previous three decades, when crises erupted in the Arab–Israeli theatre, the Security Council deployed neither troops nor diplomats, framed neither the principles of peace-making nor even the parameters of demilitarization. There were innumerable resolutions, and almost as many vetoes, but little result" (Jones 2010, 313). What continued to function were some UN practical commitments, notably UNRWA, UNDOF, UNIFIL, and UNTSO (Urquhart 1995, 579). Similarly, a Security Council report pointed out that many "contrast the Council's huge activism since 1990 on conflict and security issues all around the world, with its relative inaction on the Palestinian situation" (Security Council Report 2007). As the Security Council became the "leading global actor for initiating and supporting diplomacy between warring parties and for facilitating consent-based peacekeeping operations" and a "pre-eminent forum through its declaratory resolutions for articulating and validating global approaches to specific conflicts" (Graubart and Jimenez-Bacardi 2016, 27), the Middle East was excluded from this trend.

After the Cold War, indeed, none of the actors observed really foresaw a substantial role for the UN any longer, even though all role identities reoriented toward "peace." Iran switched its role from the spearhead of the Muslim cause to opponent of "unjust peace" and in the late 1990s to "promoter of just and lasting peace," to the now rather firm role of regional stabilizer in the 2000s. The US reinforced its role as key broker, while Russia, Egypt, the EU, and Turkey represented themselves as contributors to peace initiatives. Saudi Arabia continued in its role as regional mediator. Except for Iran, all states observed in this book became absorbed into the US-led peace process.

From the early 2000s onward, the Bush administration found it useful to instrumentalize the UNSC to legitimize its script of peacemaking, and to garner support for its new push for "peace"-making in light of the second Intifada and its larger project of remaking the Middle East. The US's leading role at the top of a peacemaking system became even clearer with the establishment of the Quartet, as Russia, the EU, and the UN were now more directly absorbed into the US-led Middle East Peace Process. On the regional level, while the Saudi peace initiative differed in some respects from the US two-state version, it nonetheless acted as a regional backup platform for the US. The new Saudi peace proposal also sidelined the UN while voicing its direct support for the US. In 2007, the Arab Quartet (Egypt, Jordan, Saudi Arabia, and the United Arab Emirates) was founded to act as a local contact group to the Middle East Quartet. Thus, the centralization of peacemaking on the US and the sidelining of a substantial role for the UN have been almost uncontested in this third period, even though it has led neither to peace nor to regional security.

6.4.1. The Normative Framing of the Conflict at the UNSC

With the advent of the Reagan administration, the UNSC was seen as useful for playing a limited role in Lebanon, but its role in the Occupied Palestinian Territory became marginalized. In 1982, for example, the UNSC passed sixteen resolutions connected to the conflict of which fourteen were on Lebanon (the US vetoed three resolutions on Lebanon) and two on UNDOF (it vetoed one on the Israeli-occupied Syrian Golan

Heights). All three draft resolutions presented in respect to the Occupied Palestinian Territory were vetoed by the US. The US veto on any UNSC resolution mentioning the illegality of the Israeli settlements in the OPT became US standard procedure in this period. Reagan rejected framing settlements as illegal, while he did argue that "settlement activity is in no way necessary for the security of Israel and only diminishes the confidence of the Arabs that a final outcome can be freely and fairly negotiated" (Reagan 1982). Since the 1980s, and with only one exception in 2016 (see below), the US has consistently blocked resolutions that explicitly point out that settlements are illegal, while it has passed resolutions that protect civilians in the OPT. It has, therefore, tendentiously adopted the Israeli distinction between Palestinian land and people (but it has remained committed to the applicability of the Fourth Geneva Convention to the OPT). While the first Reagan administration blocked any resolution on the OPT, it was only in reaction to the first Intifada that the US allowed the UNSC to at least consider the situation again, but only related to Palestinian people, not land. The second Reagan and the Bush senior administration voted for resolutions on deportations and the killing of Palestinian students. In 1987, during the first Intifada, in Resolution 605, the UNSC "strongly deplored those policies and practices of Israel, the occupying Power, which violate the human rights of the Palestinian people in the occupied territories, and in particular the opening of fire by the Israeli army, resulting in the killing and wounding of defenseless Palestinian civilians" (UNSC 1987). In 1988 the UNSC twice ordered Israel to refrain from deportation of Palestinians in Resolutions 607 and 608 (UNSC 1988a; 1988b). On the Geneva Convention, the US has voted for dozens of resolutions that confirmed its applicability, but has tended (however not consistently) to veto those that urge Israel to accept the de jure applicability of the convention or called upon the High Contracting Parties to ensure the application of this convention by Israel. The US tendency to veto resolutions that condemn settlements as illegal and its tendency to pass resolutions that determine the Geneva Convention as applicable is inherently a contradictory policy, as the latter implies the first since the Fourth Geneva Convention prohibits the transfer of part of its own civilian population of the occupying power into the territory it occupies.

After the end of the Cold War, the US continued to let resolutions pass to protect the Palestinian population under occupation. Resolution 672 authorized a mission to be sent to Jerusalem to investigate the killing of twenty Palestinians over Temple Mount riots (UNSC 1990a). Israel declined permission to the mission, being denounced for this in Resolution 673 (UNSC 1990b). Resolution 681 requested the Secretary-General to monitor the situation of Palestinians under occupation and urged Israel to accept the de jure applicability of the Geneva Convention, calling also "upon the High Contracting Parties to the said Convention to ensure respect by Israel, the occupying Power, for its obligations under the Convention" (UNSC 1990c). Under the Clinton administration, in 1994, the UNSC adopted Resolution 904, reaffirming the applicability of the Fourth Geneva Convention and called for measures to guarantee the safety and protection of Palestinians in the occupied territory, including through a temporary international or foreign presence (UNSC 1994). However, as in the 1980s, the US did not protect the Palestinians' right to their land. In 1995, the Clinton administration vetoed a resolution that would have confirmed that the Israeli expropriation of land in East Jerusalem is invalid (UNSC 1995). In 1997, the US vetoed two resolutions, one (sponsored by Egypt and Qatar) that demanded that Israel refrain from settlement activity in East Jerusalem (UNSC 1997b) and one (sponsored by France, Portugal, Sweden, and the UK) that declared settlements illegal and an obstacle to peace (UNSC 1997a).

Furthermore, in the 1990s both the Bush senior and the two Clinton administrations excluded the UNSC from contributing to peacemaking. The Bush administration launched the Madrid Process—co-convened by the Soviet Union, which was, however, too weak to challenge the US agenda—which provided a "structural formula that created separate but parallel bilateral and multilateral tracks" (Eisenberg 2012, 90) with the latter focusing on water, refugees, the environment, economic development, and arms control. This structure provided for an international conference that effectively satisfied Israel's demands for one-on-one talks and no role for the United Nations. Syria and Lebanon refused to participate; Iran was not invited. Not the Secretary-General, but only a UN representative, could attend the conference as an observer, while the UN was a full regional participant in the multilateral negotiations. As Bennis has pointed out, Israeli participation was guaranteed through a letter of assurances which stated that "UN representatives will have no authority. He . . . may hold talks only in the hallways, note down the content of the talks, and report to the secretary general." An addendum asserted that the "United States is also required to make a commitment that the UN Security Council will not convene to discuss the [Middle East] conflict during negotiations"

(Bennis 1997, 62). Exposing the Madrid talks for this approach, the General Assembly called for the convening of an international conference under UN auspices with the participation of the PLO in 1990 and 1991.

Even more than in the Madrid talks, the UN was entirely dropped from the Oslo Accords, which did not include any international supervisory and enforcement mechanisms. Rather, the UN was "relegated to being a relief services provider, at best" (Raja Khalidi 2016, 409).[9] While hitherto established peacekeeping missions in the Middle East were kept, no UN observer, monitoring, or peacekeeping missions were deployed in the Occupied Palestinian Territory.

> The immutable US rejection of a Council role was rooted partly in US support for Israel's long-standing rejection of any internationally-mandated ombudsman position monitoring its adherence to or violation of international human rights conventions. But it also reflected the US recognition that such a resolution would finally place the Council in a position of assuming responsibility for the Palestinians living under Israeli occupation. That, for the US, represented the first step down the slippery slope towards a UN-sponsored international peace conference. US backing for Israeli rejection of such a conference remained a cornerstone of the US-Israeli alliance, and not even the new set of commitments to new Arab allies would change Washington's position. (Bennis 1997, 57)

With the onset of the second Intifada and in light of the US-led Iraq invasion in the region, the US began to hesitantly involve the UNSC again; not substantially, however, but rather as a supporter of the US's own role. In the early 2000s, the number of tabled draft resolutions and US vetoes increased, turning against resolutions—inter alia—that called for a UN observer force in the West Bank and Gaza (UNSC 2001), that condemned the Israeli killing of UN employees of the World Food Programme (UNSC 2002a), seeking to bar Israel from extending the separation wall/fence in line with an ICJ advisory opinion (UNSC 2003a), and calling on Israel to halt its Gaza operation (UNSC 2004).[10] As a flood of draft resolutions put the US under pressure, it now began to table its own resolutions, which would seek to assert, legitimize, and institutionalize a different script on the conflict.

In 2002, the UNSC adopted Resolution 1397, which demanded "the immediate cessation of all acts of violence, including all acts of terror, provocation, incitement and destruction" and reaffirmed its "vision of a region where two States, Israel and Palestine, live side by side within secure and recognized boundaries" (UNSC 2002b), repeated in Resolutions 1515 (UNSC 2003b) and 1850 (UNSC 2008) whereby the latter confirms that Gaza will be part of the Palestinian state. All these resolutions, however, do not imply a right to statehood for the Palestinians. Rather, they make Palestinian statehood subject to bilateral negotiations. The resolution on the Israeli-built separation wall, which illegally annexed Palestinian territory, was vetoed by the US.

Finally, activity by the UNSC on the issue of "terrorism" picked up in this third period. While the UNSC was blocked on the issue of terrorism during the Cold War, this changed in the 1990s when terrorism began to be instrumentalized by the US. The Security Council began to impose sanctions on states and regimes accused of sponsoring terrorism (Security Council Report 2007). In this period, a series of UNSC resolutions also instrumentalized "terrorism" in the Israel-Palestinian conflict, while never addressing the issue of state terrorism, that is, the systematic violence ingrained in the structure of the occupation. Resolution 1397 demanded "immediate cessation of all acts of violence, including all acts of terror, provocation, incitement, and destruction" (UNSC 2002b), Resolution 1402 expressed "grave concern at the further deterioration of the situation, including the recent suicide bombings in Israel and the military attacks against the headquarters of the President of the Palestine Authority" (UNSC 2002c), Resolution 1435 condemned "all terrorist acts against any civilians, including the terrorist bombings in Israel on 18 and 19 September 2002 and in a Palestinian school in Hebron on 17 September 2002" (UNSC 2002d).

6.4.2. The Normative Framing of the Conflict at the UNGA

In the face of the UNSC's inactivity in the 1980s, the UNGA—trying to expose how the UNSC was blocked on pursuing diplomacy on the conflict—convened the International Conference on the Question of Palestine at the United Nations Office in Geneva in the autumn of 1983, attended by the representatives of 137 states, as well as the PLO. It adopted the Declaration on Palestine, as well as a Programme of Action for the Achievement of Palestinian Rights (United Nations 2008).

The UNGA also continued to pass an array of resolutions that responded to the Israeli invasion in Lebanon in the early 1980s and the first Intifada in the late 1980s. In the late 1980s, in light of UNSC's inactivism, UNGA set up parameters for a resolution of the conflict, in Resolution 43/176 (UNGA 1988a), namely, the withdrawal of Israel from the Palestinian territory occupied since 1967, including Jerusalem, and from the other occupied Arab territories; guaranteeing arrangements for the security of all states in the region, including those named in Resolution 181, within secure and internationally recognized boundaries; resolving the Palestine refugee question in conformity with General Assembly Resolution 194; dismantling the Israeli settlements in the territories occupied since 1967; and guaranteeing freedom of access to Holy Places, religious buildings, and sites.

In 1988, after the declaration of the State of Palestine by PLO president Yasser Arafat, two resolutions were adopted by the UNGA. Resolution 43/176 spoke of the "security of all states in the region, including those named in Resolution 181" (UNGA 1988a), that is, an Arab and a Jewish state, was adopted by 138 votes (the US and Israel voted no, Canada and Costa Rica abstained). Resolution 43/177 acknowledged the proclamation of the State of Palestine and affirmed the need to enable the Palestinian people to exercise their sovereignty over their territory occupied since 1967 (UNGA 1988b), adopted by 104 votes with the US and Israel voting no, and thirty-six states, including the EC Twelve, abstaining.

The UNGA's role in the 1990s changed, however, notably as a result of the breakdown of the Soviet bloc, but also as the Non-Aligned Movement changed. In 1991, the UNGA revoked the Zionism is racism resolution in Resolution 46/86 (UNGA 1991) in response to US pressure.

In the early 1990s, UNGA passed resolutions in support of the Oslo peace process. From 1991 onward, the General Assembly passed annual resolutions on the illegality of the settlements, and from 1997 onward, it convened frequent emergency special sessions, expressing specific concern for Israeli settlement expansions in the West Bank including East Jerusalem and for the persistent violations by Israel of the provisions of the Fourth Geneva Convention. In 1996, it started to annually address the issue of terrorism. In 2003, the UNGA adopted a resolution that enabled the International Court of Justice (ICJ) to present an advisory opinion on the legality of the separation wall/fence (UNGA 2003; International Court of Justice 2004). In 2005, the UNGA adopted Resolution 60/7, rejecting the denial of the Holocaust, and requesting the Secretary-General to establish a program of outreach on the subject of the "the Holocaust at the United Nations" including "measures to mobilize civil society for Holocaust remembrance and education" (UNGA 2005). In 2007, in resolution 61/255, the UNGA stated that the denial of the Holocaust risks that it will be repeated (UNGA 2007a). In the same year, in Resolution 62/146, the General Assembly reaffirmed "the right of the Palestinian people to self-determination, including the right to their independent State of Palestine" (UNGA 2007b), with 176 yes votes, four abstentions,[11] and five no votes.[12] The EU member states all voted for the resolution.

6.5. After 2011: A Shift in the Framing?

Since 2011, as in the context of the Arab uprisings Palestinian bottom-up movements also exposed the inactivism of the PLO in fighting for Palestinian rights, the PLO accelerated its activity at the UN. In 2011, it issued its statehood bid at the UN, which the US announced it would block in the UNSC. In the same year, the US vetoed a resolution that would have condemned Israeli settlements as illegal (UNSC 2011). President Obama argued that "peace will not come through statements and resolutions at the United Nations" and that the "path to a Palestinian state" is through negotiations (Obama 2011). This approach was repeated in 2014, when the Obama administration vetoed a resolution with parameters tabled for the Palestinians by Jordan (UNSC 2014) (together with Australia, while UK, Nigeria, South Korea, Rwanda, and Lithuania abstained).

In response to US pressure, Palestinian president Abbas downgraded his statehood bid and instead of statehood asked the UNGA to get an upgrade from "non-member observer entity" to "non-member observer state." In 2012, UNGA accorded Palestine non-member observer state status in the United Nations (UNGA 2012) with 138 nations in favor, forty-one abstentions, and nine against, including the US. The bid had been supported by all Arab states—Egypt, for example, argued that "negotiations are not an end in themselves" (Gheit 2010, 38)—as well as Iran,[13] Turkey, Russia, and parts of the EU (see chapter 5). This gave not only more visibility to the Palestine question, but also had practical implications. Rather than seeing Palestine as occupied territory, the UN now regards it as an "Occupied State" (Falk 2016, 84). Furthermore, the PLO could now join UN treaties and specialized agencies as well as the ICC. In 2015, Palestine acceded to the Rome Statute, formally joining the

ICC and accepting its jurisdiction over alleged crimes committed in the OPT, including East Jerusalem. In 2015, the state of Palestine submitted a state referral to the ICC, requesting that the prosecutor "investigate, in accordance with the temporal jurisdiction of the Court, past, ongoing and future crimes within the court's jurisdiction, committed in all parts of the territory of the State of Palestine" (Kiswanson 2018). In 2018, it also instituted a proceeding against the United States at the International Court of Justice on the relocation of the US embassy to Jerusalem (Palestine versus United States of America). With these proceedings, the PLO is gradually returning to multilateralism as "a position of resistance" (Erakat 2016, 110), which contests the US's key role as a broker. An internationalization of the conflict can "marginalize the United States' role and seek to diminish its debilitating intervention. Multilateralism suggests radically deploying legal, popular, and media strategies to challenge the status quo" (Erakat 2016, 110).

In addition to this, the EU's differentiation policy has entered UNSC Resolution 2334. At the very end of his second presidency, President Obama did not veto UNSC Resolution 2334, which reaffirmed that settlements are a flagrant violation of international law. The resolution furthermore called "upon all States, bearing in mind paragraph 1 of this resolution [which states that settlements are a flagrant violation of international law], to distinguish, in their relevant dealings, between the territory of the State of Israel and the territories occupied since 1967" (UNSC 2016), evoking the EU's differentiation policy, which is also increasingly used by the Office of the High Commissioner for Human Rights (OHCHR). In early 2020, it published a blacklist of more than hundred companies doing business with settlements. It should also be noted that in the OHCHR the discourse is beginning to shift from highlighting individual breaches of law by the occupying power to the overall scenario of a nontemporary occupation as a pretext for annexation.[14] In 2017, in light of fifty years of occupation, the UN Special Rapporteur on the situation of human rights in the Palestinian Territory, S. Michael Lynk, argued that the occupation of the Palestinian territory is

> the longest-running military occupation in the modern world. . . . Indeed, the Israeli occupation has become a legal and humanitarian oxymoron: an occupation without end. . . . The prevailing approach of the international community has been to treat Israel as the lawful occupant of the Palestinian territory, albeit an occupant that has committed a number of grave

> breaches of international law in its conduct of the occupation, including the settlement enterprise, the construction of the Wall, the annexation of East Jerusalem and the systemic violations of Palestinian human rights. In the view of the Special Rapporteur, while the lawful occupant approach may have been the appropriate diplomatic and legal portrayal of the occupation in its early years, it has since become wholly inadequate both as an accurate legal characterization of what the occupation has become and as a viable political, diplomatic and legal catalyst. . . . The duration of this occupation is without precedent or parallel in today's world. . . . The only credible explanation for Israel's continuation of the occupation and its thickening of the settlement regime is to enshrine its sovereign claim over part or all of the Palestinian territory, a colonial ambition par excellence. Every Israeli government since 1967 has pursued the continuous growth of the settlements, and the significant financial, military and political resources committed to the enterprise belies any intention on its part to make the occupation temporary. (Lynk 2017)

While the Special Rapporteur has pointed out how what he refers to as "occu-annexation" as such is illegal under international law, United Nations Economic and Social Commission for Western Asia (ESCWA) has gone beyond this and argued that the whole situation in Israel and the Occupied Palestinian Territory might be in violation of the International Apartheid Convention (ESCWA 2017).

Thus, as the regional order is transforming decisively since 2011, what can be witnessed at the UN level is that the framing of the conflict is also showing seeds of change as the two-state paradigm becomes difficult to sustain in light of the realities of endless military rule and annexation on the ground that a decades-long peace process set in the context of the script of the "peace process" has enabled.

6.6. Epilogue

In the first period identified in chapter 5, the United Nations was used by the superpowers as a conflict management tool, mainly focused on the interstate level. The normative framing of the conflict at the UNGA shifted starkly from the partition plan, which spoke about two states, to bestowing international legitimacy on one state, while the Palestinians were dealt with in the framework of individual refugee rights, not collective rights to self-determination and statehood. The UNSC mainly dealt with the interstate dimension, but in a reactive rather than proactive way. It did, however, once pass a resolution under Chapter VII of the UN Charter with immediate effects. In the following three periods, the UNSC would never wield Chapter VII power again.

In the second period, after the 1967 war, the superpowers used the UN to prevent war, but not to make peace. The game changer in this respect has been Egypt's switch toward bilateral negotiations headed by the US. The UN and a comprehensive approach to peacemaking that could have established a security architecture guaranteed by the UN was thus sidelined, while bilateral peace treaties were negotiated, guaranteed solely by US power. The normative framing of the conflict as it emerged in the UNSC and the UNGA in this period differed starkly. The framing at the UNSC was dominated by the US. During the Carter period, the UNSC demanded the end of occupation and singled out Israeli settlements as illegal and an obstacle to peace. The one issue that all US presidents have blocked without any deviation has been the issue of Palestinian statehood. In stark contrast to this, the UNGA has come forward with a strong alternative script in this period; it has not only repeatedly confirmed the illegality of Israeli settlements and the rights of the Palestinian people under the Geneva Convention, but it has also developed the Palestinians' right to their own sovereign and independent state.

In the third period, the UN has been marginalized from peacemaking in the Middle East. Even actors such as Saudi Arabia and the EC, which still saw an important role for the UN in the 1980s, dropped this agenda after the end of the Cold War. As a result, peace treaties have remained bilateral and are not rooted in a comprehensive security architecture guaranteed by the UN. From the early 2000s onward, the US began to instrumentalize the UNSC to support its leading peace-broker role in several resolutions that promoted a two-state solution based on negotiations, not on the right of the Palestinian people to statehood. In 1988 and 2012, a stark majority of the UNGA supported the Palestinian declaration of statehood and the Palestinian nonobserver member state bid. It should, in fact, be mentioned here that the only silver lining that continuously contrasted with the US-led Camp David system has been the position of the UNGA on the right of the Palestinians to a state, which has subsequently influenced (and been influenced by) the position of the Arab states, the Soviet Union (later Russia), the EU, and the US (in declining order of influence). Thus, while much of the literature has singled out the European Union as the normative power behind the two-state solution, the real normative power in this respect might actually lie in the UN General Assembly.

In the fourth period, the UN is beginning to enter the picture again to guarantee international law at a time when the US has moved from sidelining international law to violating it, and when the realities created in the context of a decades-long peace process make the two-state paradigm infeasible. Seeds of change at the UN are driven by various actors. One is the PLO and its push to bring the UN and international law as a protective means back into the picture. The EU and its differentiation policy are also influencing the paradigmatic normative framing of the Palestine/Israel question on the international level. It frames settlements as individual breaches of international law and thus differentiates in its trade policy between products from Israel and from the settlements. In addition, there is the position of UN bodies, which might eventually also affect the framing at the UNGA. The Special Rapporteur on the situation of human rights in the Occupied Palestinian Territory has pointed out that an endless "occu-annexation" as such might constitute a violation of international law. Beyond this, UN-ESCWA has framed the whole scenario in Israel and the Occupied Palestinian Territory as apartheid in a report it was forced to retract. All these developments point to increased agency at and by the UN.

Conclusions

This book started with the question of what the roles of seven global and regional powers—Egypt, Saudi Arabia, Iran, Turkey, Russia/USSR, EC/EU, and the US—in the Israel-Palestinian conflict have been and if their roles, rather than helping to solve the conflict, have led to its perpetuation. It then inquired into the role performances of these powers and to which scripts they amounted to, while also confronting these scripts with alternative ones, particularly the authoritative normative meaning established in the form of UN resolutions on the Palestine/Israel question. While analyzing these scripts, their ruptures, and their consequences, this book has particularly highlighted how the script of the US-led peace process has become dominant since 1979, absorbing all powers observed (with the exclusion of Iran) into it and *proving resilient thanks to their continuous performance of the script for more than forty years.* This script has been dominated by (1) a divide-and-rule paradigm that has split the Middle East and sidelined the UN, which could have provided an inclusive platform for building a comprehensive security architecture in the region; and (2) a negotiations paradigm that has sidelined international law and rights and has thus denied Palestinians their individual and collective rights. *As such, this script has perpetuated conflict on both the regional level and the local level.* It has been contested by Iran and the UNGA, which have both set up alternative scripts, focused either on "apartheid"/"a one-state solution" or the never-ending occupation/a rights-based solution.

In more detail, in the period from 1948 to 1967 there were two scripts: a global one whereby the Palestine question was framed as a "refugee issue" and was managed by the superpowers through the United Nations. They used the UN only reactively as a conflict management tool, not proactively to solve the conflict. They legitimized one state, while speaking only of individual refugee rights, not of collective rights, of the Palestinians. The regional pan-Arabism script was spearheaded by Egypt on the Palestine question. This configuration of scripts did not prevent war; it arguably led to the 1967 war. The latter was a watershed: the Arab script broke down and a new global-regional script was now produced by the US that eventually became dominant as an array of other important powers began to perform it as well. A transitory period prepared the ground for the Camp David Accords and the peace process, which sidelined the UN, comprehensive diplomacy, and international law. It split the Arab world, which meant not only that the Arabs could no longer pose any meaningful threat to Israel (Heikal 1997), *but that their ability to produce an alternative script was undermined, as well.* Egypt, Saudi Arabia, Turkey, the EU, and Russia were gradually absorbed into the US script, while excluding and marginalizing Iran. It has thus set the context in which on the regional level no comprehensive and inclusive security architecture guaranteed by the UN was built that could have outlived US power in the region.

In the meaning that was attached to the "peace process" script, international law and Palestinian rights were silenced, enabling the occupation to normalize to such a degree that a contiguous Palestinian state is hardly realizable anymore. There were neither sticks to prevent the continuing creeping annexation of Palestinian land nor any incentive for Israel to end its occupation. Not even the offer of full normalization of relations by the Arab League or the European offer of a privileged partnership with the EU interested Israel. The Middle East Peace Process has, as Omar Dajani and Hugh Lovatt have pointed out, "provided Israel with effective political cover to maintain a prolonged occupation and undermine prospects for Palestinian self-determination through a two-state solution. They have also enabled Israel to externalise the political and financial costs of its unlawful practices" (Dajani and Lovatt 2017, 1).[1] The lynchpin has been the negotiations paradigm, namely, that an occupied people has to negotiate their statehood with the occupying power, which has given Israel a de-facto veto over such a state. With this approach, peace has never materialized. Indeed, one could also argue that the US-led Middle East Peace Process has not failed, but actually achieved what it has been built up for. As Mandy Turner has suggested, if the goal of peacebuilding has been "to ensure stability and implement neoliberal economic and governance strategies, then it has not failed—in fact, quite the contrary, it has largely succeeded" (Turner 2016, 442). Nonetheless, since 2011 and following, this script is challenged specifically by the US and Saudi performance, and might have entered into a second transitory period.

The two transitory periods—after 1967 until 1979, and potentially since 2011—are, indeed, equally interesting. While agency has been important in sustaining scripts, it is even more crucial in periods of transition, when meaning can change. It is in these periods that discursive struggles on the role and meaning attached to the Palestine/Israel question are able to bring about change. Following 1967, this discursive struggle was led among the Arab states and by the PLO in the UN General Assembly while the US prevented a similar discursive struggle in the UN Security Council through its vetoes. Crucially supported by the Non-Aligned Movement, the UNGA voted with overwhelming majorities for the need of the Palestinian people to exercise their sovereignty over their territory occupied since 1967 and their right to self-determination and their independent state. The UNGA has in fact been the only countercurrent that has continuously provided a legitimate, alternative silver lining in the framework of international law and comprehensive peace.

Since 2011, we might be witnessing another period of transition and discursive struggles in the international community. These surround the Palestine nonmember observer state status at the UN, the preliminary examination of the Palestine case at the ICC, and the EU's differentiation policy, which has also been adopted by UNSC Resolution 2334, while the UN Human Rights Council has begun to compile a blacklist of companies doing business in the settlements. Finally, UN bodies have also taken specific positions in this discursive struggle. The Special Rapporteur on the situation of human rights in the Palestinian Territory occupied since 1967, S. Michael Lynk, has highlighted that an endless "occu-annexation" is illegal under international law (Lynk 2017), while the United Nations Economic and Social Commission for Western Asia has gone beyond this position in its "Apartheid report" (ESCWA 2017).

Beyond these particular findings, and seen from a larger theoretical perspective, this book has shown that role performances can be investigated in relation to each other and to the scripts they amount to. This not only departs from a uni- or bilateral understanding of roles as currently dominant in role theory in various theoretical traditions, but also helps us to understand periods of continuity and periods of ruptures. Despite pivotal events such as the end of the Cold War or the two US-led invasions of Iraq, actors sustained their role performances within the script of the "peace process," which therefore remained resilient. At other points of time, they did not and we witnessed ruptures: after 1967, when the pan-Arabism script declined with its gravitational power, Egypt; or since 2011, as the "peace process" script declines with its gravitational power, the US. But the script did not only remain or fall with its gravitational power; rather, it is dependent on the performance of all its actors; it is resilient only to the extent that it is performed by all of them. This book has inquired deeply into scripts, made up of continuous role performances that (re)produce specific webs of relationships bound by meaning through a dominant framing that might sideline or silence conflicting or competing framing. Clearly the performance of the "peace process" script at the UN can be seen as a theatrical performance (Pace and Sen 2019), and, indeed, this is why the cover picture of this book shows a UN General Assembly that almost appears as a theater stage. This theatrical play of all actors involved has not served to solve the Israel-Palestinian conflict, but it has bound the performing actors *to a shared, collective performance that has provided them with "meaningful order."*

Indeed, much of what has been found in this book relates deeply and speaks to Judith Butler's writing on performative acts. The observed performances at the UN clearly appear like "ritualized, public performances" (Butler 1988, 526), which—rather than relating to the conflict on the ground—constitute identity "as a compelling illusion, an object of belief" (Butler 1988, 520). The performance serves to maintain meaning and a certain order, rather than being an expression of an "inner" identity of these states. Many of the observed actors—whether that be Egypt, Europe, or Saudi Arabia—perform in relation to the script, not in relation to what their publics think.

Furthermore, when observing the cases of Iran and Saudi Arabia specifically, Butler's concept of performing an act "that has been going on before one arrived on the scene" (Butler 1988, 526) is evident. Even while opposing the dominant script of the "peace process," Iran still performed in relation to it, and arguably played a role assigned to it in the script, even though this changed later on. Another example is Saudi Arabia in the early 1980s and early 2000s. While in both instances it came forward with its own script, both can also be seen as just another version of the US script. As Judith Butler has observed, "Actors are always already on the stage, within the terms of the performance" and scripts "may be enacted in various ways, and just as the play requires both text and interpretation" (Butler 1988, 526).

This is different for periods of ruptures and transformations. For the latter specifically, Butler has pointed out that in "its very character as performative resides the possibility of contesting its reified status" (Butler 1988, 520). Specifically, over- or underperformance of a script enters here. A radical performance makes it possible to actually displace the whole script. It makes it appear "theatrical," it "mimes and renders hyperbolic the discursive convention" (Butler 1993, 232). This may best be seen when observing over- or underperformance. At the time of writing, the current hyperbolic Saudi and US performance of the script exposes its inherent injustice by overperforming it. The EU, at the same time, underperforms or even nonperforms. Indeed, as the script of the "peace process" is hardly being performed, an array of actors currently do not know what to expect from the US and each other and so the shared, intersubjective knowledge provided by the peace process script is gone, leading to a widely shared perception of "disorder" today.

Finally, from a non-Eurocentric perspective, several findings should be highlighted here, as they also lead to some closing practical implications of this book. First, this book also showed alternative scripts that become important specifically in periods of ruptures and transition. This happened in the 1970s and the 2010s in which we can observe heightened activity at the United Nations. Indeed, for actors such as the EU or the Arab states, this book points out the importance of the UN, which should not be forgotten just because a dominant script has sidelined it for more than forty years. The UN can play an important role in both, providing a platform for building a regionally rooted security architecture and guaranteeing and safeguarding international law and rights for the Palestinians living under occupation and for Palestine refugees particularly. Thus, it is incumbent upon actors such as the European Union or the Arab states now to envisage a new role for themselves, advocating an approach to the Palestine/Israel question anchored in international law and human rights, bringing the United Nations back into the picture. If they approach this together, they could pave the way for future US administrations to eventually buy in to it.

Second, this book has clearly shown that Western states are not only diplomatic actors outside this conflict, which they are arguing to solve; rather, in this specific case, they have produced the conflict in a way that has perpetuated it, both regionally and locally. This finding should again serve as a wake-up call for the EU or the Arab states on general assumptions about their own diplomacy. It should also make academics more wary in their analysis. This analysis needs to start on the conceptual level with a critical reflection on the meaning we apply to conflicts through paradigmatic concepts that often simply reflect concepts of powerful players and are potentially glossing over what is happening on the ground. Power relationships should become central parameters in the conceptualization of conflicts, and international law and human rights central parameters in the conceptualization of peace.

Last but not least, the United Nations is a wonderful source for research. It provides vast material to investigate key issues in international politics from various perspectives that are not present in the mainstream Western political and academic discourse, which helps to move beyond paradigms, while at the same time—through UN resolutions and international law—protecting research from attack when going beyond such paradigms.

Notes

Introduction

1. There are important exceptions to this trend, most notably the comprehensive account of Raymond Hinnebusch's *The International Politics of the Middle East* (2003), which shows that the Middle Eastern system is deeply penetrated by powers such as the US.

Chapter 1

1. Neve Gordon has argued that instead of conceiving of the PA "as an autonomous body with an external existence that in some way transcends the occupation, one can tenably claim that the PA is a product of the occupation. . . . [In 1993], all of the civil institutions, including education, health, and welfare were passed from Israel to the hands of the fledgling authority . . . which reduced the occupation's political and economic cost, while continuing to hold on to most of the territory" (Gordon 2008, 20–21).

2. This legal division means that Palestinians are not entitled even to the basic safeguards guaranteed in Israeli law (such as access to a lawyer within twenty-one days) while applying disproportionate sentences, including for children. Arbitrary arrests and administrative detention without charge or trial and without a time limit have been used extensively by Israel (B'Tselem 2014).

3. On discriminatory laws applied to Palestinians in Israel, see Adalah 2017.

4. Galtung conceives of imperialism as a "sophisticated type of dominance relation which cuts across nations, basing itself on a bridgehead which the center in the Center nation established in the center of the Periphery nation, for the joint benefit of both" (Galtung 1971, 81).

Chapter 2

1. As Thomas Diez has suggested, "Meaning does not simply exist as a given, but has to be fought over and negotiated—there is a struggle over meaning: a struggle that takes place between discourses that construct and delineate meaning" (Diez 2014, 28). However, he also points out that "relationship between discourse, if by discourse we mean the context in which an articulation occurs . . . is . . . at best a mutually constitutive one. It is thus appropriate to say that discourses inform articulations, and that articulations reproduce discourses; but that is not a causal relationship in the positivist sense" (Diez 2014, 32).

2. Lori Allen argues that the UN holds power as a symbolic realm. "The UN is a site where 'the world' is imagined and where humanitarian values are espoused" (Allen 2016, 59).

Chapter 3

1. While the Treaty of Rome did not mention foreign policy objectives, these developed specifically in the 1970s as the European Political Cooperation was created, while the Single European Act of 1986 formalized intergovernmental cooperation regarding foreign policy and determined the competencies of the European Council (leading), the European Commission (assisting), and the European Parliament (observing) in European Political Cooperation. The Maastricht Treaty then set up the Common Foreign and Security Policy (CFSP) as the successor of European Political Cooperation. The Amsterdam Treaty revised the provisions regarding the CFSP, appointed the Secretary General of the Council to the High Representative of the CFSP and introduced the new troika of the High Representative, the Council presidency, and the Commission representative. The Treaty of Nice established the European Security and Defense Policy and incorporated it into the CFSP pillar. With the 2009 treaty of Lisbon, the CFSP and the European Security and Defense Policy were merged into the Common Security and Defense Policy and the pillar system was abandoned with the Common Security and Defense Policy and foreign aid policy now being part of the "shared competences." Lisbon also established the office of an EU minister of foreign affairs—the High Representative of the Union for Foreign Affairs and Security—and a European diplomatic service, the European External Action Service. As Stephan Keukeleire and Jennifer MacNaughtan suggested, it "might be more accurate to characterize EU foreign policy as existing on a continuum, going from various degrees of supranational integration, over various degrees of intergovernmental integration, to purely intergovernmental cooperation" (Keukeleire and MacNaughtan 2008, 31).

2. The Israeli-Palestinian conflict plays an important role in the opening speeches at the UNGA. Mor Mitrani (2017) argues that Israel and the Palestinian

Authority are the most named entities in UNGA speeches since 1992—Israel appears in 40 percent, the PA in almost 42 percent of the speeches.

3. Indeed, the resolution of the German parliament has not only been criticized by the UN (Salloum and Schult 2019), and potentially amounts to a breach of law as evident in a related ruling of a German court (Middle East Monitor 2019), but it has also been exposed as highly problematic by a group of German academics working on the Middle East (Die Zeit 2019).

Chapter 4

1. This relates to the UN Charter, Chapter I, Article 2, "All Members shall refrain in their international relations from the threat or use of force against the territorial integrity or political independence of any state, or in any other manner inconsistent with the Purposes of the United Nations." (United Nations 1945).

Chapter 5

1. The Arab state system came into being from the decline of the Ottoman Empire in the eighteenth century up until World War II. With formal independence, as Beverly Milton-Edwards has pointed out, "the new political elite of the Arab states in the region were forced to address the pressing issue of creating new bonds in old boundaries, while at the same time balancing the demands of old bonds in new boundaries" (Milton-Edwards 2011, 66). Thus, specifically in the early periods, states had to build up both support by local constituencies and regional peers. This was a rather difficult context as state sovereignty was frequently challenged by both internal and external actors.

2. The dire state of Egyptian-Saudi relations was most obvious in the civil war in Yemen, where republicans fought royalists, supported by Egypt and Saudi Arabia, respectively. Having overstretched Egyptian military capacities by his engagement in Yemen and the 1967 war, Nasser was forced to sign a treaty in 1967 with Prince Faisal.

3. The 1978 Camp David Accords consisted of two documents, the Framework for the Conclusion of a Peace Treaty between Egypt and Israel, which led to the 1979 peace treaty, and the Framework for Peace in the Middle East, which dealt with the Occupied Palestinian Territory but was never implemented as Egypt had given away its "carrots" by entering a separate peace treaty.

4. At the same time, through encouraging the PLO "which did not recognise any such right and rejected UNSCR 242, Egypt expressed its continued engagement in an existential struggle for Palestine, and not just for the restitution of Egyptian territory" (Stein 2012, 100). This was, however, also a convenient strategy, as it shifted the responsibility onto the shoulders of the PLO, a nonstate actor.

5. Furthermore, the spike in oil prices meant a dramatic change in the Gulf as the "three major regional states—Iran, Iraq, and Saudi Arabia—all had vastly increased amounts of military and economic power" (Gause 2013, 287). This development set the scene for a confrontation in the Gulf that would escalate from the 1980s onward.

6. Nasser had originally founded the PLO in 1964 as an organization through which he could control Palestinian activism.

7. In 2007, during a thaw in their relations, King Abdullah held discussions with Iranian president Mahmud Ahmadinejad in Mecca. Ahmadinejad, as the Saudi press reported, apparently voiced support for the initiative, even though this was later denied by Iran (Golan 2012, 426–27). In fact, however, the Saudi Peace Initiative has received support by all member states of the Organization of Islamic Cooperation, thus also by Iran, in repeated sessions.

8. The Ottoman Empire during its decline was the context in which the Israel-Palestinian conflict initially took its shape. For centuries, the Ottoman Empire had provided a "shelter" for Jews and this continued during World War II, when Turkish officials such as Selahattin Ülkümen helped Jews to escape the Holocaust at high personal cost. The Ottomans initially did not hinder Jewish migration to Palestine but later on, at the end of the nineteenth century, when the nature and the scope of Jewish immigration started to change, the Ottoman authorities and later the Young Turks began to perceive this as a dangerous development for the local balance and sought to curtail it (Kamel 2015).

9. In 2011, Iranian supreme leader, Ayatollah Ali Khamenei, stated that he rejected the statehood bid, arguing that "all land belongs to Palestinians," not just what the international community refers to the Occupied Palestinian Territory, further being quoted as saying that "we neither propose dumping the migrant Jews in the sea nor the UN arbitration, rather our proposal includes a referendum to be participated [in] by all Palestinians" (Haaretz 2011).

10. For an in-depth analysis, see Moshirzadeh 2015, 30–33.

11. In the Middle East, as the US was perceived as providing "weapons power" to Israel, Russia and the USSR were seen as providing "manpower" to Israel, not only in the first waves of immigration but also as more than one million immigrants from the post-Soviet space immigrated to Israel since the late 1980s (Maltz 2015).

12. Vladimir Lenin was initially anti-Zionist as he feared Zionism would "divert the attention of Jewish workers from communist efforts to undertake world revolution" (Freedman 2012, 325). The Executive Committee of the Communist International saw Zionism as "the expression of the exploiting, and great power oppressive strivings, of the Jewish bourgeoisie" and the Jewish Communist Party of Palestine was advised to "support the national freedom of the Arab population against the British-Zionist occupation" (Kreutz 2007, 46).

13. This is, however, contested by Bernard Lewis (1999, 25) who argued that "it is difficult to believe that Stalin, who killed countless millions in his own

concentration camps, was moved by compassion for the plight of Hitler's surviving victims. A much more likely explanation is that he saw in Jewish migration to Palestine and the struggle for a Jewish state a useful way of weakening and eventually eliminating the power of Britain, then still his principal Western rival in the Middle East."

14. The USSR also sought to pressure Syria to endorse the resolution as well. However, as Andrej Kreutz has pointed out, in spite of "substantial economic, military, and political support, the USSR was apparently unable to force Damascus to closely follow its line. The lack of correspondence between Soviet assistance and their ability to control Syrian behavior continued and became even more noticeable in the years to come" (Kreutz 2007, 48). At the same time, the USSR did not back up Syria in military and political terms to the same extent as the US backed up Israel. The Soviet-Syrian relationship was a mutually dependent one: as Egypt began to move out of the Soviet alliance system, Syria became more important for the USSR—and vice versa.

15. Galia Golan has argued that leading Politburo members and apparently also Brezhnev himself construed the Palestinians as intransigent, irresponsible, and at times dangerous to East-West relations (Golan 1990, 28).

16. As Avi Shlaim has pointed out on the Israeli position toward the war between Iran and Iraq: "Ideally, the Israelis would have liked both sides to lose this war. The second-best scenario was for Iran and Iraq to demolish one another in a long, drawn-out war of attrition. The supply of arms to Iran, which had been under a strict American embargo since the revolution, was one way of fueling the war and sustaining the stalemate. As long as Iraq remained bogged down in this conflict, it could not join forces with Syria or Jordan to form an eastern front against Israel" (Shlaim 2014, 440–41).

17. This point was made by Dimitris Boutris at a conference held at the Istituto Affari Internazionali on the EU and Area C in the Occupied Palestinian Territory, on October 4, 2017.

18. Austria, Belgium, Denmark, Cyprus, Finland, France, Greece, Ireland, Italy, Luxembourg, Malta, Portugal, Spain, and Sweden.

19. Bulgaria, Estonia, Germany, Hungary, Latvia, Lithuania, the Netherlands, Poland, Romania, Slovakia, Slovenia, and the United Kingdom.

20. The Czech Republic.

21. As Anders Persson argues, from "not having mentioned the major Palestinian terror attacks against Israel in the 1970s, the EU came to see 'the fight against all forms of terrorism' as 'paramount in the quest for a just and comprehensive peace in the Middle East' " (Persson 2018).

22. Trade rose from 150 million USD in 1998 to more than three billion USD today (Borshchevskaya 2016).

23. Friedman, Lara. 2019. "The Embassy of Hungary Seems to Think All US Jews Celebrate Its Alignment with Trump & Bibi on Jerusalem. Suggests a Remarkable/Laughable Failure of Basic Research.Pic.Twitter.Com/E8HAa9inY3."

Tweet. @LaraFriedmanDC (blog). March 18. https://twitter.com/LaraFriedmanDC/status/1107638760261459968.

24. The Lisbon Treaty of the EU (2009), Article 3, obliges the EU in its relations with the wider world to promote "the protection of human rights, in particular the rights of the child, as well as to the strict observance and the development of international law, including respect for the principles of the United Nations Charter" (European Union 2009).

25. Third parties, as has been pointed out by the International Court of Justice (2004) in its advisory opinion, have the responsibility not to aid, assist, or recognize as legal a situation arising from a breach of international law and to cooperate to bring to an end such violations.

26. Russia's image in the region has been partially harmed by this. The American Pew Research Center finds that both the US and Russia are viewed quite unfavorably in the region today, as only 29 percent and 25 percent, respectively, see the two powers favorably (Pew Research Center 2015). Russia is seen unfavorably specifically in Israel (by 74 percent) and Jordan (by 80 percent), while 52 percent of Palestinians perceive it unfavorably.

27. As Noura Erekat has pointed out, neither "the Oslo Accords nor any subsequent agreements that have flowed therefrom have been predicated on established international law, including the laws regulating occupation, human rights norms, or the series of Security Council and General Assembly resolutions regarding the conflict in particular" (Erekat 2016, 102).

28. Husam Zomlot, "Hussam Zomlot reacts to US decision to close PLO office in DC." 2018. https://www.aljazeera.com/news/2018/09/hussam-zomlot-reacts-decision-close-plo-office-dc-180910193703244.html.

29. Thus, this research also added a different perspective to much of the constructivist IR literature on the study of international norms, which has mainly taken the collective understandings of Western elites as consequential (Legro 1997, 33) and which "typically posits Western actors as the agents . . . thereby relegating non-Western actors to passive roles" (Graubart and Jimenez-Bacardi 2016, 26). In light of its post-Eurocentric perspective, this book shows the agency by both Western and non-Western actors, while it has not neglected that power is unequally distributed among them.

Chapter 6

1. The UNGA can only expel a member upon the recommendation of the UNSC.

2. It should be noted here that Palestinians have a long history of popular resistance since the 1920s; see Qumsiyeh (2010).

3. The Arab states initially showed a readiness to negotiate with Israel (Rabinovich 1991, 2012). "Each of the neighboring Arab states was prepared to

negotiate directly with Israel and to bargain about borders. On the other central issue, that of Palestinian refugees, individual Arab states had less freedom of action. Here there was a clear and consistent Pan-Arab position, binding on all the members of the Arab League. The position was that Israel alone had created the refugee problem and that it must not be allowed to evade its responsibility for solving this problem. The solution had to be along the line of UN resolutions that gave the refugees themselves the choice between returning to their homes and receiving compensation for their property from Israel. The collective position permitted individual Arab states to cooperate with the United Nations Relief and Works Agency (UNRWA) for Palestine and the Near East, but only on condition that this cooperation did not compromise the basic rights of the refugees" (Shlaim 2014, 49).

4. **In favor:** Argentina, Australia, Bolivia, Belorussian SSR, Canada, Chile, China, Colombia, Costa Rica, Cuba, Czechoslovakia, Dominican Republic, Ecuador, France, Guatemala, Haiti, Honduras, Iceland, Liberia, Luxembourg, Mexico, Netherlands, New Zealand, Nicaragua, Norway, Panama, Paraguay, Peru, Philippines, Poland, South Africa, Ukrainian SSR, USSR, United States, Uruguay, Venezuela, Yugoslavia. **Against:** Afghanistan, Burma, Egypt, Ethiopia, India, Iran, Iraq, Lebanon, Pakistan, Saudi Arabia, Syria, Yemen. **Abstained:** Belgium, Brazil, Denmark, El Salvador, Greece, Siam, Sweden, Turkey, United Kingdom.

5. This resolution was opposed by Egypt and the UK abstained.

6. About 100,000 Palestinians remained within Israel's borders and became "internally displaced Palestinians." On the population in Palestine during the Ottoman and Mandate periods, see McCarthy (1990).

7. In 1953, in response to cross-border raids, troops from the Israeli army under the command of Ariel Sharon entered the village of Qibya in the West Bank and killed Palestinian men, women, and children. Israel denied that the Israeli army had perpetrated the massacre.

8. Russian vetoes have, however, increased again in the mid-2000s, first in relation to its direct neighborhood (e.g., Georgia, Ukraine) and then also in relation to the civil war in Syria.

9. As Raja Khalidi points out, "Donors and international institutions, including UN agencies, have become the inseparable partners, if not managers, of Palestinian development, trade, fiscal, financial, and social service policies and institutions" (Raja Khalidi 2016, 410).

10. How difficult it was to receive American approval in that period is shown in the Security Council Report (2007): in 2006, as nineteen Palestinians were killed in an Israeli shelling of Beit Hanoun, Qatar proposed a resolution that called for the immediate withdrawal of Israeli forces from Gaza, making numerous amendments to balance the draft. For instance, "indiscriminate" was changed to "disproportionate"; "military assault," "aggression," and "massacre" to "military operations"; "demands" was replaced with "calls upon." The calls for a cease-fire and for the dispatch of a UN observer force were replaced by calls for

a halt of violence and for the establishment of a fact-finding mission by the UN Secretary-General. There were also some alterations to the paragraph on the role of the Quartet. Finally, the condemnation of the firing of rockets from Gaza into Israel was shifted to the preamble and an operative clause called for the firing to stop. Nonetheless, the US vetoed the draft, claiming it was "biased against Israel," "politically motivated," and failed either to "display an evenhanded characterization of the recent events in Gaza" or to "advance the cause of Israeli-Palestinian peace."

11. Australia, Cameroon, Canada, Nauru.

12. Israel, Marshall Islands, Micronesia, Palau, the United States of America.

13. While voting with approval, Iran's Supreme Leader, Ayatollah Ali Khamenei, had also stated that the Palestinians should not limit themselves to the 1967 borders as "all land" belongs to them (Haaretz 2011).

14. I owe this point to Alice Panepinto, made in an ongoing e-mail conversation after an Istituto Affari Internazionali-Gruppo di Volontariato Civile conference on the EU and Area C in the West Bank, on October 4, 2017.

Conclusions

1. See also Azhar and Pinfari 2017.

References

Abadi, Jacob. 2006. "Egypt's Policy towards Israel: The Impact of Foreign and Domestic Constraints." *Israel Affairs* 12 (1): 159–76. https://doi.org/10.1080/13537120500382040.

Abdel Meguid, Amed Esmat. 1978. "Speech by Mr. Abdel Meguid at the General Assembly Plenary Session." http://www.un.org/ga/search/view_doc.asp?symbol=A/33/PV.28.

Acharya, Amitav, and Barry Buzan, eds. 2010. *Non-Western International Relations Theory: Perspectives on and beyond Asia*. London: Routledge.

Adalah. 2017. "The Discriminatory Laws Database." 2017. https://www.adalah.org/en/content/view/7771.

Adib-Moghaddam, Arshin. 2017. *Psycho-Nationalism: Global Thought, Iranian Imaginations*. Cambridge: Cambridge University Press.

Adwan, Sami, and Dan Bar-On. 2004. "Shared History Project: A PRIME Example of Peace-Building under Fire." *International Journal of Politics, Culture, and Society* 17 (3): 513–21.

Aggestam, Lisbeth. 2006. "Role Theory and European Foreign Policy: A Framework of Analysis." In *The European Union's Roles in International Politics: Concepts and Analysis*, edited by Ole Elgström and Michael Smith, 11–29. Abingdon, Oxon: Routledge.

Ahmadinejad, Mahmoud. 2005. "Statement by Iranian President Mahmoud Ahmadinejad at the United Nations General Assembly Plenary Meeting." http://www.un.org/ga/search/view_doc.asp?symbol=A/60/PV.10.

———. 2008. "Statement by Iranian President Mahmoud Ahmadinejad at the United Nations General Assembly Plenary Meeting." http://www.un.org/ga/search/view_doc.asp?symbol=A/63/PV.6.

———. 2011. "Statement by Iranian President Mahmoud Ahmadinejad at the United Nations General Assembly Plenary Meeting." http://www.un.org/ga/search/view_doc.asp?symbol=A/66/PV.15.

Ajami, Fouad. 1978. "The End of Pan-Arabism." *Foreign Affairs*, December 1. https://www.foreignaffairs.com/articles/yemen/1978-12-01/end-pan-arabism.

Al Saud, Faisal. 1947. "Speech of Amir Faisal al Saud at the General Assembly Plenary Debate." http://www.un.org/ga/search/view_doc.asp?symbol=A/PV.89.

Al Saud, Sultan bin Abdulaziz. 2005. "Statement by Crown Prince Sultan Bin Abdulaziz Al Saudi at the United Nations General Assembly Plenary Meeting." http://www.un.org/ga/search/view_doc.asp?symbol=A/60/PV.6.

Al Sisi, Abdel Fattah. 2016. "Speech by Mr. Al Sisi at the General Assembly Plenary Meeting." http://www.un.org/ga/search/view_doc.asp?symbol=A/71/PV.9.

Alavi, Seyed Ali. 2019. *Iran and Palestine: Past, Present, Future*. Milton Park, Abingdon, Oxon: Routledge.

Al-Faisal, Saud. 1991. "Statement by Prince Saud Al-Faisal at the United Nations General Assembly Plenary Meeting." http://www.un.org/ga/search/view_doc.asp?symbol=A/46/PV.15.

Al-Jubeir, Adel Ahmed. 2017. "Minister of Foreign Affairs Speech during 70th Regular Session of the UN General Assembly." Kingdom of Saudi Arabia Ministry of Foreign Affairs. http://www.un.org/ga/search/view_doc.asp?symbol=A/72/PV.20.

Allagany, Gaafar. 1993. "Statement by Mr. Gaafar at the United Nations General Assembly Plenary Meeting." http://www.un.org/ga/search/view_doc.asp?symbol=A/48/PV.28.

Allen, Lori. 2016. "Palestine, the Third World, and the UN as Seen from a Special Commission." In *Land of Blue Helmets: The United Nations and the Arab World*, edited by Karim Makdisi and Vijay Prashad, 58–73. Berkeley: University of California Press.

Al-Sowayel, Faisal. 1967. "Speech by Mr. Al-Sowayel at the United Nations General Assembly Plenary Meeting." http://www.un.org/ga/search/view_doc.asp?symbol=A/PV.1589.

Altunişik, Meliha Benli. 2004. "Turkey's Middle East Challenges: Towards a New Beginning?" In *Turkish Foreign Policy in Post–Cold War Era*, edited by Idris Bal, 363–77. Boca Raton, FL: Brown Walker Press.

Aoun, Elena. 2003. "European Foreign Policy and the Arab-Israeli Dispute: Much Ado about Nothing?" *European Foreign Affairs Review* 8 (3): 289–312.

Arab League. 1967. "Khartoum Resolution." https://ecf.org.il/issues/issue/141.

———. 1973. "Declaration of the Arab Summit Conference at Algiers." http://www.jewishvirtuallibrary.org/declaration-of-the-arab-summit-conference-at-algiers-november-1973.

———. 1974. "40 Decisions of the Arab Summit Conference in Rabat." http://content.ecf.org.il/files/M00094_ArabLeagueSummit-Rabat1974-EnglishText_0.pdf.

———. 1982. "Text of Final Declaration at Arab League Meeting in Fez." http://www.nytimes.com/1982/09/10/world/text-of-final-declaration-at-arab-league-meeting.html?mcubz=1.

———. 2002. "Arab Peace Initiative." https://www.theguardian.com/world/2002/mar/28/israel7.

Arafat, Yasser. 1988. "Speech at UN General Assembly." http://mondediplo.com/focus/mideast/arafat88-en.

Aras, Bulent. 2009. "Turkey and the Palestinian Question." SETA Policy Brief. http://setadc.org/wp-content/uploads/2015/05/SETA_Policy_Brief_No_27_Palestinian_Question_Bulent_Aras.pdf.

Aruri, Nasser. 2003. *Dishonest Broker: The Role of the United States in Palestine and Israel.* Cambridge, MA: South End Press.

Asseburg, Muriel. 2003. "The EU and the Middle East Conflict: Tackling the Main Obstacle to Euro-Mediterranean Partnership." *Mediterranean Politics* 8 (2–3): 174–93. https://doi.org/10.1080/13629390308230011.

Asseburg, Muriel, and Nimrod Goren, eds. 2019. "Divided and Divisive. Europeans, Israel and Israeli-Palestinian Peacemaking." https://www.swp-berlin.org/fileadmin/contents/products/fachpublikationen/Asseburg_PAX_REPORT_Divided_Divisive.pdf.

Aydın-Düzgit, Senem. 2014. "Unravelling European Union Foreign Policy through Critical Discourse Analysis: Guidelines for Research." In *EU Foreign Policy through the Lens of Discourse Analysis: Making Sense of Diversity*, edited by Caterina Carta and Jean-Frédéric Morin, 133–50. Farnham: Ashgate Publishing.

———. 2019. "Can Non-Democracies Support International Democracy? Turkey as a Case Study." *Third World Quarterly* 41 (2): 1–22. https://doi.org/10.1080/01436597.2019.1636643.

Aykan, Mahmut Bali. 1993. "The Palestinian Question in Turkish Foreign Policy from the 1950s to the 1990s." *International Journal of Middle East Studies* 25 (1): 91–110. https://doi.org/10.1017/S0020743800058062.

Ayoob, Mohammed. 2014. "Turkey and Iran in the Era of the Arab Uprisings." In *The New Middle East: Protest and Revolution in the Arab World*, edited by Fawaz A. Gerges, 402–17. Cambridge: Cambridge University Press.

Azarova, Valentina. 2017. "Israel's Unlawfully Prolonged Occupation: Consequences under an Integrated Legal Framework." http://www.ecfr.eu/publications/summary/israels_unlawfully_prolonged_occupation_7294.

———. 2018. "The Secret Life of Non-Recognition: EU-Israel Relations and the Obligation of Non-Recognition in International Law." *Global Affairs* 4 (1): 23–37. https://doi.org/10.1080/23340460.2018.1507278.

Azhar, Hirah, and Marco Pinfari. 2017. "Israel-Palestine: The Mediterranean Paradox." In *The EU, Promoting Regional Integration, and Conflict Resolution*, edited by Thomas Diez and Nathalie Tocci, 57–80. New York: Palgrave Macmillan.

Azoulay, Ariella, and Adi Ophir. 2012. *The One-State Condition: Occupation and Democracy in Israel/Palestine.* Stanford: Stanford University Press.

Baconi, Tareq. 2019. "The Plan's One Silver Lining." *Twitter* (blog). https://twitter.com/tareqbaconi/status/1143058420221825024.

Bahgat, Gawdat. 2003. "The New Middle East: The Gulf Monarchies and Israel." *Journal of Social, Political, and Economic Studies* 28 (2): 123.

———. 2009. "Saudi Arabia and the Arab–Israeli Conflict in the Last Years of the Bush Presidency." *Israel Affairs* 15 (2): 180–89. https://doi.org/10.1080/13537120902734442.

Baker, James. 1989. "Statement to AIPAC." May 22. http://mfa.gov.il/MFA/ForeignPolicy/MFADocuments/Yearbook8/Pages/59%20Statement%20to%20AIPAC%20by%20Secretary%20of%20State%20Baker-.aspx.

Barbiere, Cecile. 2014. "European Parliament Passes Watered-Down Palestine Resolution." *EurActiv*, December 18. https://www.euractiv.com/section/global-europe/news/european-parliament-passes-watered-down-palestine-resolution/.

Barnett, Michael. 1998. *Dialogues in Arab Politics*. New York: Columbia University Press.

Barnett, Michael, and Raymond Duvall. 2005. "Power in International Politics." *International Organization* 59 (1): 39–75.

Barnett, Michael, and Etel Solingen. 2007. "Designed to Fail or Failure of Design? The Origins and Legacy of the Arab League." In *Crafting Cooperation: Regional International Institutions in Comparative Perspective*, edited by Amitav Acharya and Alastair Iain Johnston, 180–220. Cambridge: Cambridge University Press.

Bartal, Shaul. 2015. *Jihad in Palestine: Political Islam and the Israeli-Palestinian Conflict*. London: Routledge.

Bass, Warren. 2004. *Support Any Friend: Kennedy's Middle East and the Making of the U.S.-Israel Alliance*. Oxford: Oxford University Press.

Beaumont, Peter. 2017. "UN Sends Warning Letters to Firms That Trade in Occupied Palestinian Territories." *Guardian*, September 28. https://www.theguardian.com/world/2017/sep/28/un-human-rights-warning-letter-firms-palestine-territories-occupied-israel.

Behrooz, Maziar. 2012. "Iran after Revolution (1979–2009)." *The Oxford Handbook of Iranian History*, February. https://doi.org/10.1093/oxfordhb/9780199732159.013.0017.

Bellamy, Richard, and Dario Castiglione. 2004. "Normative Theory and the EU: Legitimising the Euro-Polity and Its Regime." In *After National Democracy: Rights, Law and Power in America and the New Europe*, edited by Lars Trägårdh, 9–40. Oñati International Series in Law and Society. Oxford: Hart.

Bengio, O. 2004. *The Turkish-Israeli Relationship: Changing Ties of Middle Eastern Outsiders*. New York: Palgrave Macmillan.

Bennis, Phyllis. 1997. "The United Nations and Palestine: Partition and Its Aftermath." *Arab Studies Quarterly* 19 (3): 47–76.

Bercovitch, Jacob, Victor Kremenyuk, and I. William Zartman. 2008. *The SAGE Handbook of Conflict Resolution*. Thousand Oaks: SAGE.

Berry, Mike, and Greg Philo. 2006. *Israel and Palestine: Competing Histories*. London: Pluto.

Bicchi, Federica. 2014. "Information Exchanges, Diplomatic Networks and the Construction of European Knowledge in European Union Foreign Policy." *Cooperation and Conflict* 49 (2): 239–59. https://doi.org/10.1177/0010836713482871.

———. 2018. "The Debate about the Occupation of Palestinian Territories on UK Campuses, from Politicization to Re-Writing the Rules." *Global Affairs* 4 (1): 89–100. https://doi.org/10.1080/23340460.2018.1507282.

Bicchi, Federica, and Benedetta Voltolini. 2018. "Europe, the Green Line and the Issue of the Israeli-Palestinian Border: Closing the Gap between Discourse and Practice?" *Geopolitics* 23 (1): 124–46. https://doi.org/10.1080/14650045.2017.1305953.

Borshchevskaya, Anna. 2016. "The Maturing of Israeli-Russian Relations." *InFocus Quarterly*, Spring. http://www.washingtoninstitute.org/policy-analysis/view/the-maturing-of-israeli-russian-relations.

Börzel, Tanja A., Assem Dandashly, and Thomas Risse. 2015. "Responses to the 'Arabellions': The EU in Comparative Perspective—Introduction." *Journal of European Integration* 37 (1): 1–17. https://doi.org/10.1080/07036337.2014.975986.

Bouris, Dimitris. 2014. *The European Union and Occupied Palestinian Territories: State-Building without a State*. London: Routledge.

Bouris, Dimitris, and Irene Fernández-Molina. 2018. "Contested States, Hybrid Diplomatic Practices, and the Everyday Quest for Recognition." *International Political Sociology* 12 (3): 306–24. https://doi.org/10.1093/ips/oly006.

Bouris, Dimitris, and Daniela Huber. 2017. "Imposing Middle East Peace: Why EU Member States Should Recognise Palestine." *IAI Istituto Affari Internazionali Commentary 17/25*, November 16. http://www.iai.it/en/pubblicazioni/imposing-middle-east-peace-why-eu-member-states-should-recognise-palestine.

Bouris, Dimitris, and Beste İşleyen. 2018. "The European Union and Practices of Governing Space and Population in Contested States: Insights from EUPOL COPPS in Palestine." *Geopolitics* 25 (2): 1–21. https://doi.org/10.1080/14650045.2018.1552946.

Boutros-Ghali, Boutros. 1979. "Speech by Mr. Boutros Ghali at the General Assembly Plenary Meeting." http://www.un.org/ga/search/view_doc.asp?symbol=A/34/PV.15.

Brynen, Rex. 2000. *A Very Political Economy: Peacebuilding and Foreign Aid in the West Bank and Gaza*. Washington, DC: US Institute of Peace Press.

B'Tselem. 2014. "Administrative Detention." 2014. http://www.btselem.org/administrative_detention.

Bush, George H. W. 1991. "Address before a Joint Session of the Congress on the Cessation of the Persian Gulf Conflict." http://www.presidency.ucsb.edu/ws/?pid=19364.

Bush, George W. 2001. "Statement by US President George Bush at the United Nations General Assembly Opening Session." http://www.un.org/ga/search/view_doc.asp?symbol=A/56/PV.44.

———. 2004. "Statement by US President George Bush at the United Nations General Assembly Opening Session." http://www.un.org/ga/search/view_doc.asp?symbol=A/59/PV.3.

Busse, Jan. 2017. *Deconstructing the Dynamics of World-Societal Order: The Power of Governmentality in Palestine*. New York: Routledge. https://doi.org/10.4324/9780203712252.

Butler, Judith. 1988. "Performative Acts and Gender Constitution: An Essay in Phenomenology and Feminist Theory." *Theatre Journal* 40 (4): 519–31. https://doi.org/10.2307/3207893.

———. 1993. *Bodies That Matter: On the Discursive Limits of "Sex."* New York: Routledge.

Buzan, Barry, and Ole Wæver. 2003. *Regions and Powers: The Structure of International Security*. Cambridge: Cambridge University Press.

Campbell, David. 2013. *Writing Security: United States Foreign Policy and the Politics of Identity*. Minneapolis: University of Minnesota Press.

Canan, Fuat. 2009. *The Impact of Europeanization on Turkish Foreign Policy: An Analysis of Period since 1999*. Saarbrücken: VDM Verlag Dr. Müller.

Caplan, Neil. 2011. *The Israel-Palestine Conflict: Contested Histories*. Chichester: John Wiley & Sons.

Caporaso, James A. 1996. "The European Union and Forms of State: Westphalian, Regulatory or Post-Modern?" *Journal of Common Market Studies* 34 (1): 29–52.

Carrington, Lord Peter Alexander Rupert. 1981. "Statement by Mr. Carrington at the United Nations General Assembly Opening Session." http://www.un.org/ga/search/view_doc.asp?symbol=A/36/PV.8.

Carter, Jimmy. 1977. "Statement by US President Jimmy Carter at the United Nations General Assembly Opening Session." http://www.un.org/ga/search/view_doc.asp?symbol=A/32/PV.18.

Cetin, Hikmet. 1993. "Statement by Mr. Cetin at the United Nations General Assembly Opening Debate." http://www.un.org/ga/search/view_doc.asp?symbol=A/48/PV.11.

Chomsky, Noam. 1997. *World Orders, Old and New*. London: Pluto Press.

———. 1999. *Fateful Triangle: The United States, Israel, and the Palestinians*. Boston: South End Press.

Christopher, Warren. 1995. "Statement by Warren Christopher at the United Nations General Assembly Opening Session." http://www.un.org/ga/search/view_doc.asp?symbol=A/50/PV.4.

Ciller, Tansu. 1996. "Statement by Deputy Prime Minister Tansu Ciller at the United Nations General Assembly Opening Session." http://www.un.org/ga/search/view_doc.asp?symbol=A/51/PV.15.

Claude, Inis L. 1966. "Collective Legitimization as a Political Function of the United Nations." *International Organization* 20 (03): 367–79. https://doi.org/10.1017/S0020818300012832.

Clinton, Bill. 1993. "Statement by US President Bill Clinton at the United Nations General Assembly Opening Session." http://www.un.org/ga/search/view_doc.asp?symbol=A/48/PV.4.

———. 1994. "Statement by US President Bill Clinton at the United Nations General Assembly Opening Session." http://www.un.org/ga/search/view_doc.asp?symbol=A/49/PV.4.

Collins, John Martin. 2012. *Global Palestine*. New York: Columbia University Press.

Conrad, Sebastian, and Shalini Randeria. 2013. "Einleitung: Geteilte Geschichten—Europa in einer postkolonialen Welt (Introduction: Shared/Divided Histories—Europe in a Postcolonial World)." In *Jenseits des Eurozentrismus: Postkoloniale Perspektiven in den Geschichts- und Kulturwissenschaften (Beyond Eurocentrism: Postcolonial perspectives in historical and cultural sciences)*, edited by Sebastian Conrad, Shalini Randeria, and Regina Roemhild. Frankfurt am Main: Campus Verlag.

Corbin, Juliet, and Anselm Strauss. 1997. *Basics of Qualitative Research: Techniques and Procedures for Developing Grounded Theory*. 3rd ed. Los Angeles: SAGE Publications.

Cronin, David. 2010. *Europe's Alliance with Israel: Aiding the Occupation*. London: Pluto Press.

Dajani, Omar, and Hugh Lovatt. 2017. "Rethinking Oslo: How Europe Can Promote Peace in Israel-Palestine." ECFR Policy Brief. http://www.ecfr.eu/publications/summary/rethinking_oslo_how_europe_can_promote_peace_in_israel_palestine_7219.

Dannreuther, Roland. 2015. "Russia and the Arab Spring: Supporting the Counter-Revolution." *Journal of European Integration* 37 (1): 77–94. https://doi.org/10.1080/07036337.2014.975990.

Del Sarto, Raffaella A. 2015. "Borders, Power and Interdependence: A Borderlands Approach to Israel-Palestine and the European Union." In *Fragmented Borders, Interdependence and External Relations*, edited by Raffaella A. Del Sarto, 3–23. Palgrave Studies in International Relations Series. Houndmills: Palgrave Macmillan UK. https://doi.org/10.1057/9781137504142_1.

Die Zeit. 2019. "Israel-Boykott: Im Kampf gegen Antisemitismus hilft das nicht." *Die Zeit*, June 4, sec. Politik. https://www.zeit.de/politik/deutschland/2019-06/israel-boykott-bds-antisemitismus-meinungsfreiheit-bundesregierung.

Diez, Thomas. 2001. "Europe as a Discursive Battleground Discourse Analysis and European Integration Studies." *Cooperation and Conflict* 36 (1): 5–38. https://doi.org/10.1177/00108360121962245.

———. 2005. "Constructing the Self and Changing Others: Reconsidering `Normative Power Europe'." *Millennium—Journal of International Studies* 33 (3): 613–36. https://doi.org/10.1177/03058298050330031701.

———. 2014. "Speaking Europe, Drawing Boundaries: Reflections on the Role of Discourse in EU Foreign Policy and Identity." In *EU Foreign Policy through the Lens of Discourse Analysis: Making Sense of Diversity*, edited by Caterina Carta and Jean-Frédéric Morin, 27–42. Farnham: Ashgate Publishing.

Diez, Thomas, and Michelle Pace. 2011. "Normative Power Europe and Conflict Transformation." In *Normative Power Europe*, edited by Richard G. Whitman, 210–25. Palgrave Studies in European Union Politics. Houndmills: Palgrave Macmillan https://doi.org/10.1057/9780230305601_11.

Dijk, Teun A. Van. 2011. *Discourse Studies: A Multidisciplinary Introduction*. Thousand Oaks: SAGE.

Doty, Roxanne. 1996. *Imperial Encounters: The Politics of Representation in North-South Relations*. Minneapolis: University of Minnesota Press.

Dyduch, Joanna. 2018. "The Visegrád Group's Policy towards Israel." SWP Comment C 54. https://www.swp-berlin.org/en/publication/the-visegrad-groups-policy-towards-israel/.

Economic and Social Commission for Western Asia (ESCWA). 2017. "Israeli Practices towards the Palestinian People and the Question of Apartheid." https://www.middleeastmonitor.com/wp-content/uploads/downloads/201703_UN_ESCWA-israeli-practices-palestinian-people-apartheid-occupation-english.pdf.

Ehteshami, Anoushiravan. 2003. "Iran-Iraq Relations after Saddam." *Washington Quarterly* 26 (4): 115–29.

———. 2009. " 'Iran's Regional Policies since the End of the Cold War." In *Contemporary Iran: Economy, Society, Politics*, edited by Ali Gheissari, 324–48. Oxford: Oxford University Press.

———. 2014. "The Foreign Policy of Iran." In *The Foreign Policies of Middle East States*, edited by Raymond Hinnebusch and Anoushiravan Ehteshami, 283–310. Boulder, CO: Lynne Rienner.

Ehteshami, Anoushiravan, and Ariabarzan Mohammadi. 2017. "Iran's Discourses and Practices in the Mediterranean." MEDRESET Working Paper No. 5. http://www.medreset.eu/saudi-arabias-qatars-discourses-practices-mediterranean/.

Eisenberg, Laura Zittrain. 2012. "Seeking Peace: The Israeli-Palestinian Peace Process: 1967–1993." In *Routledge Handbook on the Israeli-Palestinian Conflict*, edited by Joel Peters and David Newman, 81–90. London: Routledge.

Erakat, Noura. 2016. "The UN Statehood Bid: Palestine's Flirtation with Multilateralism." In *Land of Blue Helmets: The United Nations and the Arab World*, edited by Karim Makdisi and Vijay Prashad, 95–114. Berkeley: University of California Press.

Erdogan, Recep Tayyip. 2007. "Statement by Recep Tayyip Erdogan at the United Nations General Assembly Opening Session." http://www.un.org/ga/search/view_doc.asp?symbol=A/62/PV.11.

———. 2009. "Statement by Recep Tayyip Erdogan at the United Nations General Assembly Opening Session." http://www.un.org/ga/search/view_doc.asp?symbol=A/64/PV.5.

———. 2011. "Statement by Recep Tayyip Erdogan at the United Nations General Assembly Opening Session." http://www.un.org/ga/search/view_doc.asp?symbol=A/66/PV.15.

———. 2017. "Statement by Turkish President Erdogan at the United Nations General Assembly." https://gadebate.un.org/sites/default/files/gastatements/72/tr_en.pdf.

Erekat, Noura. 2016. "The UN Statehood Bid: Palestine's Flirtation with Multilateralism." In *Land of Blue Helmets: The United Nations and the Arab World*, edited by Karim Makdisi and Vijay Prashad, 95–114. Berkeley: University of California Press.

European Council. 1973. "Text of Declaration on the Middle East." http://aei.pitt.edu/5576/1/5576.pdf.

———. 1980. "Venice Declaration." http://eeas.europa.eu/archives/docs/mepp/docs/venice_declaration_1980_en.pdf.

———. 1998. "Cardiff European Council Presidency Conclusions." http://www.consilium.europa.eu/en/european-council/conclusions/pdf-1993-2003/cardiff-european-council-15-and-16-june-1998-presidency-conclusions/.

———. 1999. "Berlin European Council Presidency Conclusions." http://www.europarl.europa.eu/summits/ber2_en.htm#partIV.

———. 2012a. "Council Conclusions on the Middle East Peace Process." https://www.consilium.europa.eu/uedocs/cms_data/docs/pressdata/EN/foraff/130195.pdf.

———. 2012b. "Council Conclusions on the Middle East Peace Process." https://www.consilium.europa.eu/uedocs/cms_data/docs/pressdata/EN/foraff/134140.pdf.

———. 2015. "Council Conclusions on the Middle East Peace Process." http://www.consilium.europa.eu/en/press/press-releases/2015/07/20-fac-mepp-conclusions/.

———. 2016a. "Council Conclusions on Business and Human Rights." http://www.consilium.europa.eu/en/press/press-releases/2016/06/20-fac-business-human-rights-conclusions/.

———. 2016b. "Council Conclusions on the Middle East Peace Process." http://www.consilium.europa.eu/en/press/press-releases/2016/01/18-fac-conclusions-mepp/.

European Union. 2009. "Lisbon Treaty." http://www.lisbon-treaty.org/wcm/the-lisbon-treaty/treaty-on-european-union-and-comments/title-1-common-provisions/4-article-3.html.

Fahmy, Ismail. 1977. "Speech by Mr. Fahmy at the General Assembly Plenary Session." http://www.un.org/ga/search/view_doc.asp?symbol=A/32/PV.10.

Falk, Richard. 2016. "On Behalf of the United Nations: Serving as a Special Rapporteur of the Human Rights Council for Palestinian Territories Occupied since 1967." In *Land of Blue Helmets: The United Nations and the Arab World*, edited by Karim Makdisi and Vijay Prashad, 74–94. Berkeley: University of California Press.

Freedman, Robert. 2012. "Russia." In *Routledge Handbook on the Israeli-Palestinian Conflict*, edited by Joel Peters and David Newman, 325–35. London: Routledge.

Friedman, Thomas. 1991. "Baker Cites Israel for Settlements." http://www.nytimes.com/1991/05/23/world/baker-cites-israel-for-settlements.html.

Galtung, Johan. 1971. "A Structural Theory of Imperialism." *Journal of Peace Research* 8 (2): 81–117. https://doi.org/10.2307/422946.

Gat, Moshe. 2012. *In Search of a Peace Settlement: Egypt and Israel between the Wars, 1967–1973*. Houndmills: Palgrave Macmillan.

Gause, Gregory F., III. 2013. "The International Politics of the Gulf." In *International Relations of the Middle East*, edited by Louise Fawcett, 3rd ed., 286–303. Oxford: Oxford University Press.

Gavriely-Nuri, Dalia. 2008. "The `Metaphorical Annihilation' of the Second Lebanon War (2006) from the Israeli Political Discourse." *Discourse & Society* 19 (1): 5–20. https://doi.org/10.1177/0957926507083685.

Gheit, Ahmed Aboul. 2001. "Speech by Mr. Aboul Gheit at the United Nations General Assembly Plenary Meeting." http://www.un.org/ga/search/view_doc.asp?symbol=A/56/PV.52.

———. 2010. "UN General Assembly Opening General Debate Statement." http://www.un.org/ga/search/view_doc.asp?symbol=A/65/PV.16.

Gilbert, Martin. 2012. *The Routledge Atlas of the Arab-Israeli Conflict*. London: Routledge.

Gilligan, Carol. 1993. *In a Different Voice: Psychological Theory and Women's Development*. Reissue ed. Cambridge, MA: Harvard University Press.

Glaser, Barney, and Anselm Strauss. 1999. *The Discovery of Grounded Theory: Strategies for Qualitative Research*. Chicago: Aldine Transaction.

Golan, Galia. 1990. *Soviet Policies in the Middle East: From World War Two to Gorbachev*. New York: Cambridge University Press.

———. 2012. "Peace Plans: 1993–2012." In *Routledge Handbook on the Israeli-Palestinian Conflict*, edited by Joel Peters and David Newman, 92–106. London: Routledge.

Gordon, Neve. 2008. *Israel's Occupation*. Berkeley: University of California Press.

Gordon, Neve, and Sharon Pardo. 2015a. "Normative Power Europe Meets the Israeli-Palestinian Conflict." *Asia Europe Journal* 13 (3): 265–74.

———. 2015b. "Normative Power Europe and the Power of the Local." *Journal of Common Market Studies* 53 (2): 416–27. https://doi.org/10.1111/jcms.12162.

Gözen, Ramazan. 2004. "Turkish Foreign Policy in Turbulence of the Post-Cold War Era: Impact of External and Domestic Constraints." In *Turkish Foreign Policy in Post-Cold War Era*, edited by Idris Bal, 27–52. Boca Raton, FL: Brown Walker Press.

Grandi, Filippo. 2016. "Challenged but Steadfast: Nine Years with Palestinian Refugees and the UN Relieve and Works Agency." In *Land of Blue Helmets:*

The United Nations and the Arab World, edited by Karim Makdisi and Vijay Prashad, 318–34. Berkeley: University of California Press.

Graubart, Jonathan, and Arturo Jimenez-Bacardi. 2016. "David in Goliath's Citadel: Mobilizing the Security Council's Normative Power for Palestine." *European Journal of International Relations* 22 (1): 24–48. https://doi.org/10.1177/1354066115571762.

Gromyko, Andrei. 1947. "Hundred and Twenty-Fifth Plenary Meeting Held in the United Nations General Assembly, 124. Continuation of the Discussion on the Palestinian Question." https://unispal.un.org/DPA/DPR/unispal.nsf/0/8E9EACABC8A7E3D185256CF0005BA586.

———. 1971. "Statement by Andrei Andreevich Gromyko at the United Nations General Assembly Opening Session." http://www.un.org/ga/search/view_doc.asp?symbol=A/PV.1942.

———. 1979. "Statement by Andrei Andreevich Gromyko at the United Nations General Assembly Opening Session." http://www.un.org/ga/search/view_doc.asp?symbol=A/34/PV.7.

Gül, Abdullah. 2003. "Statement by Abdullah Gül at the United Nations General Assembly Opening Session." http://www.un.org/ga/search/view_doc.asp?symbol=A/58/PV.14.

Haaretz. 2011. "Iran Supreme Leader: Palestinian UN Statehood Bid Doomed to Fail." *Haaretz*, October 1. http://www.haaretz.com/israel-news/iran-supreme-leader-palestinian-un-statehood-bid-doomed-to-fail-1.387496.

Hansen, Lene. 2006. *Security as Practice: Discourse Analysis and the Bosnian War*. New York: Taylor and Francis.

Harnisch, Sebastian. 2011. "Role Theory: Operationalization of Key Concepts." In *Role Theory in International Relations*, edited by Cornelia Frank, Hanns W. Maull, and Sebastian Harnisch, 7–15. New York: Taylor and Francis.

Harpaz, Guy. 2007. "Normative Power Europe and the Problem of a Legitimacy Deficit: An Israeli Perspective." *European Foreign Affairs Review* 12 (1): 89–109.

Harpaz, Guy, and Asaf Shamis. 2010. "Normative Power Europe and the State of Israel: An Illegitimate EUtopia?" *Journal of Common Market Studies* 48 (3): 579–616. https://doi.org/10.1111/j.1468-5965.2010.02065.x.

Heikal, Mohamed. 1978. *The Sphinx and the Commissar: The Rise and Fall of Soviet Influence in the Middle East*. 1st US ed. New York: Harper and Row.

———. 1997. *Secret Channels: The Inside Story of Arab-Israeli Peace Negotiations*. London: HarperCollins.

Heller, Joseph. 2016. *The United States, the Soviet Union and the Arab-Israeli Conflict, 1948–67: Superpower Rivalry*. Oxford: Oxford University Press.

Hinnebusch, Raymond. 2003. *The International Politics of the Middle East*. Manchester: Manchester University Press.

Hollis, Rosemary. 2012. "Europe." In *Routledge Handbook on the Israeli-Palestinian Conflict*, edited by Joel Peters and David Newman, 336–45. London: Routledge.

Holsti, K. J. 1970. "National Role Conceptions in the Study of Foreign Policy." *International Studies Quarterly* 14 (3): 233–309. https://doi.org/10.2307/3013584.

Hooghe, Liesbet, and Gary Marks. 2001. *Multi-Level Governance and European Integration*. Governance in Europe. Lanham, MD: Rowman and Littlefield.

Huber, Daniela. 2017. "Israeli Regional Perspectives and the Mediterranean." In *Routledge Handbook of Mediterranean Politics*, edited by Richard Gillespie and Frédéric Volpi. Abingdon, Oxon: Routledge.

———. 2018. "The EU and 50 Years of Occupation: Resistant to or Complicit with Normalization?" *Middle East Critique* 27 (4): 351–64. https://doi.org/10.1080/19436149.2018.1516020.

———. 2021. "The Islamic Republic of Iran and Its Politics of Norm Competition and Engagement." In *Framing Power Europe? EU External Action on Democracy and Human Rights in a Competitive World*, edited by Raffaele Marchetti and Nicolas Levrat. Abingdon, Oxon: Routledge.

Huber, Daniela, and Lorenzo Kamel. 2016. *Arab Spring and Peripheries: A Decentring Research Agenda*. London: Routledge.

International Court of Justice. 2004. "Legal Consequences of the Construction of a Wall in the Occupied Palestinian Territory." http://www.icj-cij.org/docket/files/131/1677.pdf.

International Federation for Human Rights (FIDH). 2012. "Trading Away Peace: How Europe Helps Sustain Illegal Israeli Settlements." https://www.fidh.org/IMG/pdf/trading_away_peace_-_embargoed_copy_of_designed_report.pdf.

Ish-Shalom, Piki. 2011. "Defining by Naming: Israeli Civic Warring over the Second Lebanon War." *European Journal of International Relations* 17 (3): 475–93. https://doi.org/10.1177/1354066110366057.

Jaspal, Rusi, and Adrian Coyle. 2014. "Threat, Victimhood, and Peace: Debating the 2011 Palestinian UN State Membership Bid." *Digest of Middle East Studies* 23 (1): 190–214. https://doi.org/10.1111/dome.12041.

Jepperson, Ronald, Alexander Wendt, and Peter Katzenstein. 1996. "Norms, Identity, and Culture in National Security." In *The Culture of National Security: Norms and Identity in World Politics*, edited by Peter J Katzenstein, 33–75. New Directions in World Politics. New York: Columbia University Press.

Jones, Bruce. 2010. "The Security Council and the Arab-Israeli Wars: 'Responsibility without Power.'" In *The United Nations Security Council and War: The Evolution of Thought and Practice since 1945*, edited by Vaughan Lowe, Adam Roberts, Jennifer Welsh, and Dominik Zaum, 298–323. Oxford: Oxford University Press.

Jung, Dietrich, ed. 2004. *The Middle East and Palestine: Global Politics and Regional Conflict*. New York: Palgrave Macmillan.

Jupille, Joseph and James Caporaso. 1998. "States, Agency, and Rules: The EU in Global Environmental Politics." In *The European Union in the World Community*, edited by Carolyn Rhodes, 213–31. Boulder, CO: Lynne Rienner.

Kamel, Lorenzo. 2015. *Imperial Perceptions of Palestine: Orientalism and Colonialism in the Holy Land*. London: I.B. Tauris.

Kerr, Malcolm H. 1971. *The Arab Cold War: Gamal 'Abd al-Nasir and His Rivals, 1958–1970*. 3rd ed. London: Oxford University Press.

Keukeleire, Stephan, and Sharon Lococq. 2016. "Operationalizing the Decentring Agenda: Constructing an Outside-in Approach towards EU Foreign Policy Analysis." European Consortium for Political Research Conference Paper. https://ecpr.eu/Events/PaperDetails.aspx?PaperID=27057&EventID=105.

Keukeleire, Stephan, and Jennifer MacNaughtan. 2008. *The Foreign Policy of the European Union*. New York: Palgrave Macmillan.

Khalatbary, Abbas Ali. 1971. "Statement by Mr. Abbas Ali Khalatbary at the United Nations General Assembly Plenary Meeting." http://www.un.org/ga/search/view_doc.asp?symbol=A/PV.1940.

———. 1975. "Statement by Abbas Ali Khalatbary at the United Nations General Assembly Plenary Meeting." http://www.un.org/ga/search/view_doc.asp?symbol=A/PV.2361.

Khalidi, Raja. 2016. "The United Nations, Palestine, Liberation, and Development." In *Land of Blue Helmets: The United Nations and the Arab World*, edited by Karim Makdisi and Vijay Prashad, 409–29. Berkeley: University of California Press.

Khalidi, Rashid. 2007. *The Iron Cage: The Story of the Palestinian Struggle for Statehood*. Repr. ed. Boston: Beacon Press.

———. 2013. *Brokers of Deceit: How the U.S. Has Undermined Peace in the Middle East*. Boston: Beacon Press.

Kharrazi, Kamal. 1997. "Statement by Iranian Foreign Minister Kamal Kharrazi at the United Nations General Assembly Plenary Debate." http://www.un.org/ga/search/view_doc.asp?symbol=A/52/PV.6.

———. 2000. "Statement by Iranian Foreign Minister Kamal Kharrazi at the United Nations General Assembly Plenary Debate." http://www.un.org/ga/search/view_doc.asp?symbol=A/55/PV.16.

Khatami, Seyed Mohammad. 1998. "Statement by Iranian President Seyed Mohammad Khatami at the United Nations General Assembly Plenary Meeting." http://www.un.org/ga/search/view_doc.asp?symbol=A/53/PV.8.

Kinkel, Klaus. 1994. "Statement by Mr Kinkel at the United Nations General Assembly Opening Session." http://www.un.org/ga/search/view_doc.asp?symbol=A/49/PV.6.

Kissinger, Henry. 1973. "Statement by Henry Kissinger at the United Nations General Assembly Opening Session." http://www.un.org/ga/search/view_doc.asp?symbol=A/PV.2124.

———. 1974. "Statement by Henry Kissinger at the United Nations General Assembly Opening Session." http://www.un.org/ga/search/view_doc.asp?symbol=A/PV.2238.

———. 1976. "Statement by Henry Kissinger at the United Nations General Assembly Opening Session." http://www.un.org/ga/search/view_doc.asp?symbol=A/31/PV.11.

Kiswanson, Nada. 2018. "What Can Palestinians Expect from the ICC?" *Al Jazeera*, May 28. https://www.aljazeera.com/indepth/opinion/palestine-icc-israel-war-crimes-180527113534760.html.

Konecny, Martin. 2018. "EU Must Stand up to Trump's Middle East 'Peace Plan.'" *EUobserver*, October 30. https://euobserver.com/opinion/143251.

Kostiner, Joseph. 2009. "Saudi Arabia and the Arab–Israeli Peace Process: The Fluctuation of Regional Coordination." *British Journal of Middle Eastern Studies* 36 (3): 417–29. https://doi.org/10.1080/13530190903338946.

Kreutz, Andrej. 2007. *Russia in the Middle East: Friend or Foe?* Westport, CT: Praeger Security International.

Kurtzer, Daniel, and Scott Lasensky. 2008. *Negotiating Arab-Israeli Peace: American Leadership in the Middle East*. Washington, DC: United States Institute for Peace Press.

Labelle, Maurice, Jr. 2011. "'The Only Thorn': Early Saudi-American Relations and the Question of Palestine, 1945–1949." *Diplomatic History* 35 (2): 257–81. https://doi.org/10.1111/j.1467-7709.2010.00949.x.

Laqueur, Walter, and Barry Rubin. 2008. *The Israel-Arab Reader: A Documentary History of the Middle East Conflict: Seventh Revised and Updated Edition*. New York: Penguin.

Lavrov, Sergei. 2007. "Statement by Mr. Lavrov at the United Nations General Assembly Opening Session." http://www.un.org/ga/search/view_doc.asp?symbol=A/62/PV.11.

———. 2017. "Statement by H.E. Mr. Sergey V. LAVROV, Minister of Foreign Affairs of the Russian Federation, at the 72nd Session of the UN General Assembly." https://gadebate.un.org/sites/default/files/gastatements/72/ru_en.pdf.

———. 2018. "Address by Mr. Sergey Lavrov, Minister for Foreign Affairs of the Russian Federation to the UN General Assembly." https://undocs.org/en/A/73/PV.12.

Legro, Jeffrey W. 1997. "Which Norms Matter? Revisiting the 'Failure' of Internationalism." *International Organization* 51 (1): 31–63. https://doi.org/10.1162/002081897550294.

LeVine, Mark. 2009. *Impossible Peace: Israel/Palestine since 1989*. London: Zed Books.

Lewis, Bernard. 1999. *Semites and Anti-Semites: An Inquiry into Conflict and Prejudice*. New York: W. W. Norton.

Lynch, Marc. 1999. *State Interests and Public Spheres: The International Politics of Jordan's Identity*. New York: Columbia University Press.

———. 2006. *Voices of the New Arab Public: Iraq, al-Jazeera, and Middle East Politics Today*. New York: Columbia University Press.

Lynk, S. Michael. 2017. "Situation of Human Rights in the Palestinian Territories Occupied since 1967. Advance Unedited Version." Office of the High Commissioner for Human Rights. www.ohchr.org/Documents/Countries/PS/A_72_43106.docx

MadaMasr. 2016. "Egypt Votes for Rival UNSC Resolutions on Syria from Russia and France." October 9. https://www.madamasr.com/en/2016/10/09/news/u/egypt-votes-for-rival-unsc-resolutions-on-syria-from-russia-and-france/.

Madani, Nizar Obaid. 1998. "Statement by Mr. Madani at the United Nations General Assembly Plenary Meeting." http://www.un.org/ga/search/view_doc.asp?symbol=A/53/PV.20.

Makdisi, Karim. 2018. "Palestine and the Arab–Israeli Conflict: 100 Years of Regional Relevance and International Failure." MENARA Working Paper No. 27. http://www.menaraproject.eu/portfolio-items/palestine-and-the-arab-israeli-conflict-100-years-of-regional-relevance-and-international-failure/.

———. 2019. "Contested Multilateralism: The United Nations and the Middle East." MENARA Working Paper no. 31. http://www.menaraproject.eu/portfolio-items/contested-multilateralism-the-united-nations-and-the-middle-east/.

Makdisi, Karim, and Vijay Prashad. 2016. *Land of Blue Helmets. The United Nations and the Arab World*. Berkeley: University of California Press.

Makdisi, Ussama. 2010. *Faith Misplaced: The Broken Promise of U.S.-Arab Relations: 1820–2001*. New York: PublicAffairs.

Maltz, Judy. 2015. "A Special Haaretz Interactive Project Marking 25 Years since the Soviet Union Let the Jewish People Go." *Haaretz*. http://www.haaretz.com/st/c/prod/eng/25yrs_russ_img/.

Manners, Ian. 2018. "Theorizing Normative Power in European Union-Israeli/Palestinian Relations: Focus of This Special Issue." *Middle East Critique* 27 (4): 321–34. https://doi.org/10.1080/19436149.2018.1510578.

Manners, Ian, and Richard Whitman. 2003. "The 'Difference Engine': Constructing and Representing the International Identity of the European Union." *Journal of European Public Policy* 10 (3): 380–404.

Martins, Bruno Oliveira. 2015. " 'A Sense of Urgency': The EU, EU Member States and the Recognition of the Palestinian State." *Mediterranean Politics* 20 (2): 281–87. https://doi.org/10.1080/13629395.2015.1046268.

Mattern, Janice Bially. 2004. *Ordering International Politics: Identity, Crisis and Representational Force*. New York: Routledge.

Matthews, Elizabeth. 2011. *The Israel-Palestine Conflict: Parallel Discourses*. Abingdon, Oxon: Routledge.

McCarthy, Justin. 1990. *The Population of Palestine: Population History and Statistics of the Late Ottoman Period and the Mandate*. New York: Columbia Univ Press.

McKinlay, Andy, Chris McVittie, and Rahul Sambaraju. 2012. " 'This Is Ordinary Behaviour': Categorization and Culpability in Hamas Leaders' Accounts of the Palestinian/Israeli Conflict." *British Journal of Social Psychology* 51 (4): 534–50. https://doi.org/10.1111/j.2044-8309.2011.02021.x.

Mead, George. 1967. *Mind, Self, and Society: From The Standpoint of a Social Behaviorist: 1*. Edited by Charles Morris. Rev. ed. Chicago: University of Chicago Press.

Mearsheimer, John J., and Stephen M. Walt. 2007. *The Israel Lobby and U.S. Foreign Policy*. New York: Farrar, Straus and Giroux.

Medvedev, Dmitry. 2009. "Statement by President Dmitry Medvedev at the United Nations General Assembly Opening Session." http://www.un.org/ga/search/view_doc.asp?symbol=A/64/PV.4.

Middle East Monitor. 2019. "Victory as German Court Rules Anti-BDS Motion Breaches Principle of Equality." *Middle East Monitor*, September 18. https://www.middleeastmonitor.com/20190918-victory-as-german-court-rules-anti-bds-motion-breaches-principle-of-equality/.

Middle East Quartet. 2002. "A Performance-Based Roadmap to a Permanent Two-State Solution to the Israeli-Palestinian Conflict." http://www.un.org/news/dh/mideast/roadmap122002.pdf.

———. 2016. "Report of the Middle East Quartet." http://www.un.org/News/dh/infocus/middle_east/Report-of-the-Middle-East-Quartet.pdf.

Miller, Jean Baker. 1987. *Toward a New Psychology of Women*. 2nd ed. Boston: Beacon Press.

Milton-Edwards, Beverley. 2011. *Contemporary Politics in the Middle East*. 3rd ed. Cambridge: Polity.

Ministry of Foreign Affairs of the Russian Federation. 2017. "Press Release on Russia-Egypt Draft UN Security Council Press Statement on Intra-Palestinian Reconciliation Blocked by US." http://www.mid.ru/foreign_policy/news/-/asset_publisher/cKNonkJE02Bw/content/id/2958590.

Mitchell, Timothy. 2013. "Die Welt als Ausstellung." In *Jenseits des Eurozentrismus: Postkoloniale Perspektiven in den Geschichts- und Kulturwissenschaften (Beyond Eurocentrism: Postcolonial perspectives in historical and cultural sciences)*, edited by Sebastian Conrad, Shalini Randeria, and Regina Roemhild, 438–65. Frankfurt am Main: Campus Verlag.

Mitrani, Mor. 2013. "(Re-)Telling Societal Beliefs: Changing Narratives in Israel's Political Discourse Regarding Transition to Peace." *International Journal of Conflict Management* 24 (3): 245–64. https://doi.org/10.1108/IJCMA-12-2012-0090.

———. 2017. "The Discursive Construction of the International Community: Evidence from the United Nations General Assembly." KFG Working

Paper. http://www.polsoz.fu-berlin.de/en/v/transformeurope/publications/working_paper/wp/wp78/WP_78_WEB_new.pdf.

Mitzen, Jennifer. 2006. "Ontological Security in World Politics: State Identity and the Security Dilemma." *European Journal of International Relations* 12 (3): 341–70. https://doi.org/10.1177/1354066106067346.

Mohseni, Payam. 2013. "The Islamic Awakening: Iran's Grand Narrative of the Arab Uprisings." *Crown Center Middle East Brief* 71. https://www.brandeis.edu/crown/publications/meb/MEB71.pdf.

More, Anne Le. 2008. *International Assistance to the Palestinians after Oslo: Political Guilt, Wasted Money*. London: Routledge.

Morozov, Viatcheslav, ed. 2013. *Decentring the West: The Idea of Democracy and the Struggle for Hegemony*. Farnham, Surrey: Routledge.

Morsi, Mohamed. 2012. "Speech by Mr. Morsi at the United Nations General Assembly Plenary Session." http://www.un.org/ga/search/view_doc.asp?symbol=A/67/PV.9.

Moshirzadeh, Homeira. 2007. "Discursive Foundations of Iran's Nuclear Policy." *Security Dialogue* 38 (4): 521–43. https://doi.org/10.1177/0967010607084999.

———. 2015. "International Relations in Iran and Its Discursive Dynamics." *Iranian Review of Foreign Affairs* 5 (4): 5–45.

Moussa, Amre. 1992. "Speech of Mr. Moussa at the United Nations General Assembly Plenary Meeting." http://www.un.org/ga/search/view_doc.asp?symbol=A/47/PV.12.

———. 1998. "UN General Assembly Opening General Debate Statement." https://documents-dds-ny.un.org/doc/UNDOC/GEN/N98/858/88/PDF/N9885888.pdf?OpenElement.

Mubarak, Hosni. 1983. "Speech of Mr. Mubarak at the United Nations General Assembly Plenary Meeting." http://www.un.org/ga/search/view_doc.asp?symbol=A/38/PV.10.

Mueller, Patrick. 2013. "Europe's Foreign Policy and the Middle East Peace Process: The Construction of EU Actorness in Conflict Resolution." *Perspectives on European Politics and Society* 14 (1): 20–35. https://doi.org/10.1080/15705854.2012.732397.

Müller, Patrick, and Yazid Zahda. 2018. "Local Perceptions of the EU's Role in Peacebuilding: The Case of Security Sector Reform in Palestine." *Contemporary Security Policy* 39 (1): 119–41. https://doi.org/10.1080/13523260.2017.1399624.

Muravchik, Joshua. 2013. "The UN and Israel: A History of Discrimination." *World Affairs Journal*, December.

Musu, C. 2010. *European Union Policy towards the Arab-Israeli Peace Process: The Quicksands of Politics*. Basingstoke: Palgrave Macmillan.

Nasser, Gamal Abdel. 1955. *Egypt's Liberation; The Philosophy of the Revolution*. Washington DC: Public Affairs Press.

———. 1960. "General Assembly Plenary Debate Speech by Mr. Nasser, President of the United Arab Republic." http://www.un.org/ga/search/view_doc.asp?symbol=A/PV.873.

Nayak, Meghana, and Eric Selbin. 2010. *Decentering International Relations*. London: Zed Books.

Newman, David. 1989. "Civilian and Military Presence as Strategies of Territorial Control: The Arab-Israel Conflict." *Political Geography Quarterly* 8 (3): 215–27. https://doi.org/10.1016/0260-9827(89)90039-6.

———. 1996. "Shared Spaces—Separate Spaces: The Israel-Palestine Peace Process." *GeoJournal* 39 (4): 363–75. https://doi.org/10.1007/BF02428499.

Nicolaïdis, Kalypso A., Berny Sèbe, and Gabrielle Maas. 2015. "Echoes of Empire: The Present of the Past." In *Echoes of Empire: Memory, Identity and the Legacy of Imperialism*, edited by Kalypso A. Nicolaidis, Berny Sèbe, and Gabrielle Maas, 1–18. London: I.B. Tauris.

Nikolov, Krassimir. 2017. "Partnership after Peace? An Optimist's View on the EU's Future Special and Privileged Relations with the State of Israel and Palestine." http://bdi.mfa.government.bg/data/DJ/DJ_19_2017.pdf.

Nonneman, Gerd. 2007. "Determinants and Patterns of Saudi Foreign Policy: 'Omnibalancing' and 'Relative Autonomy' in Multiple Environments." In *Saudi Arabia in the Balance: Political Economy, Society, Foreign Affairs*, edited by Gerd Nonneman and Paul Aarts, 315–351. New York: New York University Press. https://www.academia.edu/4112908/_Determinants_and_patterns_of_Saudi_foreign_policy_omnibalancing_and_relative_autonomy_in_multiple_environments_.

Nuseibeh, Hazem Zaki. 1982. *Palestine and the United Nations*. New York: Quartet Books.

Obama, Barack. 2009. "Remarks by President Obama in Address to the United Nations General Assembly." http://www.un.org/ga/search/view_doc.asp?symbol=A/64/PV.3.

———. 2011. "Remarks by President Obama in Address to the United Nations General Assembly." https://obamawhitehouse.archives.gov/the-press-office/2011/09/21/remarks-president-obama-address-united-nations-general-assembly.

———. 2013. "Remarks by President Obama in Address to the United Nations General Assembly." http://www.un.org/ga/search/view_doc.asp?symbol=A/68/PV.5.

Öberg, Marko Divac. 2005. "The Legal Effects of Resolutions of the UN Security Council and General Assembly in the Jurisprudence of the ICJ." *European Journal of International Law* 16 (5): 879–906. https://doi.org/10.1093/ejil/chi151.

Oliphant, Roland. 2018. "With Israel Embassy Move US Forfeits Authority in the Middle East, Says Turkey's Recep Tayyip Erdogan." *Telegraph*, May 14. https://www.telegraph.co.uk/news/2018/05/14/israel-embassy-move-us-forfeits-authority-middle-east-says-turkeys/.

Onar, Nora Fisher, and Kalypso Nicolaïdis. 2013. "The Decentring Agenda: Europe as a Post-Colonial Power." *Cooperation and Conflict* 48 (2): 283–303. https://doi.org/10.1177/0010836713485384.

Owen, Roger. 2004. *State, Power and Politics in the Making of the Modern Middle East*. 3rd ed. London: Routledge.

Özal, Turgut. 1985. "Statement by Mr. Turgut Ozal, Prime Minister of the Republic of Turkey, at the United Nations General Assembly Plenary Meeting." http://www.un.org/ga/search/view_doc.asp?symbol=A/40/PV.45.

Pace, Michelle. 2007. "The Construction of EU Normative Power." *Journal of Common Market Studies* 45 (5): 1041–64. https://doi.org/10.1111/j.1468-5965.2007.00759.x.

———. 2008. "The EU as a 'Force for Good' in Border Conflict Cases?" In *The European Union and Border Conflicts: The Power of Integration and Association*, edited by Thomas Diez, Mathias Albert, and Stephan Stetter, 173–202. Cambridge: Cambridge University Press.

———. 2009. "Paradoxes and Contradictions in EU Democracy Promotion in the Mediterranean: The Limits of EU Normative Power." *Democratization* 16 (1): 39–58. https://doi.org/10.1080/13510340802575809.

Pace, Michelle, and Ali Bilgic. 2017. "Trauma, Emotions, and Memory in World Politics: The Case of the European Union's Foreign Policy in the Middle East Conflict." *Political Psychology*, December 11. https://doi.org/10.1111/pops.12459.

Pace, Michelle, and Roberto Roccu.2020. "Imperial Pasts in the EU's Approach to the Mediterranean" *Interventions* 22 (6): 671–685. https://doi.org/10.1080/1369801X.2020.1749702.

Pace, Michelle, and Somdeep Sen. 2019. *The Palestinian Authority in the West Bank: The Theatrics of Woeful Statecraft*. London: Routledge.

Pallister-Wilkins, Polly. 2015. "Bridging the Divide: Middle Eastern Walls and Fences and the Spatial Governance of Problem Populations." *Geopolitics* 20 (2): 438–59. https://doi.org/10.1080/14650045.2015.1005287.

Pappé, Ilan, and Jamil Hilal. 2010. *Across the Wall: Narratives of Israeli-Palestinian History*. London: I.B. Tauris.

Pardo, Sharon, and Neve Gordon. 2018. "Euroscepticism as an Instrument of Foreign Policy." *Middle East Critique* 27 (4): 399–412. https://doi.org/10.1080/19436149.2018.1516338.

Parsi, Trita. 2019. "America's Effort to Isolate Iran Will Backfire." *National Interest*, February 12. https://nationalinterest.org/feature/americas-effort-isolate-iran-will-backfire-44342.

Parsons, Nigel, and Mark B. Salter. 2008. "Israeli Biopolitics: Closure, Territorialisation and Governmentality in the Occupied Palestinian Territories." *Geopolitics* 13 (4): 701–23. https://doi.org/10.1080/14650040802275511.

Permanent Mission of France to the UN in New York. 2019. "Joint Statement by Belgium, France, Germany, Poland and the UK." France ONU. March

26. https://onu.delegfrance.org/Our-position-on-the-status-of-the-Golan-Heights-is-well-known.

Persson, Anders. 2014. *The EU and the Israeli–Palestinian Conflict 1971–2013: In Pursuit of a Just Peace*. Lanham, MD: Lexington Books.

———. 2017. "Shaping Discourse and Setting Examples: Normative Power Europe Can Work in the Israeli–Palestinian Conflict." *Journal of Common Market Studies*, August 7. n/a-n/a. https://doi.org/10.1111/jcms.12578.

———. 2018. "Introduction: The Occupation at 50: EU-Israel/Palestine Relations since 1967." *Middle East Critique* 27 (4): 317–20. https://doi.org/10.1080/19436149.2018.1492222.

Peters, Joel. 1998. "The Arab-Israeli Multilateral Peace Talks and the Barcelona Process: Competition or Convergence?" *International Spectator* 33 (4): 63–76. https://doi.org/10.1080/03932729808456834.

———. 2010. "Europe and the Israel–Palestinian Peace Process: The Urgency of Now." *European Security* 19 (3): 511–29. https://doi.org/10.1080/09662839.2010.534135.

Pew Research Center. 2015. "Russia, Putin Held in Low Regard around the World." http://www.pewglobal.org/2015/08/05/russia-putin-held-in-low-regard-around-the-world/.

Pinfari, Marco. 2009. *Nothing but Failure? The Arab League and the Gulf Cooperation Council as Mediators in Middle Eastern Conflicts*. Crisis States Working Papers Series No. 2. http://citeseerx.ist.psu.edu/viewdoc/download?doi=10.1.1.630.5422&rep=rep1&type=pdf.

Pogodda, Sandra, Oliver Richmond, Nathalie Tocci, Roger Mac Ginty, and Birte Vogel. 2014. "Assessing the Impact of EU Governmentality in Post-Conflict Countries: Pacification or Reconciliation?" *European Security* 23 (3): 227–49. https://doi.org/10.1080/09662839.2013.875533.

Primakov, Yevgeny. 1996. "Statement by Evgenii Primakov at the United Nations General Assembly Opening Session." http://www.un.org/ga/search/view_doc.asp?symbol=A/51/PV.6.

———. 1997. "Russian Proposal for a Code of Peace and Security in the Middle East." http://ecf.org.il/media_items/365.

Quandt, William B. 2005. *Peace Process: American Diplomacy and the Arab-Israeli Conflict since 1967*. 3rd ed. Washington, DC: Brookings Institution Press; Berkeley: University of California Press.

Quigley, John. 2005. *The Case for Palestine: An International Law Perspective*. Rev. ed. Durham, NC: Duke University Press.

———. 2013. *The Six-Day War and Israeli Self-Defense: Questioning the Legal Basis for Preventive War*. Cambridge: Cambridge University Press.

Qumsiyeh, Mazin B. 2010. *Popular Resistance in Palestine: A History of Hope and Empowerment*. London: Pluto Press.

Rabbani, Mouin. 2017. "Blog." *MEDRESET* (blog). 2017. http://www.medreset.org/.

Rabinovich, Itamar. 1991. *The Road Not Taken: Early Arab-Israeli Negotiations*. New York: Oxford University Press.

———. 2012. *The Lingering Conflict: Israel, The Arabs, and the Middle East 1948–2012*. Washington, DC: Brookings Institution Press.

Radosh, Allis, and Ronald Radosh. 2009. *A Safe Haven: Harry S. Truman and the Founding of Israel*. New York: HarperCollins.

Ramazani, Rouhollah K. 2013. *Independence without Freedom: Iran's Foreign Policy*. Charlottesville: University of Virginia Press.

Rawshandil, Jalīl, and Nathan Chapman Lean. 2011. *Iran, Israel, and the United States: Regime Security vs. Political Legitimacy*. Santa Barbara, CA: ABC-CLIO.

Reagan, Ronald. 1982. "Reagan Plan." https://ecf.org.il/issues/issue/158.

———. 1983. "Statement by US President Ronald Reagan at the United Nations General Assembly Opening Session." http://www.un.org/ga/search/view_doc.asp?symbol=A/38/PV.5.

———. 1985. "Statement by US President Ronald Reagan at the United Nations General Assembly Meeting on the Occasion of the Commemoration of the Fortieth Anniversary of the United Nations." http://www.un.org/ga/search/view_doc.asp?symbol=A/40/PV.48.

Reuters. 2013. "Source: Saudi Arabia Scrapped UN Speech in Protest over Syria, Israel–Diplomacy & Politics–Jerusalem Post." October 3. https://www.jpost.com/Diplomacy-and-Politics/Source-Saudi-Arabia-scrapped-UN-speech-in-protest-over-Syria-Israel-327765.

Riad, Mahmoud. 1967. "Speech by Mr. Riad at the General Assembly Plenary Meeting."

Robinson, Fiona. 2006. "Methods of Feminist Normative Theory: A Political Ethic of Care for International Relations." In *Feminist Methodologies for International Relations*, edited by Brooke Ackerly, Maria Stern, and Jacqui True, 221–40. Cambridge: Cambridge University Press. http://dx.doi.org/10.1017/CBO9780511617690.014.

Rouhani, Hassan. 2013. "Statement by Iranian President Hassan Rouhani at the United Nations General Assembly Plenary Meeting." http://www.un.org/ga/search/view_doc.asp?symbol=A/68/PV.6.

———. 2016. "Address by Mr. Hassan Rouhani, President of the Islamic Republic of Iran to UNGA." https://undocs.org/en/A/71/PV.14.

———. 2017. "Address by Mr. Hassan Rouhani, President of the Islamic Republic of Iran." http://www.un.org/ga/search/view_doc.asp?symbol=A/72/PV.7.

Rowley, Christina, and Jutta Weldes. 2012. "Identities and US Foreign Policy." In *U.S. Foreign Policy*, edited by Michael Cox and Doug Stokes, 2nd ed., 178–92. New York: Oxford University Press.

Roy, Sara. 1995. *The Gaza Strip: The Political Economy of De-Development*. Washington, DC: Institute for Palestine Studies.

Ruggie, John Gerard. 1993. "Territoriality and Beyond: Problematizing Modernity in International Relations." *International Organization* 47 (1): 139–74.

Saad-Ghorayeb, Amal. 2011. "Understanding Hizbullah's Support for the Asad Regime." Conflicts Forum. www.conflictsforum.org/wp-content/uploads/2012/03/Monograph-HizbullahSupportAsad1.pdf.

Sadat, Anwar el. 1975. "Address by Mr. Mohamed Anwar El-Sadat, President of the Arab Republic of Egypt." http://www.un.org/ga/search/view_doc.asp?symbol=A/PV.2388.

Said, Edward W. 1988. *Orientalism*. New York: Vintage Books.

Sakkaf, Omar. 1972. "Speech by Mr. Sakkaf at the General Assembly Plenary Meeting." http://www.un.org/ga/search/view_doc.asp?symbol=A/PV.2057.

———. 1974. "Speech by Mr. Sakkaf." http://www.un.org/ga/search/view_doc.asp?symbol=A/PV.2253.

Salem, Walid. 2005. "The Anti-Normalization Discourse in the Context of Israeli-Palestinian Peace-Building." *Palestine–Israel Journal of Politics, Economics, and Culture; East Jerusalem* 12 (1): 100–109.

Salloum, Raniah, and Christoph Schult. 2019. "Resolution Zu BDS-Boykottbewegung: Uno Rügt Antisemitismus-Beschluss des Bundestags." *Spiegel Online*, October 25, sec. Politik. https://www.spiegel.de/politik/deutschland/vereinte-nationen-uno-ruegt-antisemitismus-beschluss-des-bundestags-a-1293375.html.

Salmon, Jean. 1989. "Declaration of the State of Palestine." *Palestine Yearbook of International Law Online* 5 (1): 48–82. https://doi.org/10.1163/221161489X00033.

Sarsar, Saliba. 2004. "The Question of Palestine and United States Behavior at the United Nations." *International Journal of Politics, Culture, and Society* 17 (3): 457–70.

Sayigh, Yezid. 2007. "Inducing a Failed State in Palestine." *Survival* 49 (3): 7–39. https://doi.org/10.1080/00396330701564786.

Sbragia, Alberta. 1992. "Thinking about the European Future: The Uses of Comparison." In *Euro-Politics: Institutions and Policymaking in the New European Community*, edited by Alberta Sbragia, 257–91. Washington, DC: Brookings Institution.

Scham, Paul, Walid Salem, and Benjamin Pogrund. 2005. *Shared Histories: A Palestinian-Israeli Dialogue*. Walnut Creek, CA: Left Coast Press.

Schulze, Kirsten E. 2013. *The Arab-Israeli Conflict*. London: Routledge.

Sela, Avraham. 1997. *The Decline of the Arab-Israeli Conflict: Middle East Politics and the Quest for Regional Order*. Albany: State University of New York Press.

Sen, Somdeep. 2018. "Writing the 'Refugee Crisis': Proposals for Activist Research." In *Syrian Refugee Children in the Middle East and Europe: Integrating the*

Young and Exiled, edited by Michelle Pace and Somdeep Sen, 101–12. Milton Park, Abingdon, Oxon: Routledge.

Serralvo, Jose. 2016. "Government Recognition and International Humanitarian Law Applicability in Post-Gaddafi Libya." In *Yearbook of International Humanitarian Law Volume 18, 2015*, edited by Terry D. Gill, 3–41. The Hague: T.M.C. Asser Press. https://doi.org/10.1007/978-94-6265-141-8_1.

Shlaim, Avi. 2014. *The Iron Wall: Israel and the Arab World*. London: Penguin.

Shukairy, Ahmad. 1958. "Speech by Mr. Shukairy at the General Assembly Plenary Debate." http://www.un.org/ga/search/view_doc.asp?symbol=A/PV.766.

Shultz, George. 1985. "Statement by Mr. Shultz at the United Nations General Assembly Opening Session." http://www.un.org/ga/search/view_doc.asp?symbol=A/40/PV.4.

Simonet, Henri. 1977. "Statement by Mr. Henri Simonet Minister for Foreign Affairs of Belgium President of the Council of the European Community and of European Political Co-Operation." http://aei.pitt.edu/5579/1/5579.pdf.

Smith, Karen. 2003. *European Union Foreign Policy in a Changing World*. Cambridge: Polity.

Spiegel, Steven. 1985. *The Other Arab-Israeli Conflict*. Chicago: University of Chicago Press.

———. 2012. "The United States, 1948–1993." In *Routledge Handbook on the Israeli-Palestinian Conflict*, edited by Joel Peters and David Newman, 295–307. London: Routledge.

Stein, Ewan. 2012. *Representing Israel in Modern Egypt: Ideas, Intellectuals and Foreign Policy from Nasser to Mubarak*. London: I.B.Tauris.

Stoel, Max van der. 1976. "Statement by Mr. van Der Stoel." http://www.un.org/ga/search/view_doc.asp?symbol=A/31/PV.7.

Suchkov, Maxim A. 2018. "Moscow Updates Playbook on Making Israel, Iran Happy." *Al-Monitor*, June 1. https://www.al-monitor.com/pulse/originals/2018/06/russia-playbook-making-israel-iran-happy.html.

Tartir, Alaa. 2017. "The Palestinian Authority Security Forces: Whose Security?" *Al-Shabaka* (blog). https://al-shabaka.org/briefs/palestinian-authority-security-forces-whose-security/.

———. 2018. "The Limits of Securitized Peace: The EU's Sponsorship of Palestinian Authoritarianism." *Middle East Critique* 27 (4): 365–81. https://doi.org/10.1080/19436149.2018.1516337.

Tartir, Alaa, and Timothy Seidel, eds. 2018. *Palestine and Rule of Power: Local Dissent vs. International Governance*. New York: Palgrave Macmillan.

Tawake, Sandra. 2000. "Transforming the Insider-Outsider Perspective: Postcolonial Fiction from the Pacific." *Contemporary Pacific* 12 (1): 155–75.

Terzi, Özlem. 2010. *The Influence of the European Union on Turkish Foreign Policy*. Farnham: Routledge.

Tessler, Mark. 1990. "The Intifada and Political Discourse in Israel." *Journal of Palestine Studies* 19 (2): 43–61. https://doi.org/10.2307/2537412.

Teti, Andrea. 2004. "A Role in Search of a Hero: Construction and the Evolution of Egyptian Foreign Policy, 1952–67." *Journal of Mediterranean Studies* 14 (1–2): 77–105.

Tickner, Arlene B., and David L. Blaney, eds. 2012. *Thinking International Relations Differently*. New York: Routledge.

Tilley, Virginia, ed. 2012. *Beyond Occupation: Apartheid, Colonialism and International Law in the Occupied Palestinian Territories*. London: Pluto Press.

Tocci, Nathalie. 2009. "Firm in Rhetoric, Compromising in Reality: The EU in the Israeli–Palestinian Conflict." *Ethnopolitics* 8 (3–4): 387–401. https://doi.org/10.1080/17449050903086989.

———. 2013. "The Middle East Quartet and (In)Effective Multilateralism." *Middle East Journal* 67 (1): 29–44.

Tonutti, Alessandro. 2013. "Feasting on the Occupation: Illegality of Settlement Produce and the Responsibility of EU Member States under International Law." Al Haq. http://www.alhaq.org/publications/publications-index/item/feasting-on-the-occupation-illegality-of-settlement-produce-and-the-responsibility-of-eu-members-states-under-international-law.

Trump, Donald. 2017. "Remarks by President Trump to the 72nd Session of the United Nations General Assembly." The White House. https://www.whitehouse.gov/briefings-statements/remarks-president-trump-72nd-session-united-nations-general-assembly/.

———. 2018. "Remarks by President Trump to the 73rd Session of the United Nations General Assembly." The White House. https://www.whitehouse.gov/briefings-statements/remarks-president-trump-73rd-session-united-nations-general-assembly-new-york-ny/.

Tür, Özlem. 2012. "Turkey and Israel in the 2000s—From Cooperation to Conflict." *Israel Studies* 17 (3): 45–66. https://doi.org/10.2979/israelstudies.17.3.45.

Turner, Mandy. 2012. "Completing the Circle: Peacebuilding as Colonial Practice in the Occupied Palestinian Territory." *International Peacekeeping* 19 (4): 492–507. https://doi.org/10.1080/13533312.2012.709774.

———. 2016. "Peacebuilding in Palestine: Western Strategies in the Context of Colonialization." In *Land of Blue Helmets: The United Nations and the Arab World*, edited by Karim Makdisi and Vijay Prashad, 430–47. Berkeley: University of California Press.

Tusk, Donald. 2016. "Address by President Donald Tusk at the 71st United Nations General Assembly." https://www.consilium.europa.eu/en/press/press-releases/2016/09/21/tusk-speech-unga/.

———. 2017. "Address by President Donald Tusk at the 72nd United Nations General Assembly." http://www.consilium.europa.eu/en/press/press-releases/2017/09/20/tusk-speech-un-general-assembly/.

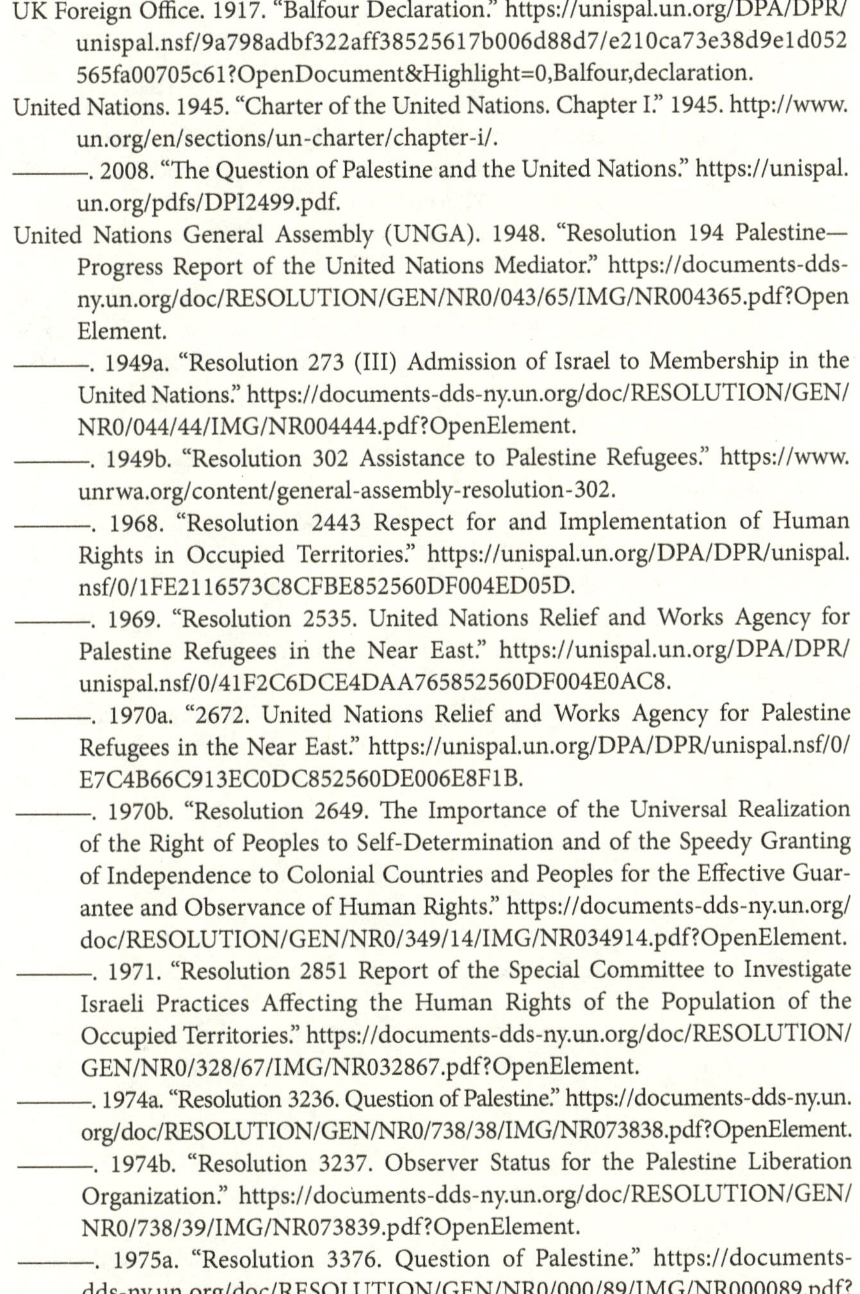

UK Foreign Office. 1917. "Balfour Declaration." https://unispal.un.org/DPA/DPR/unispal.nsf/9a798adbf322aff38525617b006d88d7/e210ca73e38d9e1d052565fa00705c61?OpenDocument&Highlight=0,Balfour,declaration.

United Nations. 1945. "Charter of the United Nations. Chapter I." 1945. http://www.un.org/en/sections/un-charter/chapter-i/.

———. 2008. "The Question of Palestine and the United Nations." https://unispal.un.org/pdfs/DPI2499.pdf.

United Nations General Assembly (UNGA). 1948. "Resolution 194 Palestine—Progress Report of the United Nations Mediator." https://documents-dds-ny.un.org/doc/RESOLUTION/GEN/NR0/043/65/IMG/NR004365.pdf?OpenElement.

———. 1949a. "Resolution 273 (III) Admission of Israel to Membership in the United Nations." https://documents-dds-ny.un.org/doc/RESOLUTION/GEN/NR0/044/44/IMG/NR004444.pdf?OpenElement.

———. 1949b. "Resolution 302 Assistance to Palestine Refugees." https://www.unrwa.org/content/general-assembly-resolution-302.

———. 1968. "Resolution 2443 Respect for and Implementation of Human Rights in Occupied Territories." https://unispal.un.org/DPA/DPR/unispal.nsf/0/1FE2116573C8CFBE852560DF004ED05D.

———. 1969. "Resolution 2535. United Nations Relief and Works Agency for Palestine Refugees in the Near East." https://unispal.un.org/DPA/DPR/unispal.nsf/0/41F2C6DCE4DAA765852560DF004E0AC8.

———. 1970a. "2672. United Nations Relief and Works Agency for Palestine Refugees in the Near East." https://unispal.un.org/DPA/DPR/unispal.nsf/0/E7C4B66C913EC0DC852560DE006E8F1B.

———. 1970b. "Resolution 2649. The Importance of the Universal Realization of the Right of Peoples to Self-Determination and of the Speedy Granting of Independence to Colonial Countries and Peoples for the Effective Guarantee and Observance of Human Rights." https://documents-dds-ny.un.org/doc/RESOLUTION/GEN/NR0/349/14/IMG/NR034914.pdf?OpenElement.

———. 1971. "Resolution 2851 Report of the Special Committee to Investigate Israeli Practices Affecting the Human Rights of the Population of the Occupied Territories." https://documents-dds-ny.un.org/doc/RESOLUTION/GEN/NR0/328/67/IMG/NR032867.pdf?OpenElement.

———. 1974a. "Resolution 3236. Question of Palestine." https://documents-dds-ny.un.org/doc/RESOLUTION/GEN/NR0/738/38/IMG/NR073838.pdf?OpenElement.

———. 1974b. "Resolution 3237. Observer Status for the Palestine Liberation Organization." https://documents-dds-ny.un.org/doc/RESOLUTION/GEN/NR0/738/39/IMG/NR073839.pdf?OpenElement.

———. 1975a. "Resolution 3376. Question of Palestine." https://documents-dds-ny.un.org/doc/RESOLUTION/GEN/NR0/000/89/IMG/NR000089.pdf?OpenElement.

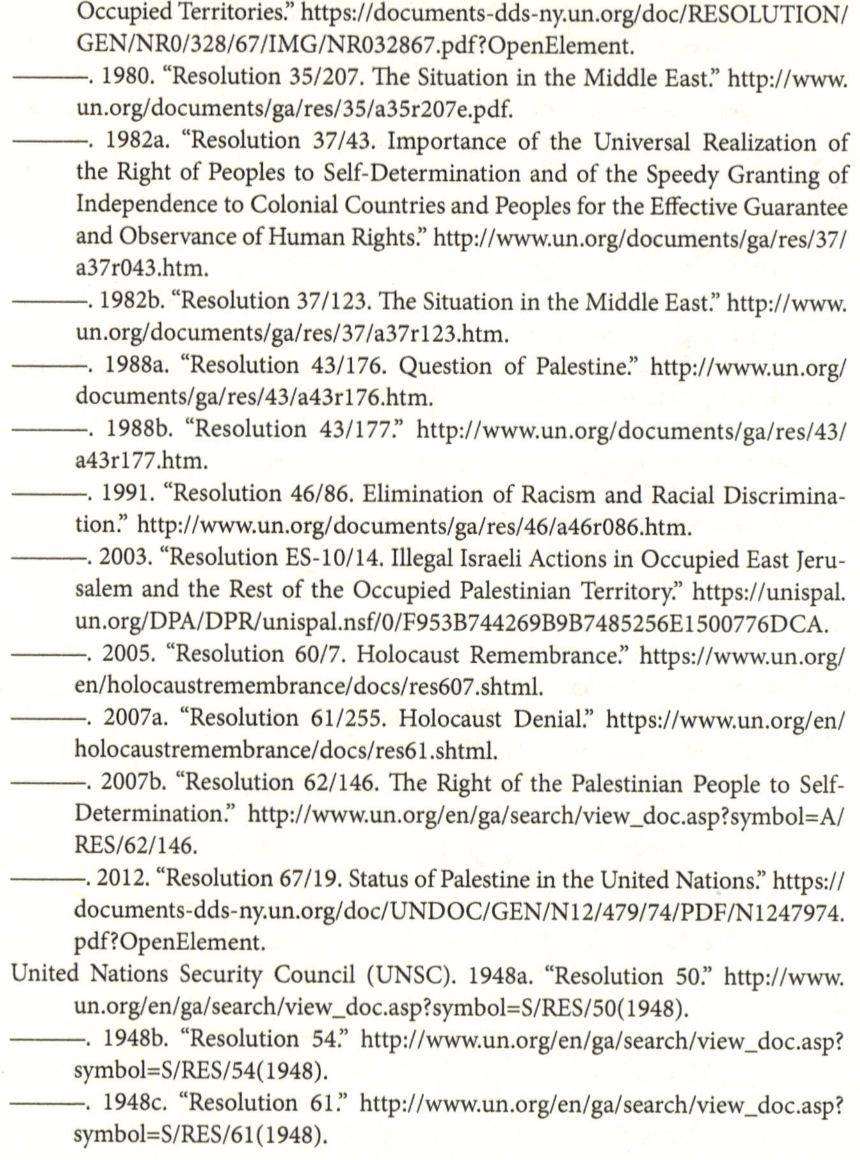

———. 1975b. "Resolution 3379. Elimination of All Forms of Racial Discrimination." https://unispal.un.org/DPA/DPR/unispal.nsf/0/761C1063530766A7052566A2005B74D1.

———. 1976. "Resolution 31/106. Report of the Special Committee to Investigate Israeli Practices Affecting the Human Rights of the Population of the Occupied Territories." https://documents-dds-ny.un.org/doc/RESOLUTION/GEN/NR0/328/67/IMG/NR032867.pdf?OpenElement.

———. 1980. "Resolution 35/207. The Situation in the Middle East." http://www.un.org/documents/ga/res/35/a35r207e.pdf.

———. 1982a. "Resolution 37/43. Importance of the Universal Realization of the Right of Peoples to Self-Determination and of the Speedy Granting of Independence to Colonial Countries and Peoples for the Effective Guarantee and Observance of Human Rights." http://www.un.org/documents/ga/res/37/a37r043.htm.

———. 1982b. "Resolution 37/123. The Situation in the Middle East." http://www.un.org/documents/ga/res/37/a37r123.htm.

———. 1988a. "Resolution 43/176. Question of Palestine." http://www.un.org/documents/ga/res/43/a43r176.htm.

———. 1988b. "Resolution 43/177." http://www.un.org/documents/ga/res/43/a43r177.htm.

———. 1991. "Resolution 46/86. Elimination of Racism and Racial Discrimination." http://www.un.org/documents/ga/res/46/a46r086.htm.

———. 2003. "Resolution ES-10/14. Illegal Israeli Actions in Occupied East Jerusalem and the Rest of the Occupied Palestinian Territory." https://unispal.un.org/DPA/DPR/unispal.nsf/0/F953B744269B9B7485256E1500776DCA.

———. 2005. "Resolution 60/7. Holocaust Remembrance." https://www.un.org/en/holocaustremembrance/docs/res607.shtml.

———. 2007a. "Resolution 61/255. Holocaust Denial." https://www.un.org/en/holocaustremembrance/docs/res61.shtml.

———. 2007b. "Resolution 62/146. The Right of the Palestinian People to Self-Determination." http://www.un.org/en/ga/search/view_doc.asp?symbol=A/RES/62/146.

———. 2012. "Resolution 67/19. Status of Palestine in the United Nations." https://documents-dds-ny.un.org/doc/UNDOC/GEN/N12/479/74/PDF/N1247974.pdf?OpenElement.

United Nations Security Council (UNSC). 1948a. "Resolution 50." http://www.un.org/en/ga/search/view_doc.asp?symbol=S/RES/50(1948).

———. 1948b. "Resolution 54." http://www.un.org/en/ga/search/view_doc.asp?symbol=S/RES/54(1948).

———. 1948c. "Resolution 61." http://www.un.org/en/ga/search/view_doc.asp?symbol=S/RES/61(1948).

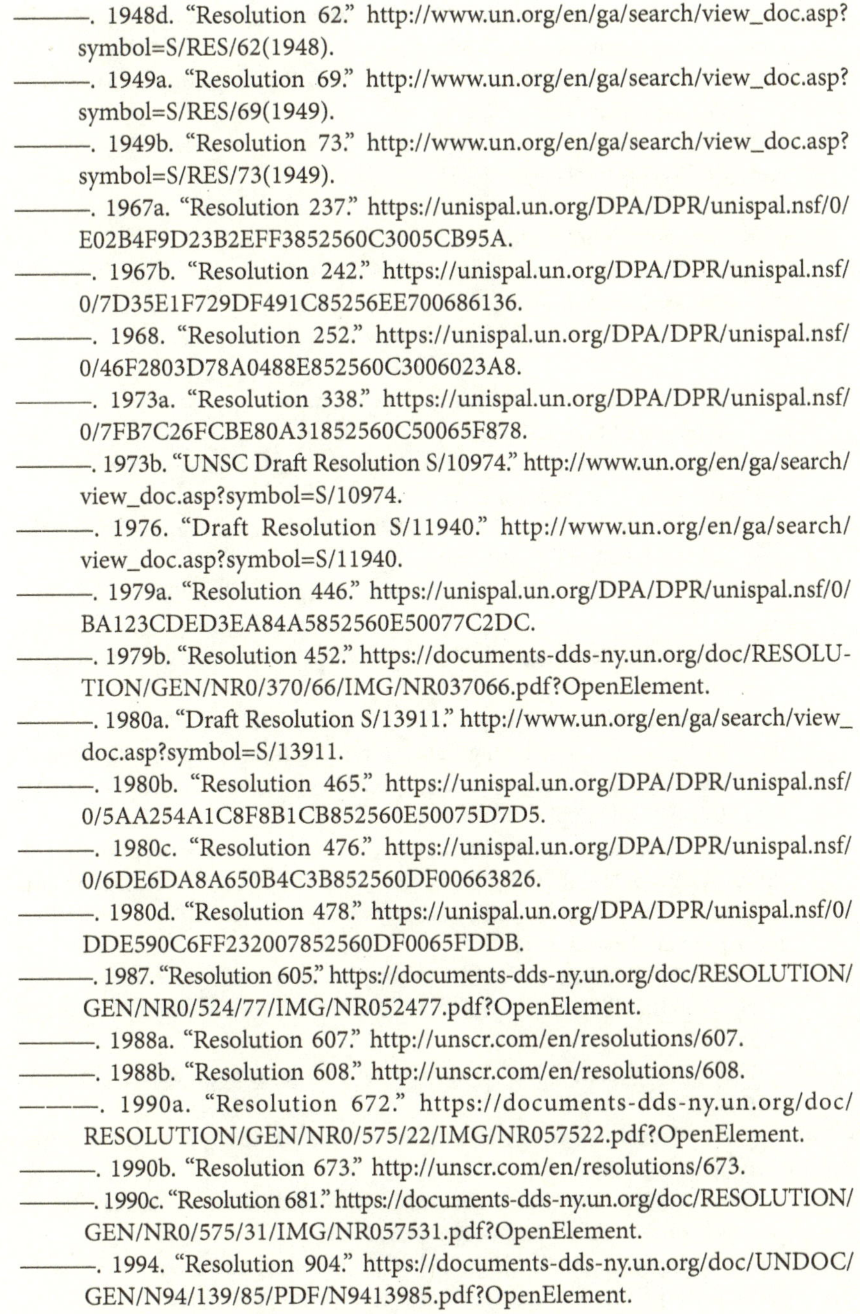

———. 1948d. "Resolution 62." http://www.un.org/en/ga/search/view_doc.asp?symbol=S/RES/62(1948).

———. 1949a. "Resolution 69." http://www.un.org/en/ga/search/view_doc.asp?symbol=S/RES/69(1949).

———. 1949b. "Resolution 73." http://www.un.org/en/ga/search/view_doc.asp?symbol=S/RES/73(1949).

———. 1967a. "Resolution 237." https://unispal.un.org/DPA/DPR/unispal.nsf/0/E02B4F9D23B2EFF3852560C3005CB95A.

———. 1967b. "Resolution 242." https://unispal.un.org/DPA/DPR/unispal.nsf/0/7D35E1F729DF491C85256EE700686136.

———. 1968. "Resolution 252." https://unispal.un.org/DPA/DPR/unispal.nsf/0/46F2803D78A0488E852560C3006023A8.

———. 1973a. "Resolution 338." https://unispal.un.org/DPA/DPR/unispal.nsf/0/7FB7C26FCBE80A31852560C50065F878.

———. 1973b. "UNSC Draft Resolution S/10974." http://www.un.org/en/ga/search/view_doc.asp?symbol=S/10974.

———. 1976. "Draft Resolution S/11940." http://www.un.org/en/ga/search/view_doc.asp?symbol=S/11940.

———. 1979a. "Resolution 446." https://unispal.un.org/DPA/DPR/unispal.nsf/0/BA123CDED3EA84A5852560E50077C2DC.

———. 1979b. "Resolution 452." https://documents-dds-ny.un.org/doc/RESOLUTION/GEN/NR0/370/66/IMG/NR037066.pdf?OpenElement.

———. 1980a. "Draft Resolution S/13911." http://www.un.org/en/ga/search/view_doc.asp?symbol=S/13911.

———. 1980b. "Resolution 465." https://unispal.un.org/DPA/DPR/unispal.nsf/0/5AA254A1C8F8B1CB852560E50075D7D5.

———. 1980c. "Resolution 476." https://unispal.un.org/DPA/DPR/unispal.nsf/0/6DE6DA8A650B4C3B852560DF00663826.

———. 1980d. "Resolution 478." https://unispal.un.org/DPA/DPR/unispal.nsf/0/DDE590C6FF232007852560DF0065FDDB.

———. 1987. "Resolution 605." https://documents-dds-ny.un.org/doc/RESOLUTION/GEN/NR0/524/77/IMG/NR052477.pdf?OpenElement.

———. 1988a. "Resolution 607." http://unscr.com/en/resolutions/607.

———. 1988b. "Resolution 608." http://unscr.com/en/resolutions/608.

———. 1990a. "Resolution 672." https://documents-dds-ny.un.org/doc/RESOLUTION/GEN/NR0/575/22/IMG/NR057522.pdf?OpenElement.

———. 1990b. "Resolution 673." http://unscr.com/en/resolutions/673.

———. 1990c. "Resolution 681." https://documents-dds-ny.un.org/doc/RESOLUTION/GEN/NR0/575/31/IMG/NR057531.pdf?OpenElement.

———. 1994. "Resolution 904." https://documents-dds-ny.un.org/doc/UNDOC/GEN/N94/139/85/PDF/N9413985.pdf?OpenElement.

———. 1995. "Draft Resolution S/1995/394." http://www.un.org/en/ga/search/view_doc.asp?symbol=S/1995/394.

———. 1997a. "Draft Resolution S/1997/199." http://www.un.org/en/ga/search/view_doc.asp?symbol=S/1997/199.

———. 1997b. "Draft Resolution S/1997/241." http://www.un.org/en/ga/search/view_doc.asp?symbol=S/1997/241.

———. 2001. "Draft Resolution S/2001/1199." http://www.un.org/en/ga/search/view_doc.asp?symbol=S/2001/1199.

———. 2002a. "Draft Resolution S/2002/1385." http://www.un.org/en/ga/search/view_doc.asp?symbol=S/2002/1385.

———. 2002b. "Resolution 1397." https://www.un.org/press/en/2002/sc7326.doc.htm.

———. 2002c. "Resolution 1402." http://www.un.org/en/ga/search/view_doc.asp?symbol=S/RES/1402(2002).

———. 2002d. "Resolution 1435." http://www.un.org/en/ga/search/view_doc.asp?symbol=S/RES/1435(2002).

———. 2003a. "Draft Resolution S/2003/980." http://www.un.org/en/ga/search/view_doc.asp?symbol=S/2003/980.

———. 2003b. "Resolution 1515." https://www.un.org/press/en/2003/sc7924.doc.htm.

———. 2004. "Draft Resolution S/2004/783." http://www.un.org/en/ga/search/view_doc.asp?symbol=S/2004/783.

———. 2007. "Special Research Report No. 4: The Middle East 1947–2007: Sixty Years of Security Council Engagement on the Israel/Palestine Question." http://www.securitycouncilreport.org/special-research-report/lookup-c-glKWLeMTIsG-b-3748287.php?print=true.

———. 2008. "Resolution 1850." http://www.securitycouncilreport.org/atf/cf/%7B65BFCF9B-6D27-4E9C-8CD3-CF6E4FF96FF9%7D/IP%20SRES1850.pdf.

———. 2011. "Draft Resolution S/2011/24." https://www.un.org/en/ga/search/view_doc.asp?symbol=S/2011/24.

———. 2014. "Draft Resolution S/2014/916." http://www.securitycouncilreport.org/atf/cf/%7B65BFCF9B-6D27-4E9C-8CD3-CF6E4FF96FF9%7D/s_2014_916_v2.pdf.

———. 2016. "Resolution 2334." https://www.un.org/webcast/pdfs/SRES2334-2016.pdf.

———. 2017. "Security Council Resolutions." 2017. http://www.un.org/en/sc/documents/resolutions/.

Urquhart, Brian. 1995. "The United Nations in the Middle East: A 50-Year Retrospective." *Middle East Journal* 49 (4): 572–81.

US National Security Council. 1977. "Paper Prepared in the National Security Council." https://history.state.gov/historicaldocuments/frus1977-80v08/d54.

Valbjørn, Morten, and André Bank. 2012. "The New Arab Cold War: Rediscovering the Arab Dimension of Middle East Regional Politics." *Review of International Studies* 38 (1): 3–24. https://doi.org/10.1017/S0260210511000283.

Velayati, Ali Akbar. 1982. "Statement by Mr. Velayati at the United Nations General Assembly Plenary Session." http://www.un.org/ga/search/view_doc.asp?symbol=A/37/PV.27.

———. 1983. "Statement by Mr. Velayati at the United Nations General Assembly Plenary Meeting." http://www.un.org/ga/search/view_doc.asp?symbol=A/38/PV.13.

———. 1984. "Statement by Mr. Velayati at the United Nations General Assembly Plenary Meeting." http://www.un.org/ga/search/view_doc.asp?symbol=A/39/PV.15.

———. 1986. "Statement by Mr. Velayati at the United Nations General Assembly Plenary Session." http://www.un.org/ga/search/view_doc.asp?symbol=A/41/PV.19.

———. 1991. "Statement by Mr. Velayati at the United Nations General Assembly Plenary Meeting." http://www.un.org/ga/search/view_doc.asp?symbol=A/46/PV.5.

———. 1993. "Statement by Mr. Velayati at the United Nations General Assembly Plenary Meeting." http://www.un.org/ga/search/view_doc.asp?symbol=A/48/PV.14.

———. 1994. "UN General Assembly Opening General Debate Statement." http://www.un.org/ga/search/view_doc.asp?symbol=A/49/PV.5.

———. 1996. "Statement by Mr. Velayati at the United Nations General Assembly Plenary Meeting." http://www.un.org/ga/search/view_doc.asp?symbol=A/51/PV.4.

Voltolini, Benedetta. 2015. *Lobbying in EU Foreign Policy-Making: The Case of the Israeli-Palestinian Conflict*. London: Routledge.

Waever, Ole. 1996. "European Security Identities." *Journal of Common Market Studies* 34 (1): 103–32. https://doi.org/10.1111/j.1468-5965.1996.tb00562.x.

———. 2009. "Discursive Approaches." In *European Integration Theory*, edited by Antje Wiener and Thomas Diez, 2nd ed., 197–215. Oxford: Oxford University Press.

Walker, R. B. J. 1993. *Inside/Outside: International Relations as Political Theory*. Cambridge: Cambridge University Press.

Walt, Stephen M. 1990. *The Origins of Alliance*. Ithaca, NY: Cornell University Press.

Weizman, Eyal. 2012. *Hollow Land: Israel's Architecture of Occupation*. London: Verso Books.

Weldes, Jutta, and Diana Saco. 1996. "Making State Action Possible: The United States and the Discursive Construction of 'The Cuban Problem,' 1960–1994."

Millennium—Journal of International Studies 25 (2): 361–95. https://doi.org/10.1177/03058298960250020601.

Wendt, Alexander. 1999. *Social Theory of International Politics*. Cambridge: Cambridge University Press.

Wessels, Wolfgang. 1997. "An Ever Closer Fusion? A Dynamic Macropolitical View on Integration Processes." *Journal of Common Market Studies* 35 (2): 267–99.

Westad, Odd Arne. 2007. *The Global Cold War: Third World Interventions and the Making of Our Times*. Rev. ed. Cambridge: Cambridge University Press.

Wildeman, Jeremy. 2018. "EU Development Aid in the Occupied Palestinian Territory, between Aid Effectiveness and World Bank Guidance." *Global Affairs* 4 (1): 115–28. https://doi.org/10.1080/23340460.2018.1507285.

Wodak, Ruth, and Michael Meyer. 2009. *Methods for Critical Discourse Analysis*. London: SAGE.

Yacobi, Haim, and David Newman. 2008. "The EU and the Israel-Palestine Conflict." In *The European Union and Border Conflicts: The Power of Integration and Association*, edited by Thomas Diez, Mathias Albert, and Stephan Stetter, 173–202. Cambridge: Cambridge University Press.

Yazdi, Ebrahim. 1979. "Statement by Mr. Yazdi at the United Nations General Assembly Plenary Session." http://www.un.org/ga/search/view_doc.asp?symbol=A/34/PV.21.

Yost, Charles Woodruff. 1970. "Statement by Charles Woodruff Yost at the United Nations General Assembly Opening Session." http://www.un.org/ga/search/view_doc.asp?symbol=A/PV.1854.

Zahedi, Ardeshir. 1968. "Statement by Mr. Zahedi at the United Nations General Assembly Plenary Meeting." http://www.un.org/ga/search/view_doc.asp?symbol=A/PV.1695.

Index

www.ingramcontent.com/pod-product-compliance
Lightning Source LLC
LaVergne TN
LVHW050152080826
844660LV00002B/178

* 9 7 8 1 4 3 8 4 8 1 5 9 3 *